To
Chad
Enjoy

Pop Smoke, Birds Inbound

The Forgotten Soldier

A Novel by

Rick R .Garcia

authorHOUSE®

AuthorHouse™
1663 Liberty Drive
Bloomington, IN 47403
www.authorhouse.com
Phone: 1 (800) 839-8640

Published by AuthorHouse 06/06/2016

ISBN: 978-1-5049-7626-8 (sc)
ISBN: 978-1-5049-7627-5 (e)

Library of Congress Control Number: 2016901437

Contents

Preface

I survived the 'Nam, but not the battle.
Rick R. Garcia

Pop Smoke, Birds Inbound is an extraordinary journey providing insight into the mind and soul of an only son born to Hispanic parents and caught up in the 1969 draft lottery. It chronicles a young man who was shipped far away to "the land of Hush-a-bye" to fight in the most controversial war the United States ever participated in: the Vietnam War. But *Pop Smoke, Birds Inbound* isn't about the ugly side of that war.

Pop Smoke, Birds Inbound is a factual account of one soldier's triumphs and failures *between* firefights—an incredible story of survival, from living to loving. It's a unique side of the Vietnam War never before described in such vivid detail. It is my story.

Although the events, dates, and characters are uncommonly accurate due to a journal I kept during my tour of Southeast Asia, the names have been changed to protect the privacy of individuals. All areas, maps, place names, and facts have been verified by today's technology.

The Vietnam War put a once-proud nation in turmoil. During the height of the conflict, the antiwar movement caused civil unrest in America. Young men evaded the draft by fleeing to Canada, claiming conscientious objector status, homosexuality, or marriage with child.

It was a time when hippies made their presence in society, the sexual revolution boomed, the drug culture killed, and a new breed of music took on a decisively unique flavor, marking the generation for years to come.

Victim of the draft, I was inducted into the US Army on August 20, 1970. Confident that the "sole survivor" policy, reinstated in 1964, would prevent me from going to battle, I chose to honor my obligation and serve my country. Besides, America's involvement in the Vietnam War had peaked during the 1968 Tet Offensive. US ground forces were gradually being withdrawn as part of a policy known as Vietnamization, aimed at ending America's involvement in the war.

Despite peace efforts made by President Lyndon B. Johnson to end the war, young men were still dying, and I wanted no part of that. Soldiers were returning to America not as heroes, but as "baby killers." The nation desperately lacked the symbolism of heroism, glory, and patriotism. Soldiers returned with emptiness and moral uncertainty.

After the completion of eight weeks of intense AIT (advance infantry training), I was issued orders to report to Oakland Army Base, gateway to Southeast Asia. Eventually, I would be assigned to Blackfoot Platoon, Company Bravo, Second Battalion, Eighth Regiment, First Cavalry Division, within which the majority of this story takes place.

Although the Vietnam War had come to an end, grunts continued to battle the hostility within. As a survivor, I understood their pain. Regardless of the opposition, I understood freedom came with a price.

Although the war ended in victory for North Vietnam, there were no winners. The Vietnam conflict was a bloody war in which 58,000 blacks, Hispanics, and poverty-stricken whites sacrificed their lives, not to mention the million South Vietnamese, NVA, and Viet Cong insurgents.

I was awarded the Vietnam campaign ribbon, Combat Infantry badge, three Bronze Stars, and two Air Medals. I received two Silver Star recommendations. The commendations would only be tarnished by the defeat.

The horrific Vietnam experience will always be embedded in my thoughts. For the soldiers who paid the ultimate price, I can only grieve—especially for Joey, killed while on patrol.

For years, I managed the painful memories of a war I could never forget. It wasn't that the experience didn't affect me—I just dealt with it differently.

My Return

On April 23, 1975, as I was sipping a cup of Mom's freshly brewed coffee, Dad summoned me to the living room. A *CBS News* special report on the Vietnam War was about to air.

Dad, a proud World War II veteran, focused his eyes on the black-and-white television console. Footage of NVA (North Vietnamese Army) tanks rumbling down Highway 1 were being broadcast. Anchor Walter Cronkite sadly announced that Xuan Loch had fallen to the NVA in the last major battle of the war. A hundred thousand NVA soldiers were advancing on Saigon. The war that the United States had tried to end with peace and honor was instead about to end in bitter defeat for the people of South Vietnam.

CBS switched the broadcast to President Ford addressing Tulane University students and faculty. "The war in Vietnam is finished, as far as America is concerned," he announced.

With regret, I looked away from the TV set as Walter Cronkite closed his commentary. "Vietnam will fall to North Vietnam within the week, and that's the way it is."

The enduring image of the bloody Vietnam War was about to end. All that remained were the painful memories an ungrateful nation would never forget. Emotionally affected over the outcome of the war, I decided to visit the final resting place of a soldier whose memory was engraved in my heart.

"Where you going?" asked Dad.

"Cemetery," I replied, walking out the front door.

As I drove through the gates of the Union Avenue Cemetery, a light drizzle collected on my windshield. Parking next to the tree that marked his grave, I headed for his final resting place.

His headstone had recently been cleared of debris. All that remained was a small bouquet of wilted carnations. Suddenly a strong gust of wind rustled the trees, knocking over the bouquet. The dark clouds indicated a storm arriving soon. Staring at the sacred landscape, I stepped back in time.

Episode One

Destination Vietnam

January 22, 1971. After completing advanced infantry training, I made the best of a thirty-day leave. With an MOS (military occupation school) of 11B20 (light weapons infantry), I had military orders to report to Oakland Army Base Deportation Center for overseas processing.

As a sole surviving son, I remained confident that I wouldn't be sent to the front line. Besides, the recently inaugurated thirty-seventh president of the United States was going to put an end to the war that politicians conveniently labeled a "conflict."

My parents accompanied me. Dad placed the gearshift of his 1963 Dodge Dart in reverse and pulled out of the driveway. A neighbor was seated in his favorite chair, enjoying an early morning cup of coffee before heading for his ranch. He waved. As if I were one of his own, he was troubled about me going to Vietnam.

The home on Wilkins and Liggett brought back painful memories of the death of a popular neighborhood boy killed in the 1968 Tet offensive.

"All Along the Watch Tower" played on the radio as Dad turned onto Union Avenue. Ignoring Mom's nurturing words, I clutched the dollar bill my grandmother had given me for good luck.

*****

My predicament could have been avoided entirely if I had remained in college. My decision to leave the community

1

college eventually sent me to Vietnam. Due to poor choices and lack of effort, I had struggled through the previous semester, falling below a 2.0 grade point average.

A recent promotion from salad chef to evening cook at a local restaurant allowed me to consider time off from school. After I discussed my options with the deferment officer, Miss White, she agreed I would be able to retain my deferment as long as I returned to school in the fall.

Besides employment, time off from school gave me an opportunity to pursue a life of drinking and drugs. Gambling that the war would end before the fun ran out, I didn't take the draft seriously. Unfortunately, I lost. Within two weeks, the official selective service envelope arrived at my door—I had been drafted.

Rushing back to the campus, I headed for the deferment office to investigate.

"Can I help you?" asked an elderly woman standing at the counter.

"Can I speak with Miss White?" I asked.

"I'm the new deferment officer," answered the unfamiliar face.

"Where's Miss White?" I asked.

"She took a position at a junior college up north. Can I help you?"

"I received a draft notice, and according to Miss White, my deferment was in place until next fall."

"What's your name?"

"Garcia."

"Let me pull your file."

The newly appointed deferment officer returned, shuffling through the paperwork in my file.

"Why didn't you return to school, Mr. Garcia?"

"I made arrangements to take a semester off," I replied truthfully.

"There's nothing in your file that indicates that, so when you didn't return to school, I dropped your deferment. Sorry, there's nothing I can do for you now," said the deferment officer sympathetically.

"There has to be something you can do. I don't want to go to Vietnam!" I pleaded.

"I will only reinstate your deferment if you enroll in a minimum of ten and a half units. Until then, there is nothing I can do."

I spent the entire day pleading with instructors to allow me to enroll in their classes. The majority of instructors claimed I had missed too many days and wouldn't be able to make up the work. I desperately explained their decision could place me in grave danger, but they refused.

With one last opportunity, I presented a document to the medical examiner at the induction center. The family urologist had written it, verifying evidence of a urethra stricture. Hoping to be classified 4-F (unfit for military duty), I watched as the medical examiner reviewed the document.

"Sorry, but this isn't a valid medical condition to classify you 4-F. But I'll file it in the circular file," said the medical examiner, tossing the letter into the trash can.

Ironically, after reporting to Fort Ord, I received a notice from the Selective Service Board stating that if I submitted form SS No. 109, verifying my return to college in the fall, my student deferment would be reinstated. Unfortunately, it was too late—I had been inducted in the US Army.

Making matters worse, I had recently ended a summer romance with a girl named Lisa and was feeling a little homesick. I wasn't concerned about serving my country. I was afraid of being killed in Vietnam.

There was a small glimmer of hope when I stepped off the bus and into the Fort Ord processing center. After I filled out the required forms, the processing clerk asked about my previous employment. "What did you do in civilian life?"

"I was a cook," I replied.

"Would you like to cook for the army?" the clerk asked.

"Absolutely, if it will keep me from going to Vietnam," I replied.

"It probably won't, but it will keep you off the front line."

"If I'm a sole surviving son, will that get me into cook school?" I replied.

"The only way I can guarantee cook school is to enlist for three years, whether you are a sole surviving son or not."

The clerk handed over the enlistment form, along with a pen. I was ready to sign but paused. "What are my chances of going to cook school if I don't enlist for three years?" I asked.

"Your chances are still good, considering the army always needs experienced spoons."

"Then no, thanks, I'll take my chances being assigned to cook school. Besides, being a sole survivor, I probably won't have to serve on the front line," I replied, returning the form to the clerk.

I wasn't going to spend any more time in the military than I was obliged to. I decided to let destiny rule my fate.

***

After the graduation ceremony from basic training, the head drill instructor stood in front of Company B and announced the graduates' duty stations. "Everyone listen up. The following individuals have been assigned to light weapons infantry!"

The first name on the list was mine. Determined to know why I had been assigned to an infantry unit, I approached the drill sergeant. "Drill sergeant, there's been a mistake. I should be going to cook school."

The senior drill sergeant tilted his head and, with a big grin on his face, replied sarcastically, "The only cooking you're going to be doing is in the jungle. Now enjoy your weekend."

"But I'm a sole surviving son," I said.

"Don't sweat the small stuff, Garcia. Get on the bus."

First platoon's drill sergeant thought it was amusing that I had been assigned to an infantry unit and laughed. "I better not see your ass in Vietnam, old-timer," I said sarcastically.

"Don't worry, Garcia; you'll see me there. I'm going back in thirty days for a second tour."

There was no justification for my being assigned to a light weapons infantry unit. My military test scores qualified me for warrant officer training. So why was I headed for advanced infantry training?

*****

Turning onto Skyway Drive, Dad drove by the air force fighter jet on display and entered the short-term parking lot. Retrieving my duffel bag from the trunk of the car, I headed for the terminal with Mom and Dad at my side.

Awaiting my arrival was a soldier named Jet. Jet and I had become acquainted at the Fresno induction center. Seated at his side were his mother and newly wedded wife.

With very little conversation, Jet and I waited to board a small commuter plane. Mom had a deeply troubled look on her face; she seemed desperate, holding back the tears. Dad kept his emotions to himself, but he also seemed troubled.

The announcement came over the speaker: "Flight 937 to San Francisco International Airport is now boarding." It was time to leave loved ones behind.

Mom embraced me with a loving hug. Holding me tightly, she couldn't hold back the tears any longer.

"Everything is going to be all right. Besides, I have the dollar Grandmother gave me for good luck," I said to her, displaying the dollar bill. I gave her a kiss on her cheek and turned to Jet. "Are you ready, troop?"

"I'm ready if you're ready, troop."

Handing over my airline ticket to the agent, I headed for the commuter plane. I hesitated at the top of the stairs and waved one last time. With her head resting on Dad's shoulder, Mom slowly raised her hand and waved good-bye.

Episode Two

Oakland Deportation Center

The flight to San Francisco was rough but fairly short. I had a can of beer and a bag of peanuts, and then the stewardess informed everyone to fasten their seat belts. The pilot made his descent into San Francisco International Airport as the flight crew prepared to land in bad weather.

After a shaky landing, Jet and I departed the plane and headed for baggage claim. A tall, attractive female was awaiting our arrival. Dressed in impressive blue air force attire, she held a sign that read Oakland Army Base Deportation Center. Jet and I followed her directions to the exit. Outside the terminal, we were greeted by a high-ranking army sergeant. "Anyone going to Oakland Army Base Deportation Center?"

"Yes, we are," Jet answered.

"There's several ways to get there, gentlemen. You can take a cab, which will cost you money. You can take a limousine, which will also cost you money. Or you can wait for the military bus. It's free."

We were in no hurry. Jet and I decided to wait for the bus.

Thirty minutes later, bus transportation arrived. Everyone climbed aboard, and the driver headed for the Oakland Army Base. "How did you get a job driving a military bus?" I asked, taking a seat behind the driver.

"I'm assigned to the motor pool, so I guess I just got lucky," he replied.

He took the route over the Oakland Bay Bridge. I never thought I would see this part of the country from the window of a bus. A sign at the entrance of the base read, "Oakland Army Base Welcomes You."

After driving past concrete barracks and a mess hall facility, the bus arrived at the processing center. A soldier was standing nearby, awaiting our arrival. It was Little Joey, a soldier Jet and I had taken a liking to.

"Dig those cool fatigues," I said.

"Where did you get that cool hat?" asked Jet.

"It's a boonie hat. After you check in, you'll be fitted with jungle fatigues, jungle boots, and a boonie hat," said Little Joey excitedly.

With military records in hand, Jet and I waited in the cool Oakland breeze to be called into the orderly's office for processing. Unexpectedly, a door flew open. Two army MPs briskly escorted a Hispanic soldier in handcuffs into a waiting military vehicle. The soldier was forced into the backseat, and the vehicle sped away.

"What the hell did he do?" Jet asked.

"That's a soldier who refused to go to Vietnam," replied a soldier standing by the door.

"Next!" hollered the clerk.

I entered the orderly room and handed the clerk my orders. Investigating every page, the clerk reviewed the documentation. I was concerned he would discover that an article fifteen had been removed from the file. I had taken out the military citation issued against me for bad behavior.

After examining the entire file, the clerk placed it with the others. "Any questions?"

"Yes, I'm a sole surviving son. Will I still be going to Vietnam?"

"That's something you need to take up with your company commander at your next duty station. Next!" shouted the clerk.

Jet and I were each issued a pillow and blanket along with a barracks assignment. We were also given instructions to report to the yard with our duffel bags. We headed for the barracks to drop off our belongings.

We climbed three flights of stairs to get to our barracks. We selected our bunks and dropped off the pillows and blankets. We returned to the yard and joined a group of soldiers.

A staff sergeant arrived and addressed the group. The group was escorted across the base to a large warehouse. Everyone was instructed to turn in their clothing. Each man received seven new pairs of jungle fatigues, socks, underwear, jungle boots, and an olive drab boonie hat.

Everyone was instructed to change into a set of jungle clothing and place the remainder in their duffel bags. The light poly-cotton material wasn't suited to the cool Bay Area weather, but it was ideal for the high temperatures in Vietnam.

Final orders of the day were to return to the yard each morning for an 8:00 a.m. roll call until assigned to a flight manifest. On the way to the barracks, I recognized an individual from my hometown.

"When did you arrive?" I asked.

"This morning," RJ replied. "Hey, did you hear what happened to Jo Jo?"

"No, what happened?"

"After three months of being AWOL (absent without leave), Jo Jo decided to report for duty. Unfortunately when he arrived at the deportation center, he was placed under arrest.

"What happened to him?" I asked curiously.

9

"He was placed in cuffs and escorted back to Fort Ord," RJ explained.

"He's lucky," I replied.

"Why is that?" asked Jet.

"Although he's going to spend time in the brig, he probably won't go to Vietnam," I replied.

"I guess going AWOL paid off for Jo Jo," said Jet.

Jet and I dropped off our newly issued clothing and headed downstairs. RJ introduced his friend, Shake, and we picked up Little Joey too. The five of us headed for the nearest EM club (enlisted men's club).

When I discovered the officers' club, I decided I would try to get in. "Come on, let's get a drink," I said to the guys.

"Are you crazy? The officers' club is for officers, and you're not an officer," said Jet.

"You never know unless you try. Besides, what are they going do to us? Send us to Vietnam?"

A well-built sergeant was standing at the door, checking ID cards. When the soldier was distracted by an attractive brunette wearing a short skirt, I saw the opportunity to slip by.

"Hey! Soldier, where do you think you're going?"

"I just arrived and would like to get a drink," I replied.

"Let's see some military ID," said the sergeant.

"I don't have any ID on me," I replied.

"Sorry, can't let you in without ID," said the sergeant.

"Come on, Sergeant, we're going to Vietnam."

"So is everyone else in this club," said the sergeant.

"I guess rank has its privileges. Let's go, guys."

"Where now?" asked Shake.

"We can always get a drink at the EM club. We just have to find it," I said.

"Yeah, and we can have shots of Old Grand-Dad," said Shake.

"What the hell is Old Grand-Dad?" Little Joey asked.

"The best bourbon you'll ever taste," replied Shake.

Everyone agreed and headed for the EM club on the other side of the base. After a long walk, we entered the club and ordered drinks. Shake ordered a round of beers along with a shot of Old Grand-Dad whiskey for everyone. I placed four quarters in the jukebox and played the latest singles.

I took a drink of beer as I watched Shake devour a pickled egg, washing it down with the whiskey shot. I must have been crazy to drink shots when I had a 7:00 a.m. wakeup call. There had to be a better way to enjoy the evening.

It was our first night on the base, and the evening was young. Willing to take chance, I came up with an idea.

"I'll be back," I whispered to Jet.

"Where are you going?"

"There has to be a way to get into the officers' club," I said, hurrying out the door.

A short time later, I returned with a pair of sunglasses and sergeant stripes pinned to my fatigue shirt collar.

"Where did you get the stripes?" Little Joey asked.

"Yeah, and why the sunglasses?" asked Jet.

"I bought the sergeant stripes at the PX (postal exchange), and the sunglasses are a disguise so the bouncer won't recognize me."

"Can't you get in trouble for impersonating a sergeant?" Shake asked.

"Only if you impersonate an officer," I responded.

"Yeah, Garcia is only impersonating a sergeant. Let's go, troops!" shouted Jet.

Hoping the sergeant stripes would get us past the bouncer, we headed back to the officers' club. There was a different bouncer at the door when we arrived. "Wish me luck," I said to the guys as I approached.

"Good evening, Sergeant," said the bouncer, glaring at my E5 stripes. "Are these soldiers your guests?"

"Yeah, I'm taking them out for a drink before we get shipped to Vietnam," I replied nervously.

"Have a great time, Sergeant," said the bouncer with a suspicious grin.

Eager to have a good time, everyone rushed into the club. The sound of a popular San Francisco group filled the room. Little Joey, RJ, and Shake found a table and ordered drinks. Jet and I made our way to the bar. The place was filled to capacity. I searched the club for a single dance partner, and fixed my eyes on two attractive brunettes swaying their heads to the music. "Watch this. I'll show you how it's done."

"Yeah, right," Jet replied, sipping on his cocktail.

"Can I join you?" I said to one of the girls.

"I guess it will be all right."

"My name is Ricky. What's yours?" I asked.

"I'm Tina, and this is Dawn."

"The music sounds great. Would one of you like to dance?"

"I wouldn't, but Dawn will dance with you," she replied.

I took Dawn's hand and led her to the dance floor. I admired her shapely backside as we danced to a popular tune. The smell of Chanel No. 5 brought back memories of a romance with a girl in high school. When the music ended, I escorted Dawn back to her table. I tried to get Jet's attention to join us.

"Would you like my friend to join us?" I asked.

The girls glanced at Jet standing at the bar.

"He's cute. What's his name?"

"Jet," I said.

"We would love for Jet to join us, but my husband is a little jealous, and he is coming this way," said Tina.

"Is there a problem?" asked a tall lieutenant, glaring at my sergeant stripes.

"No, sir. I was just leaving," I replied. It was in my best interest to avoid a confrontation with the officer, since I was in the club illegally.

"What happened, lover boy?" Jet asked, laughing, as I took a seat at the bar.

"How did I know her husband was an officer?" I replied.

"Maybe because we're in an officers' club," Jet answered.

Jet and I continued to enjoy the entertainment until a soldier dressed in army dress greens took a seat at the end of bar. He was wearing an impressive assortment of medals and ribbons, and it was obvious he had just returned from Vietnam. Curious to know about the war I walked over and introduced myself. "Excuse me, sir. Can I buy you a beer?"

The soldier slowly turned his head and glared into my eyes. "Certainly, but don't call me sir. I work for a living," he quietly replied.

"I hope you don't mind me asking, but what's it like in Vietnam?" I asked.

"Which time? I just returned from my third tour. Twice with the Marines and once with the army. I'm going back as soon as my thirty-day leave is up."

"Your medals are impressive. What's the one with the wreath around the rifle?" I asked

"It's a CIB (combat infantry badge). What's your MOS, cherry?" the soldier asked.

"11B20, light weapons infantry," I replied.

"You'll get one if you are fortunate enough to come back," said the soldier.

"I thought we were pulling out of Vietnam," I said.

"Yeah, that's what they say, but where I was stationed, there are still major firefights going on."

"Where were you stationed?"

"Thua Thien, in the north central coast region of Vietnam," replied the soldier.

"Why do you want go back to Vietnam after three tours?"

"Because I love the country. You'll understand when you get there," he answered, taking another sip of his beer.

Why would any soldier want to return to a bloody war in which thousands of young Americans had already lost their lives? In my neighborhood there were three families who had buried a child killed in the Vietnam War.

The conversation with the decorated soldier only confirmed my worst fear—there were young men still dying over there.

Shaken by the conversation, I decided to return to the barracks. Besides, it was midnight, and the club would be closing soon.

"Did you and your friends enjoy the club tonight, Sergeant?" asked the bouncer.

"I had a great time. Too bad I have to go to Vietnam," I replied.

"Good luck, Sergeant."

"Thanks. I'm going to need it," I replied.

Walking into the brisk ocean air, the guys and I headed back to the barracks. Shake led the way, calling out cadences as we marched in single file.

Five black soldiers heard us calling out cadences and headed in our direction. Shake wasn't going to yield the right of way, and neither were the five black soldiers. In the inevitable collision, Shake drove his shoulder into a black soldier's chest.

The two soldiers exchanged punches as the rest of us kept the others from getting involved. Shake defended himself against his opponent's attempt to use a hand-to-hand combat taught in basic training. The technique was useless against Shake, who picked up the soldier and slammed him to the ground.

One of the soldiers struck RJ in the arm with a cane. Jet wrestled the soldier to the ground, only to be attacked by another. With both sides evenly matched, there was no alternative for anyone but to get involved in the altercation.

Little Joey jumped on the back of the soldier attacking Jet. Like a bull rider, Little Joey hung on with one hand, punching the soldier in the back of the head with the other. The biggest was coming at me like a freight train. RJ slammed the soldier on the head with a trash can lid. When the military police arrived on the scene, everyone scurried for the barracks.

Exhausted and sore, Jet and I climbed into our bunks for the night.

"Here we are, going to Vietnam to fight a war, and we choose to fight among ourselves," I said to Jet.

"I guess if we all got along, there wouldn't be any need for war," he replied.

***

15

Besides waking up with a serious hangover and a few bumps and bruises, Jet and I quickly discovered falling out for formation meant work detail. Anyone not assigned to that day's flight manifest was subject to spending the morning working. American troops were being shipped to Vietnam, and the military insisted on placing us on work detail.

After the morning roll call, Jet and I, along with others, were assigned to the enlisted men's club, wiping down tables, sweeping, and mopping the bar room floor. The smell of leftover booze and cigarettes gagged me as I swept. This was no place to be with a hangover, especially at eight in the morning. Our detail ended at noon, and we were free to go.

Since it would take a week before our names would be placed on a flight manifest, Jet and I decided not to show up for formation the following morning. Accompanied by Little Joey, we headed for the unoccupied barracks. The empty barracks provided a safe area to hang out until the formation was dismissed. The empty barracks were seldom patrolled, so it was unlikely the military police would find us.

The empty barracks provided a clear view of the grounds as the officer announced the morning flight manifest. The empty bunks were a testament to all the previous soldiers who had once occupied the barracks before being shipped over to Vietnam.

After the morning formation, everyone headed down the stairs to enjoy the day. We managed to avoid work detail until the fifth morning. Everyone agreed it was in our best interest to attend the morning formation, anticipating our names could be on the day's manifest.

That morning, everyone who had arrived at the deportation center on January 22 had been assigned to a flight manifest. After a short briefing, the group was instructed to return to the yard with their pillows, blankets, and personal belongings.

The soldiers were escorted to a holding hangar labeled Building No. 2. Several groups were ahead of mine. We were instructed to proceed to section G. We had strict orders to remain in the area and were not permitted to talk to anyone outside the group.

***

January 30. Everyone was up and eager to learn of the day's activities. Confined to the area, we had to wait for the officer in charge to escort us to breakfast.

After breakfast, the group of soldiers assigned to section F were transferred to their final holding area. Sections E and G remained in the building. Everyone anticipated our group would be on a plane by tomorrow.

After lunch, section E was escorted out of the building. Only section G remained. Another group would be arriving soon.

Late in the afternoon, the officer in charge instructed us to pack our things because the group was being transferred to the final holding area. Everyone secured their duffel bags and waited.

The officer in charge returned to escort my group to our final destination before leaving the States. As we entered the large hanger, the group ahead of us were boarding buses.

Everyone took a bunk and settled in. This was the only opportunity to make a phone call. I decided to call Mom one last time. I dialed and waited. Mom answered the call, surprised to hear my voice.

"Hi, Mom, this is the last time I'll be able to talk to you, so I thought I would call," I said.

"Don't say, 'last time.' You'll be back in no time," Mom replied in a sad voice.

"What difference does it make?"

"It makes a difference to me," said Mom.

"Is Dad home from work?"

"He's still at work. He should be home soon."

My eyes filled with tears as I said good-bye to the woman who nurtured and protected me for twenty years. She was devastated, knowing there was nothing she could do to keep me out of harm's way. I had caused this heartache, and there was nothing I could do to keep her from worrying about me.

"What's the matter?" asked Jet.

"I just talked with Mom," I replied.

"That's why I didn't call home," said Jet.

***

Later that in evening, I was lying on my bunk when the transportation arrived to take us to the airport. After a short briefing, the group was instructed to board the buses.

Following the others, I stepped out into the cool, damp night. I boarded the first bus and took the first available seat. The officer in charge boarded the bus last, and the driver closed the door.

The driver took the route across the Oakland Bay Bridge, heading for Travis Air Force Base. Glancing out the window, I focused on the reflection of the lights on the water as we drove over the bridge. The rhythm of the tires rolling over the expansion joints was in synch with my heartbeat.

The driver turned into the entrance to the base, where a 747 Pan American jetliner was awaiting our arrival. The jet engines were idling as we were given clearance to board. Airline stewardesses were awaiting our arrival at the front and rear exits of the plane.

Jet and I entered the cabin and took the first two empty seats. I took the aisle seat and Jet took the middle seat. Little Joey, RJ, and Shake were seated nearby.

The pilot welcomed us aboard flight 229 to Southeast Asia and announced that we would be making refueling stops in Anchorage, Alaska, and Yokota Air Force Base, Japan, before reaching our final destination: Bien Hoa Air Force Base, sixteen miles from Saigon.

The pilot revved the engines and slowly taxied down the runway. With the jetliner in position for takeoff, the tower gave the pilot clearance, and he went full throttle.

At 12:01 a.m., the jetliner lifted off the runway. The lights were turned down in the cabin. I could only wonder which soldiers would return and which would not. The plane dipped its wing and headed for Anchorage. Although friends were seated nearby, I could only feel desolation and despair.

Episode Three

Tan Son Nhut Processing Center

January 31. After flying the entire day, the jetliner touched down at Bien Hoa Air Force Base. We arrived on the same calendar day the plane departed from Travis Air Force Base. Unfortunately, time in-country didn't start until we arrived in country.

"Welcome to Indochina, gentlemen," announced the pilot. "On behalf of our flight crew, we would like to wish each and every one of you a safe return."

A soldier wearing starched jungle fatigues boarded the jetliner. Taking the microphone he made an announcement. "Welcome to Vietnam. In case of a mortar attack while departing the plane, immediately hit the ground and low crawl to the nearest wall. You are in a combat zone."

"Did he say mortar attack?" I whispered.

"That's what he said," Jet answered, staring out the window.

Everyone retrieved their personal belongings and departed the plane. When I stepped outside the cabin, I was hit with a blast of hot air. The plane had departed Travis Air Force Base when the outdoor temperature was 53 degrees Fahrenheit. Now I was in 116 degree brain-scorching heat.

The new arrivals were quickly escorted to a military bus without air conditioning, parked outside the airline terminal. When the bus was filled to capacity, the driver headed to the Tan Son Nhut Processing Center.

The drive revealed the beauty and filth of a country I had never seen before. The smell of human waste and diesel filled the air. A bus was parked on the side of the road, waiting for an elderly Vietnamese woman who was urinating. Water buffalo roamed freely as peasant farmers planted rice in their fields. Bicycles, scooters, and three-wheeled taxis crowded the highway, along with an occasional American-made automobile.

Highway 1 merged the countryside with a manufacturing district, reflecting America's involvement in the war. A sign indicated we were nearing the processing center compound.

As the driver approached the compound, armed guards waved him through the gates. Concertina wire was strung along the top of a chain-link fence, along with green sandbags.

The bus came to a stop next to a tent surrounded by sandbags stacked three feet high. A sergeant wearing a name tag with the name Williams boarded the bus.

"Welcome to your home for the next year," said the sergeant. "Grab your duffel bags and take a seat under the tent."

I climbed off the bus and located my duffel bag. Following the others, I took a seat.

"The first thing we're going to do today is fill out forms," said Sergeant Williams. "These forms are important, so make sure they filled out accurately and legibly."

"Is it always this hot?" I asked.

"This is nothing. It gets hotter," replied Sergeant Williams.

With the completion of the first form, I designated Mom as the beneficiary of my death benefit.

After completing several other forms, we new arrivals were escorted to the infirmary. Medics explained the importance of taking the malaria medication. "Gentlemen, you have two choices!" shouted the medic. "Take it or don't take it. I don't care, but I strongly suggest you start today. The malaria pills must be taken every day. You will be issued two types of pills.

The white pill is to be taken Monday through Saturday. The big orange pill is to be taken on Sunday only. There are some side effects, so don't be alarmed. Your body will adjust to it."

"What kind of side effects?" Jet asked.

"Diarrhea," said the sergeant with a sarcastic smirk on his face.

"That's shitty," said Jet, getting a laugh from the crowd.

The next stop was the dental clinic. Everyone's teeth were treated with fluoride to help prevent cavities, in case you weren't able to brush on a daily basis.

The final stop of the day was finance. Everyone stood outside to get out of the heat. When it was my turn, I was asked to turn in my US currency.

"What for?" I asked.

"We have to exchange MPC (military payment currency) for US currency. It's the only form of money allowed in Vietnam," replied the finance clerk.

I reached into my pocket and pulled out two twenty-dollar bills along with the dollar given to me for good luck. I handed over the twenties, but refused to give the clerk the dollar.

"The dollar, please," said the finance clerk.

"Sorry, I can't. It's the dollar my grandmother gave me for good luck, and I will never part with it," I answered.

The finance clerk returned two twenties in MPC.

MPC looked more like Monopoly money than official currency. Printed on durable paper with layers of lines, created colorful banknotes. The military created MPC to reduce profiteering and eliminate the use of the US dollar in local villages. The piastre was the official Vietnamese currency, with a value of two hundred piastres to one US dollar. I was going to miss the good old American greenback.

"When you reach your new duty station, you will fill out a form that will determine how much pay you can draw every payday. You will get paid once a month in Vietnam," said the clerk.

"How much do I need?" I asked.

"That's up to you. Everyone draws a small amount, and the remainder of your pay goes into savings," replied the clerk.

When everyone had exchanged their money for MPC, we were issued a pillow and blanket, along with a barracks assignment. Exhausted from the first day's unbearable heat, I decided to relax in the barracks until dinner. All the bunks were covered with mosquito nets—malaria was taken seriously in this country.

At dinnertime, everyone headed for the mess hall. Surprisingly, the food was appetizing. My plate filled with an assortment of entrées, I enjoyed dinner. Uncertain where I would be tomorrow, I returned to the barracks for the evening.

***

February 2. On my second day in-country, I was awakened by a 6:00 a.m. wake-up call. The humidity had dampened my fatigue shirt. I pulled out a clean pair of jungle fatigues and headed for a shower. The showers were located at the end of the barracks. I was going to have to adapt to my new living conditions.

Showered and dressed, I was ready for the second day of processing. I met Jet at the mess hall for an early breakfast.

"Two eggs over medium," I ordered.

"Certainly. Where's your plate, soldier?" replied the spoon.

Expecting two eggs cooked to order, I instead got a heaping spoonful of shit on a shingle (white gravy with chipped beef) dumped onto my plate.

"There's your two eggs over medium, soldier. What the hell do you think this is—a coffee shop?" said the spoon jokingly.

The schedule for the day was to report to the yard at 8:00 a.m. promptly. Eager to learn our new duty assignment, we headed to where the other soldiers were gathered. We assumed all of us would remain together. Jet and I waited eagerly to hear our new duty assignment.

At 8:35 a.m., a staff sergeant appeared in front of the formation and addressed the crowd. "Listen up, everyone. The following individuals have been assigned to the First Cavalry Division."

Everyone listened with enthusiasm as the sergeant identified the soldiers. When the entire list had been read, Jet and I were the only soldiers selected from our group. Little Joey, RJ, and Shake had been excluded.

The sergeant dismissed the formation and introduced a representative from the First Cavalry Division.

"You should consider yourself fortunate to serve with the First Cavalry. The Cavalry is one of the most decorated combat divisions in the history of the United States Army. The Cavalry served in World War II and Korea, and then transferred to Vietnam in 1965. The history of the Cavalry dates back to the American Civil War and the Indian Wars. It is remembered most for the disastrous military engagement with the Sioux Nation at the Battle of the Little Bighorn. Although their yellow, triangular patch is impressive, there's a tragic story behind the patch.

The legend is that the horse's head, cut off diagonally at the neck, represents the horse that was never ridden. The diagonal stripe represents the line that was never crossed. And the color speaks for itself—yellow. The Cavalry has since regained its colors and is now referred to as the Air Cavalry Division. Gentlemen, turn in your pillows and secure your belongings. You are about to enter the gates of the First Team Academy."

Jet and I turned in our pillows and returned to the barracks to secure our duffel bags. When we returned, our friends were waiting to say good-bye.

"I wish I were going with you," said Little Joey sadly.

"I wish you were too," I replied.

"This is my parents' address. When you reach your duty station, write my dad. He will send you my military address."

Uncertain of our futures, the three of us pledged to get together when we returned to the States. Jet and I boarded the bus, waving to our friends left behind.

The driver returned to the air force base, entering through the main entrance. Rows of protected buildings clearly indicated the possibility of incoming artillery.

A bright yellow cavalry patch painted on the side of a metal building indicated we had arrived at the First Team Academy. We were greeted by an academy member. Everyone was eager to learn about our new duty station.

"Welcome to the First Team Academy Training Center, where you will undergo seven days of intense RVN (Republic of Vietnam) training. You will be confined to the area while you're in training. The only time you will be allowed to leave the compound is when you are assigned to green-line guard. Any questions, gentlemen? If not, follow me to the orderly's office."

I entered the orderly's office and was promoted to E3 (private first class). The military was never generous, so I wondered why I had suddenly been promoted two pay grades. "That sounds great, but why?" I asked.

"In order to serve in a combat zone, you have to be a minimum E3 pay grade," replied the orderly.

"I knew there had to be a reason," I replied sarcastically.

"Next!" shouted the orderly.

"Wait a minute. I'm a sole surviving son!" I shouted in desperation.

"Sorry, your orders are cut."

"I can't believe this is happening to me. It's a law that has been in effect since World War II. Why isn't anyone listening to me?"

"Sorry, there's nothing I can do about it," replied the orderly.

Jet and I were assigned to a barracks and directed to a storage facility to turn in all of our personal belongings. Anything that wasn't military issue would remain in storage.

"Why can't we keep our personal belongings?" asked Jet.

"Where you're headed, you won't need personal belongings. Here's your claim ticket. Don't lose it. It's the only way to retrieve your belongings," said the storage attendant.

"How do they expect me not to lose this ticket?" wondered Jet.

"I don't know. I don't plan on being in the field very long," I replied.

"Yeah, right, let's get some lunch," said Jet.

Jet and I dropped off our duffel bags and headed for the mess hall. First in line, we waited for the mess hall to open. Unexpectedly, two soldiers jumped to the front of the line.

"Hey, what's going on?" I said.

26

"Step aside, cherry, time in-country," said one of the soldiers, rushing into the mess.

"What the hell was that about?" Jet asked.

"I don't know. I guess it has something to do with how long you've been in Vietnam," I replied.

There wasn't much of a selection and the food wasn't very appetizing. Like the sleeping conditions, the chow was becoming progressively less desirable. Was it because we getting closer to the battlefield?

After dinner, everyone was required to attend a mandatory formation in front of the stage.

"The following individuals have been assigned to green-line guard for the night," announced the First Team staff member.

"What the hell is green-line guard?" Jet asked.

"The green line is the perimeter of the entire base. Anything beyond that belongs to the enemy," replied the First Team staff member.

Unfortunately, my name, along with three others, was on the list. Jet escaped green-line guard for the night and returned to the barracks. I was instructed to report to the armory.

I was assigned to bunker number four and issued a weapon, along with three rounds of ammo. This was alarming, since the only thing I could accomplish with three rounds was commit suicide.

The base was on yellow alert due to a recent attack. Although there had been no casualties, I was concerned about an attack while I was on guard. Bunker number four was located directly behind the First Team barracks. There were only two soldiers per bunker. It was going to be a long night.

The soldier sharing guard duty with me volunteered to take the first watch. I agreed to pull the second, beginning at midnight. With very little conversation between us, I decided to sleep.

Suddenly I was awakened by a loud blast. "What the hell was that?" I asked.

"It's an illumination round. Bunker number five called it in. Someone saw movement in the wood line," said the soldier.

"Is it the enemy?" I wondered nervously.

"It's probably just a shadow," the soldier calmly replied.

Episode Four

First Team Academy

February 3. Although there were scary moments, I survived my first night of green-line guard. Returning to the barracks, I joined Jet for an early morning mess hall breakfast. It was the first of seven days of RVN training. Having recently completing two months of RVN training stateside, the First Team Academy staff was about to cram eight weeks' worth of jungle warfare know-how into seven days for its newest recruits.

Unfortunately, the first day of training turned out to be disastrous for two soldiers. We were warned not to pick up anything off the ground. One soldier ignored the warning and reached for a discharged dupper round (grenade). As he examined the shiny object, it exploded in his hand, seriously wounding him and a soldier nearby. A dupper round must make sixteen revolutions before detonating. The soldier must have picked up the round in its final rotation.

The two soldiers lay on the ground in agonizing pain, but alive. They were lucky to have survived the blast. They were treated in the field and taken to the hospital at Bien Hoa Air Force Base. Once stable, they were medevaced (medically evacuated) to Yokota Air Force Base to recuperate. Both soldiers received Purple Hearts and were discharged from the army. Their tours ended before they started.

***

The first day of RVN training was dedicated to the art of guerrilla warfare. To defend against the enemy's unconventional style of war, deception was imperative. It was important to understand the country's terrain, along with the extreme weather conditions. We were fighting an enemy on their own terms.

The second day of training consisted of rifle and grenade range practice. I fired the M-16 with confidence and accuracy. I launched a dozen grenades into the air as if they were baseballs. By day's end, I dreaded using these destructive weapons to kill someone.

The third day was dedicated to demonstrations of military air support. Making a low pass, a Cobra gunship displayed its destructive arsenal of weapons. Known among us as "Blue Max," the versatile attack weapon was used throughout Vietnam. No matter how determined the force, the enemy always feared the wrath of a Cobra's rockets, miniguns, grenades and antitank weapons. The enemy referred to this gunship as "Whispering Death."

The second demonstration of the day was provided by an army ground attack aircraft known as "Rash Bird." The pilot demonstrated an arsenal of firepower capabilities. Next came a demonstration of a Huey OH-6, known as "Loach." The lightweight single-engine helicopter was used for personal transport, attack missions, and jungle observation.

The fourth day of training consisted of insertion and extraction maneuvers from a UH-1 helicopter. The First Team Academy demonstrated how to properly board a helicopter from a LZ (landing zone) and depart a helicopter from a PZ (pickup zone). This model of Huey, generally referred to as "slicks" or "birds," was a turbine-powered helicopter that proved to be a valuable source of transportation for the First Cavalry Division.

The remaining three days of training consisted of instruction on NDPs (night defensive perimeters), ambushes, and booby traps. The majority of the casualties occurred in company-size engagements, and the army had adopted a new strategy. The enemy working in groups as small as five or six, and the war had turned from large-scale battles into small firefights and ambushes.

Instruction on M-18 claymores, trip flares, automatic ambushes, and booby traps provided valuable night defense against a determined enemy force, warning us if the enemy penetrated a perimeter.

Alphas were an automatic ambush consisting of a series of M-18 claymores daisy-chained together with detonation cord. The blasting cap was in the last claymore, wired to a battery. Two wires from an extension cord were wrapped separately around two plastic spoons and secured back to back with a rubber band. Trip wire was secured to a plastic knife through a hole in the handle and inserted between the two spoons. The trip wire was secured to a tree on the other side of the trotter (traveled enemy trail).

At night when the enemy traveled on the trotter, they would trip the wire. The knife would slide through the two spoons, making a positive connection and detonating all the claymores. The outcome was bad news for the enemy.

The NVA and Viet Cong were notorious for creating their own booby traps, especially punji pits and bamboo whips. Dipped in human feces, bamboo spikes were a menace to American troops.

The Viet Cong were known for booby traps made out of US ammunition. Captured M-33 grenades were placed in C-ration cans with the safety pin removed. The cans were mounted on the side of a tree trunk. A wire was tied to the striker lever and strung across a well-traveled trotter.

Another menace to soldiers was created from a single M-60 machine gun round placed into a piece of bamboo. Seated on top of a nail, the round was embedded into the ground with the tip exposed. When a GI stepped on the round, the weight of his foot pushed the shell casing against the nail, exploding the round and severely injuring a foot.

Claymores in enemy hands were just as effective against the American troops. Detonating claymores at eye level caused maximum damage to a patrol. Communist mines were also a menace to Americans. The "Bouncing Betty," a bounding mine detonated at eye level, inflicted maximum damage above the waist.

The seventh and final day of RVN training was dedicated to education on patrolling in the jungle. The First Team demonstrated proper technique in navigating trotters and searching for signs of the enemy. At the end of the day, I could only wonder if any of this training would give me the advantage against an enemy we were fighting in their own backyard.

After dinner, a mandatory formation was called to issue duty assignments. Jet and I were confident we would remain together and finally have a place to call home.

A high-ranking officer stood on the stage to make the announcement. "At ease, gentlemen. I have some bad news for some of you. Recently one of our infantry units hit the shit. For the new grunts in country, that means they just got their asses kicked by the enemy. Six soldiers were killed and sixteen others were seriously wounded. Unfortunately, some of you are going to replace those soldiers. All right, listen up. The following individuals have been reassigned to Bravo Company, Second Battalion, Eighth Regiment, First Cavalry Division."

The officer read the names in alphabetical order. I lowered my head, praying my name wouldn't be called.

Unfortunately, my name was included in the list. Jet's was not. Although I would remain with seven familiar faces, they were merely acquaintances. I rushed over to see if Jet's name had been overlooked. The officer glanced through his list, confirming Jet's name wasn't on it.

That's when I realized I was heading for a combat zone and there was nothing I could do about it. In desperation I decided to write a letter to my congressman.

US Congressman
Washington, DC

Dear Congressman,

I hope this letter finds you well. As for myself, I am currently serving in Vietnam, just about to go into combat. I hope with the power invested in your office, you can help me with my dilemma. I am the only son born to my parents, and if I am killed in combat, there will be no one to carry on the family name. According to military regulations, a sole surviving son does not have to serve in a combat zone. I am not opposed to serving in Vietnam, I just don't want to be killed.

I hope you can find it in your heart to help me. I look forward to hearing from you or your office as soon as possible.

Sincerely,
Ricky R. Garcia, Private First Class
Company B, 2nd of the 8th, 1st Cavalry Division,
Blackfoot Platoon

***

February 10. The soldiers assigned to Bravo Company were awakened by an early wake-up call, to be flown to battalion headquarters. Knowing I was headed for combat, I hadn't gotten much sleep. Jet was seated on his bunk as I packed my duffel bag.

"I guess this is it, troop," said Jet sadly.

"Don't worry. When this is over, we'll have a beer and tell each other war stories," I replied, giving Jet a hug. Not knowing if I would ever see my friend again, I slung my duffel bag over my shoulder and headed for the bus waiting to transport us to the airport.

There was an eerie silence as I entered the bus. Besides myself, assigned to Blackfoot Platoon were JC and Duggy from Minnesota, Cole from South Dakota, and Bart, Holt, and Stanney from Iowa. Knowing we were the replacements for six recently lost soldiers was weighing heavy on everyone's minds. I was at the crossroads of my future, with a long and lonely road ahead of me.

Before the break of dawn, we arrived at Bien Hoa Airport. Our instructions were to head into the terminal and wait for our flight manifest to be called. Without Jet or Little Joey, I was alone.

Shortly after eight, our flight manifest was called. I picked up my duffel bag and followed the others to the tarmac, where an AC-140 transport with engines idling was waiting for us to board. In a nearby hangar, I witnessed six coffins draped in American flags being lifted into a cargo plane to be transported to the States. I could only pray that I wouldn't suffer the same fate.

I took the first available seat and prepared for takeoff. The pilot revved the engines and began to taxi down the runway. The pilot went full throttle, and like a wooden ship on the ocean, the military transport creaked as it lifted off the runway.

Episode Five

Fire Base Fontaine

February 10. With landing gear fully extended, the pilot approached a clay runway. The C-140 transport touched down, taxiing to the end of the runway. A convoy of "deuce and a half" trucks rolled up next to the transport plane as the flight crew lowered the ramp. A deuce and a half was a two and a half ton military truck used in day-to-day activities.

Everyone made their way down the ramp and boarded the waiting trucks. The convoy rolled through the countryside, making its way to Fire Base Mace. The drivers slowed their vehicles, as they passed a Vietnamese village. Vietnamese children ran alongside the convoy, begging for food, as villagers waved.

A soldier seated next to me tossed a C-ration can at one of the village children, nearly injuring him. I felt obligated to say something. "Hey, you could have hurt that kid."

"He's a gook. He's probably going to grow up to be VC anyway," said the soldier.

"Yeah, but right now he's just a kid," I said.

The convoy came to a stop while a water buffalo crossed the road. Nearby rice paddies indicated the villagers were peasant farmers. The beauty of their country made it difficult to believe a war was being fought nearby.

Guarding the entrance of the fortified fire base were several armed guards. The convoy came to a stop in front of the supply room. An overweight supply sergeant with a cigar in his mouth was awaiting our arrival.

"Welcome to Vietnam, FNGs. For the new guys in-country, that means 'fucking new guys.' The first thing you're going to do is place all your fatigues on the supply room floor, including your boots and underwear," said the supply sergeant, lighting his cigar with his shiny Zippo lighter.

"Including my underwear?" asked Holt.

"Yes, including your underwear. You're grunts now. Where you're headed, you won't need underwear," replied the sergeant.

"I don't know about you, but I need a change of underwear every day," I said to Holt.

"Not in the jungle," said the sergeant sarcastically.

All of us dumped our jungle warfare clothing on the supply room floor. The supply sergeant issued each man a weapon, along with a rucksack, poncho, poncho liner, rubber air mattress, canteens, wool night shirt, olive drab towel, steel pot (helmet), and small plastic bottle.

"What's in the plastic bottle?" asked Bart.

"Read the label; it's insect repellent. We call it bug juice," replied the supply sergeant. "You'll need it to keep the mosquitoes from eating you alive. All right, listen up. Your current field location for second battalion is Fire Base Fontaine, located near Ap Rung, south of Highway 1. It's about a two-hour ride, so get ready to rock and roll."

Equipped with a rucksack and weapon, I climbed aboard the convoy. The drivers fired up their engines and made their way through the gate. The five-truck convoy was escorted by a jeep, armed with a 50-caliber machine gun. Everyone inhaled diesel fumes as the convoy passed villages and hamlets.

We feared an enemy attack at any moment. The drive was stressful, but scenic. When the convoy arrived at Ap Rung, the escort jeep slowed to turn onto a dirt road. Heading south, we approached a village situated next to a creek. Children waved bags of *consai* (homegrown marijuana) as village hookers groomed their hair.

Two villagers standing in the wood line caught my attention as the convoy crossed the creek. The black pajamas made me wonder if they were Viet Cong. Less than a hundred meters from the fire base, a loud blast lifted the rear of the deuce and a half, throwing everyone from their seats.

The convoy came to a complete stop. Some soldiers took cover under the bench seat, and others climbed off the truck.

"Anyone hurt?" shouted the driver.

"What the hell happened?" shouted Duggy.

"It looks like we rolled over a land mine. What's the damage?"

"The tire is blown off the rim!"

"I think we can make it to the fire base. Let's get moving," said the driver, climbing back into the cab and starting the engine.

With everyone back on the truck, the driver accelerated. Looking back at the crater in the road, I realized I had just had my first encounter with the enemy.

Guard bunkers, with three layers of sandbags, protected the entrance to Fire Base Fontaine. When the entire convoy was inside the fire base, the damaged truck came to a stop next to a shady canopy. The grunts sitting in the shade glared at us as we climbed off the back of the truck.

"FNGs wait here. I need to locate the company commander," said the company clerk.

I entered the shade of a large canvas tent, catching the attention of the cook. "Breakfast is over, cherry. Lunch is served at noon. Now get lost."

"Sorry, I'm new around here," I replied.

"What's your MOS, cherry?"

"11B20."

"Damn, I was hoping you were the new cook."

"I cooked in civilian life," I replied.

"That's not going to do me any good. What's your name, cherry?"

"Garcia. What's yours?"

"Sam, but everyone calls me Sam the Spoon."

Curious to understand my new duty assignment, I began to explore the fire base. Conveniently located next to the mess hall were the officers' quarters. Nearby was a wooden platform constructed out of trees from the jungle. It was equipped with field radios and antennas. A communications officer directed air traffic.

Three layers of sandbags stacked on a metal culvert and a six foot high chain-link fence secured the ammo dump. Seated in the shade of a canopy was a group of grungy-looking grunts enjoying a game of high-stakes poker.

Located near the ammo dump was a small wooden shack. The smell of urine indicated it was the latrine. Known as "the shitter," the shack provided five holes in a plank of wood that emptied into diesel barrels. A hatch door in the back of the shack gave access for disposing of the contents in the barrels.

On the farthest side of the fire base were artillery and mortars. The barrels of three 105 cannons shone majestically in the sun, capable of providing fire support up to 11,000 meters. Set up nearby was mortar platoon, providing close-in fire support.

Hooches along the perimeter housed the grunts securing the fire base. Outside the fire base was an oiled-down pad providing a level landing area for helicopters. Three rows of barbed and concertina wire prevented the enemy from penetrating the perimeter during the night.

After a brief tour, I returned to the convoy. The company clerk was addressing the FNGs as the driver of the truck was tightening the final nut on the spare tire.

"All right, FNGs, listen up. The new guys going to the field tomorrow are now in the hands of the supply sergeant. He'll tell you what to do. See you on log day," said the company clerk, referring to the day he'd be back to resupply us, as he climbed into the cab of the truck.

"FNGs assigned to Bravo Company, come with me!" shouted the supply sergeant.

The replacements followed the supply sergeant to the ammo dump, where he began opening boxes of C-rations and LRPs (long range patrol food packets), along with cans of ammunition, grenades, and claymore mines.

"Your company is currently in the field and will be resupplied tomorrow. You have one night to get your shit together, because you'll be joining them in the morning. Make sure you have a three-day supply of food and water, and plenty of ammo. You're going to need it. Your platoon is working in a hot AO (area of operation)."

"How much ammo do I need?" asked Bart.

"Boy, your shit is weak," said the supply sergeant sarcastically. He distributed two bandoliers of M-16 ammo and 250 rounds of M-60 ammo to each of us.

40

"Why does everyone have to carry 250 rounds of machine-gun ammo?" asked Bart.

"Because when you hit the shit, you're going to be grateful you have it," said the supply sergeant.

He retrieved a C-ration box and an LRP package and held them up in the air. "Pack enough of these to last three days."

"How much is a three-day supply?" asked Cole.

"Plan on three meals a day, usually two cans of C-rations and an LRP if you want a hot meal. As far as water is concerned, grunts usually carry a five-quart, a two-quart, and a one-quart canteen," said the supply sergeant.

"What the hell is a LRP?" asked Holt.

"An LRP is a long range patrol meal. It's the only hot meal you're going to get in the field. Just add boiling water. They taste great. I eat them all the time on the fire base."

"Where can we fill our canteens with water?" asked Bart.

"The water tank is located by the entrance to the fire base."

I packed my rucksack with plenty of C-rations and LRPs, along with the rest of the things I had been issued. I attached the claymore and machine gun ammo and lifted the rucksack. I managed to place the heavy rucksack on my back but struggled to stay on my feet. The weight shifted to one side, and I fell to the ground. The supply sergeant laughed as he helped me to my feet.

After everyone was supplied with food and ammo, the supply sergeant searched the fire base for a place to sleep. All the hooches were claimed by Alpha Company, but the supply sergeant manage to locate two empty hooches that would house eight of us for the night.

41

The entire evening I lay awake, watching illumination rounds light up the fire base and listening to the thump of mortar rounds being launched into the jungle, along with an occasional barrage of 105 artillery shells. The only thought on my mind was going into combat in the morning.

Episode Six

Joining Blackfoot

February 15. Awakened by chatter, I climbed out my hooch and joined the group of soldiers standing over a 105 artillery shell.

"Where the hell did that come from?" I asked.

"The dinks launched it into the fire base early this morning," replied an onlooker.

"What's a dink?" asked Holt curiously.

"Boy, your shit is weak. It's another name for Charlie, dumb shit," replied Duggy. Both words referred to the Viet Cong.

"Thank God it didn't explode," replied Holt.

Cole agreed. "No shit, we'd all be dead."

"All right, you renegades, what's this cluster fuck all about?" said Alpha Company's CO.

"What's a cluster fuck?" asked Holt.

"Boy, you better get your shit together before you get out in the field," said the CO sarcastically. "A cluster fuck is a bunch of grungy grunts like you standing around staring at a dud artillery shell. The demolition crew is on their way, so let's clear the area."

I was concerned about Holt. Holt wasn't able to process information like others. Why Holt had been sent to the front line was just as mysterious as the enemy's ability to launch one of our own 105 artillery rounds into the fire base. This was my second day on the fire base, and I had just experienced my second encounter with the enemy.

The arrival of the convoy meant it was time to prepare for my first mission. The company clerk gathered the replacements

43

and ordered everyone to head for the LZ. Given my full load of ammunition, a direct hit and I would go up like an explosion in a fireworks factory.

I don't think any soldier can prepare for battle. Although we had been trained in guerilla warfare, the army neglected to explain the psychological effects of war, especially the constant fear of death.

What was known was that, on February 7, 1971, Blackfoot Platoon engaged a determined and hostile enemy force. The outcome that day was sixteen casualties, ten line ones and six line twos. In plain English, that meant ten soldiers were wounded and six soldiers were killed. That day ended in victory for the enemy and defeat for the Americans.

It was a devastating loss for Bravo Company, especially for the individuals who survived the battle. How was such an outcome possible?

In 1971, the United States was withdrawing troops. The war that had peaked during the 1968 Tet offensive was slowly coming to an end, but for the eight replacement soldiers assigned to Bravo Company, it was just beginning.

"FNGs, get your shit on! The birds are on their way!" shouted the supply sergeant.

In the distance, I could hear the faint rumbling of rotor blades, a sound that would haunt me for the rest of my life. A gaggle of five Huey helicopters banked overhead and approached the LZ.

"Pop smoke, birds inbound! Garcia, Duggy, Bart, and Cole, you're on the first bird. The remaining soldiers will follow on the second!" shouted the supply sergeant, pulling the ring from a canister of yellow smoke and tossing it to the ground.

The supply sergeant stood in the center of the oiled-down landing zone, guiding in the first helicopter. The bird came in with its nose slightly tilted upward, bouncing off the hard surface. The pilot glared over his shoulder as the door gunner motioned for us to board.

I struggled with my rucksack. A strong gust of wind from the rotor blades made it difficult to stay on my feet. The company clerk tossed a red sack labeled "US Mail" into the cabin as the four of us approached the helicopter. We lowered our heads so as not to get our heads chopped off by the blades.

With a nudge from the door gunner, I managed to position myself on the cabin floor, bracing my feet on the skid. The pilot pulled back on the control lever clearing the trees. Seeing the look of despair on my face, the door gunner assured me I wasn't going to fall out of the cabin.

The gaggle of helicopters headed for a logging road at the base of a nearby mountain range. Blackfoot Platoon was eager to be resupplied. As the first helicopter approached, members of the platoon were standing off to the side. When both skids of the helicopter were securely on the ground, a soldier rushed in and retrieved the red mail sack.

I stepped off the skid and was directed toward a Hispanic soldier standing off to the side of the road. Reeking of body odor, the soldier instructed us to wait for the remaining new arrivals.

The pilot immediately lifted off the logging road to return to the fire base. The second helicopter arrived with Holt, JC, and Stanney, along with boxes of C-rations and LRPs.

"Welcome to Blackfoot, cherries. My name is Sergeant Tomas, acting platoon leader. For now, you FNGs are assigned to John's squad. He's the Puerto Rican over there picking his ass."

It appeared our new squad leader had a missing tooth, and the gap was prominent. Shaking his head as we approached, John clearly wasn't too happy to see us.

"Hell, no! I'm not taking no FNGs," he said angrily.

"The platoon leader assigned us to your squad," said Duggy.

"Go talk to Joe. I don't want the responsibility of breaking in any fucking new cherries."

"Who's Joe?" asked Bart.

"Joe's the one standing over there by the red mail sack," said John.

The seven of us followed John over to Joe's position, but he wasn't happy to see us either. "What the hell do you want?"

"John said we were assigned to your squad?" asked Duggy.

"Like hell you are! I don't need any fucking cherries in my squad!" shouted Joe, staring Duggy in the eye.

"Hold the fucking noise down," said the platoon leader.

"I'm not taking any fucking cherries!"

"I don't care who gets the cherries, just have them ready to move out in ten mikes (minutes)."

"All right, cherries, come with me," said John. "I hope you FNGs have plenty of ammo."

"I have more than I can carry," Bart replied.

"You FNGs better have your shit together. It's going to take time to get you combat effective. Even with you cherries, the platoon is below maximum strength. We just lost four of our best men, and now I have to go into combat with a bunch of cherries. You cherries wait over there until I figure out what I'm going to do with you," said John.

Another helicopter arrived with the water supply. The door gunner rolled the rubber blivet out of the cabin. Two soldiers promptly rolled the blivet over to the side of the road. Joe attached a stainless-steel valve to the end and filled his five-quart.

The last bird arrived with several duffel bags of clean clothes, along with six cases of sodas. I looked on as soldiers packed their rucksacks with C-rations and LRPs.

The experienced grunts in the platoon didn't appear to be too concerned about the enemy, because after a quick change of jungle fatigues, the majority of grunts settled down to read their mail.

Static from the field radio signaled an incoming call. The RTO (radio operator) handed the platoon leader the handset and responded. After a brief conversation, the platoon leader met with his two team leaders.

"Hey, FNGs, I have a job for you," said our new team leader. "Put the dirty jungle fatigues in the duffel bags, and pick up all the unused C-rations and LRPs, along with the mail sack and water blivet. When the backlog bird arrives, load all the crap on the helicopter. This will be your responsibility until the next FNGs arrive. Now get going. We're moving out in five."

The final bird of the day touched down, and we loaded everything not consumed back onto the bird. We watched with regret as the helicopter cleared the treetops and headed back to the fire base. The time had come to battle the most feared predator known to man—the enemy.

"Pop smoke, birds inbound!" shouted Sergeant Tomas.

"Get your shit on, FNGs. The birds are on their way. Listen up. Four of the new guys on the first bird. The rest of you are on bird five with me. And blouse up those damn fatigues, cherries! You're fucking grunts now, so look like it!" said John, heading for the dirt road.

"What the hell did he say?" asked Bart.

"I think he said you're riding on helicopter number four. I don't have a clue what he meant about blousing your fatigues," said Duggy.

Another gaggle of helicopters approached the logging road, landing simultaneously. With a bad feeling in my gut, I climbed aboard helicopter five. Five helicopters lifted off the road, flying along the base of the mountain range.

With a panoramic view of the jungle and no protection from ground fire, the birds skimmed over the treetops. My only thought was taking a round and going down.

"All right, FNGs we're going in!" screamed John. "If we draw fire when we hit the ground, pull the emergency release on your rucksack and hit the ground firing!"

I braced my feet on the skid and drew a deep breath as the helicopter touched down. John stepped off the skid and ran for the wood line. The rest of us followed. The gaggle quickly lifted off. Both squad leaders secured the perimeter.

"Keep a lookout for dinks. I'm not going to get my shit blown away because of a fucking cherry," cried the squad leader.

John casually walked up to Duggy, handing him the M-60 machine gun. "Hey big guy, you're the new machine gunner, and Bart is your assistant machine gunner," he said.

"What the hell am I supposed to do with this?" asked Duggy.

"Don't worry, you'll learn."

"If anyone is capable of carrying the machine gun, it's you," said Bart.

"Just make sure you have plenty of ammo when we hit the shit," said Duggy jokingly. He appeared to be comfortable with his new position, but wasn't too thrilled about his assistant.

"Listen up, FNGs!" shouted John. "I'm only going to tell you once. Our missions are search and destroy. Because of the constant threat of enemy ambushes, we have to be ready to kill Charlie before he kills us. Forget that crap you learned in RVN training. This is the way it's done in the field.

"At the front of the line is the point team. The point team consists of the point man, slack man, and platoon leader. Point demands a jungle-wise grunt, because there's no room for mistakes. The slack position also requires a jungle-wise grunt. His job is to look out for the point man and help break brush. The third man is our platoon leader. Good or bad, the platoon leader makes all the decisions.

"Behind the platoon leader is the platoon RTO, followed by the squad leader and his gun team. Bringing up the rear is drag position. Besides protecting the rear, he is responsible for an accurate pace count. Don't think the drag position is the safest position because you're in the rear. The enemy will allow the point team past the prime killing zone in order to inflect maximum damage.

"All right, FNGs, fall in behind me. Garcia, you're in the rear, next to drag, and pay attention. I don't want my shit blown away because of some inexperienced cherry."

"John, the platoon leader wants you up front," said the squad RTO.

"I'll be there in a minute," John replied. "FNGs, be prepared to move out when I get back."

After briefing with his team leaders, the platoon leader addressed the platoon.

"Listen up, everyone. There's been a change in mission. Besides working in a fucking hot AO, we now have to search for a pilot who fell out of his helicopter. I hope you have a strong stomach, because when we find him, he's going to smell like death-sucking lemon."

Sergeant Tomas gave the order to move out, and the point team headed down the road. My eyes were focused on the wood line. With an overwhelming feeling of fear, I wondered if I would leave Vietnam alive.

I was relieved when the point team linked up with an APC (armored personnel carrier). Sergeant Tomas ordered the platoon to spread out and set up for the evening.

"Garcia, set up over there by those two APCs," said John.

"Why between and not behind the APCs?" I said.

"Don't worry. If we hit the shit, you can run and hide. You fucking cherry! Just do what I tell you!"

I looked on curiously as the jungle-wise grunts began their ritual of setting up for the night, laying out their ponchos and poncho liners on top of their deflated air mattresses.

Just before nightfall, a long-haired grunt wearing a handkerchief around his forehead walked over and kneeled down beside me. "I'm Hoskie. I hope Joe didn't scare you today. He's got a lot on his mind, just like everyone else who survived the ambush. Once you get to know everyone, you'll see that they're a great group of guys.

"Let me tell you a little about some of the guys who are still with us. See the guy scratching his ass? That's Edsel, but we call him Hillbilly. He earned his nickname because he's from the hills of Virginia. He might act like a hillbilly, but he's probably the most educated and generous guy in the platoon.

"The young man talking with the LPC crew is Cartwright. He's a jungle-wise grunt who will probably take over point for second squad. The big guy eating out of a C-ration can is Chico. He's a Native American from North Dakota. He's doesn't say much, but don't piss him off.

"The skinny white guy sitting on his steel pot and wearing wire-rim sunglasses, that's Lenny. He's from Virginia. The grunt with the handset in his ear is Rider. He took over as the point team's RTO. The guy with curly red hair and freckles is Tucker. That guy over there is Peter Gun. I call him Avocado because his last name sounds the green fruit.

"The soldier with the curly blond hair is Scotty. He just returned to the field. He's been in the rear since the ambush. The two black soldiers playing a game of spades are Theo from Mississippi and Kelly Hicks from North Carolina. All the blacks in the platoon like to be addressed as "Brother."

"You already met the platoon squad leaders, Joe and John, along with Sergeant Tomas, the new acting platoon leader. The remainder of the grunts who survived the ambush with wounds not serious enough to send them home will return to field later."

"Why are the new guys treated so poorly? You would think they would be grateful to have replacements," I said.

"Don't take it personally. As soon as you prove yourself, you'll become one of us—a grunt. You have to remember we recently got the shit kicked out of us. We lost six men. It was definitely the scariest day of my life. The enemy was determined to kill every one of us that day," said Hoskie, shaking his head.

"What happened out there?" I asked.

Hoskie got comfortable and then began explaining the events that led to the ambush.

"February sixth, late in the afternoon, the company was combat assaulted into the field. This was the usual means of transportation to the field. It was a stressful ride for everyone because we had just returned from a three-day stand-down, and most of us were nursing major hangovers. Being combat assaulted into an unsecured LZ covered with thick brush made it difficult for the pilots to land. Not knowing if the LZ was booby-trapped, the pilots hovered above the ground as we jumped off.

"In order for us to maintain an element of surprise, the LZ hadn't been prepped. Aztec Platoon was combat assaulted into the field two clicks (kilometers) to the east. With entire company safely on the ground, Blackfoot moved into the wood line first, followed by the main CP (command post). Cheyenne would follow. There wasn't much daylight left, so platoon leader Lieutenant Pick quickly located a position and set up for the night. I took a position near the rocks, overlooking the valley, and settled down for the night.

"During the evening, everyone heard voices coming from the valley floor. At the time, no one understood why the enemy was being so careless. It was like the enemy was intentionally trying to get us to go down there.

"Lieutenant Pick made the decision to call in artillery. I listened as the lieutenant and the forward observer called for a marking round. The marking round exploded above, pinpointing the enemy's position. A minute later, artillery shells pounded the enemy's position.

"Screaming and shouting indicated the enemy was scrambling for cover. When the last shell was fired, everyone settled down for the night, with anticipation of checking out the damage in the morning. Everyone was confident the enemy had fled the area.

"The following morning, the lieutenant was ordered to send a squad down into the valley to assess the damage. First squad would stay behind to guard the equipment while Cheyenne Platoon patrolled the ridge. Aztec, working two clicks to the east, was in radio contact with the Main CP, which remained linked with Cheyenne. I had no desire to go down into the valley, especially knowing we had recently been ambushed in a similar situation.

"The point team, consisting of the platoon leader and two second-tour grunts, followed by the second squad gun team, moved cautiously down the hillside. The patrol came to a halt when lieutenant discovered a well-traveled trotter running alongside a creek and notified the CO immediately.

"The point team continued to follow the trotter until the discovery of communication wire strung through the trees halted the patrol. That alone should have been a sign to pull back, but the Main CP ordered Lieutenant Picket to move ahead with caution. Doc, the platoon medic, offered to cut the wire with his boot scissors, but word was passed back to leave it alone.

"The point team waited as the point man moved into a clearing. The remaining point team members moved up slowly as word was passed back that the point team was going to recon the area by fire. A few seconds later, a barrage of M-16 and M-60 rounds was dispersed into the jungle.

"Expecting it was safe to proceed, the platoon leader ordered the point team to move forward. That's when a loud blast sent a shock wave through the jungle, followed by a heavy

53

volume of AK-47 fire. Everyone hit the ground, scrambling for cover. Not knowing where the fire was coming from, all we could do was stay down.

"The point man went down instantly with a severely damaged leg and massive internal injuries. The slack man's arm was shattered by shrapnel, and he was stunned by the explosion. The platoon leader took the full force of the blast and died instantly. The gun team leader ran forward, trying to stabilize the situation, and took a B-40 rocket in the chest. His body lay on the jungle floor, a bloody, mangled mess, and he died soon after. The machine gunner was killed instantly trying to get his gun into operation. Unfortunately, the soldier had only been in-country a month.

"We were in serious trouble with no way out. Within seconds of the explosion, we were fully engaged in a firefight against a determined enemy force. With our leadership out of action and fire coming from all directions, we lay paralyzed in the middle of a killing zone. The enemy was attacking our flanks. The rest of us knew we had to act fast or die. Several of us laid down a base of suppressive fire to try and turn back the enemy."

Hoskie drew a deep breath.

"It seemed like hours that I lay huddled next to the tree that kept me from being killed. In reality, it was only a few minutes. Shortly after, Cheyenne and the Main CP arrived to assist with fire support and additional leadership. Aztec Platoon was ordered to provide additional fire support, but came in from the wrong direction and took on enemy fire.

"The CO ordered Cheyenne to approach the ambush from the rear to regain fire superiority. Enemy fire was making it difficult to counterattack. We continued to lay down a suppressive base of fire as Cheyenne moved ahead. The battalion commander was in the air, coordinating ground movement, along with the brigade commander giving advice. The medevac team had been dispersed and was en route. Low-observation Huey helicopters were in the air, trying to locate the enemy's position. Max circled above, waiting for the word to provide close-in fire support.

"Cheyenne's point team arrived at the rear of the ambush, only to meet a barrage of AK-47 fire, instantly killing their point man. Cheyenne's first squad leader discovered a sniper in the tree. As he was trying to position himself to take a shot, he took a round in the heart.

"The low-observation helicopter door gunner had mistaken some of Cheyenne's men for the enemy and dropped a Willy Pete (white phosphorus grenade) on top of the squad. One of Cheyenne's men was severely burned and ran through the jungle in agony.

"Although the enemy was faced with overwhelming fire superiority and outnumbered, they refused to withdraw. This was an unusual defense for the enemy. What were they protecting? Usually, the enemy would ambush American troops, then flee the area, leaving a sniper or two to keep us pinned down.

"Max was able to finally provide close-in fire support to help break contact. The medevac arrived and dropped a jungle penetrator. The slack man, who had been hit in the chest and was drowning in his own blood, was selected to be pulled out first. Due to enemy ground fire, the medevac pilot was about to abort the mission. The Huey pilot placed his aircraft between the medevac and the ground fire, shielding the extraction.

"Finally, after six horrible hours, the situation was stabilized. We were able to secure the area and start pulling back the dead and wounded. Aztec Platoon arrived to our relief, along with Alpha and Delta Companies. Delta Company had been operating to the north and had to hump most of the day to get to us. When it was obvious Bravo Company couldn't handle the situation, Alpha Company was airlifted into the nearest LZ.

"With very little daylight, the remaining members of Blackfoot returned to the base camp at the top of the hill. The bodies that couldn't be airlifted out of the field were placed in the center of the camp. The new leadership called in an air strike on the enemy's position, and the rest of us settled in for a restless night. I got out of my blood-soaked shirt and slipped into a wool night shirt.

"Recapping the day's horrific events, we lost six men, four in Blackfoot and two in Cheyenne. The platoon leader was killed instantly at the beginning of the ambush, and the point man died from his wounds before he could be extracted. The gun team leader took a direct hit in the chest from a B-40 rocket. The machine gunner was killed trying to get his M-60 into operation. The point team's slack man was hit in the chest by AK-47 fire but somehow survived. Cheyenne lost their squad leader to sniper fire and another man to ground fire.

"That evening, Alpha and Delta Companies, along with Aztec Platoon, provided perimeter security while Blackfoot and Cheyenne slept.

"We were all thinking of the lifeless bodies in the center of the perimeter. Morning couldn't come soon enough.

"Early in the morning, we were visited by the brass from brigade and division, who were reconstructing the events of the prior day. Apparently, the enemy had detonated a claymore mine suspended from a tree. When Blackfoot Platoon couldn't break contact, Aztec Platoon was called in to provide additional fire support. Unfortunately, they entered from the wrong azimuth and took on heavy enemy fire. Aztec pulled back, finding a different route but taking longer to regain fire superiority. The medevac took a round in the transmission and was forced to land at Fire Base Fontaine. The battalion commander's Huey was also hit and had to make an emergency landing on Highway 1.

"Battalion filled the critical leadership positions and evacuated the rest of our dead and wounded. Battalion replaced our expended ammo and ordered Bravo Company to continue the mission. The brass returned to the rear."

"With that many casualties, why wasn't Blackfoot extracted from the field?" I asked.

"Are you kidding? Although Blackfoot lost half their platoon and had their leadership completely wiped out, the rest of us had to pull it together and remain combat effective. That's the way it is out there, Garcia. I'm just grateful I was one of the lucky ones."

Hoskie's incredible interpretation of the events that had taken place on February 7 made me wonder if I was worthy of being a member of Blackfoot.

"By the way, the enemy isn't the only thing you have to watch out for," Hoskie whispered.

"What else could there possibly be?" I asked nervously.

"The jungle," replied Hoskie.

"I don't understand."

"I was told that one night that a grunt in Aztec Platoon was attacked by a large leopard. The soldier screamed as the giant cat mauled his body."

"Did he die?" I asked.

"Fortunately, the following morning his squad leader found him unconscious outside the perimeter. The soldier had lost a tremendous amount of blood, but he survived."

I was surprised Hoskie had taken the time to talk with me. I learned a lot from the grunt wearing the handkerchief wrapped around his forehead. Probably more than I wanted to know. After hearing Hoskie's incredible story, all I could do was wonder how I was going to survive the next 318 days.

John came by, assigning guard times for the night. "Garcia, you're assigned the 2:00 a.m. guard time."

"For how long?" I asked.

"Everyone pulls an hour of guard duty," he replied.

"How will I know it's my time to pull guard?"

"The previous guard will come over and wake you. Grab your weapon and quietly locate the guard station. Search for the illuminated watch sitting on top of the radio. The illuminated watch is there to help you find the guard position and let you know what time it is. Don't leave the guard station until your guard is over. Your call sign is 7-6 Juliette, first squad is 7-6 Romeo, and the main CP is 7-6 Hotel. When you hear your call sign, press the button on the side of the receiver and respond with, 'This is 7-6 Juliette, over.' Answer briefly and accurately. Do not mention any names or our position, and don't fall asleep. The dinks might sneak up on you and cut your throat," said John, convincingly.

"Yes, sir," I replied.

"Don't call me sir, damn it. I work for a living. Get familiar with the surroundings so you don't end up out there in the jungle. Someone might mistake you for a gook and blow your shit away. Got it?"

"What if I see the enemy?" I asked.

"Light the bastards up," replied John.

Eager to get a little rest, I started blowing up my air mattress. Joe immediately rushed over. "What are you doing, cherry? You can't blow up your air mattress. It makes too much damn noise. The dinks can hear you a mile away!"

"No one said anything to me. I didn't know any better!"

"Damn FNGs are going to get me killed," said Joe, angrily walking away.

That evening, when everyone was settled down for the night, I was lying on my back, staring up at the sky. The stars were glistening brighter than I had ever seen. An aircraft was flying over at a high altitude.

John came by and crouched on one knee. "What you staring at, Garcia?"

"I see a plane flying across the sky," I said.

"It's probably a freedom bird," said John. "That's what we call the jetliner that's going to take us back to the world someday. Don't worry, Garcia. You won't be taking one for a long time."

"That's encouraging."

"Sorry, that's the way it is."

It was 2:00 a.m. when Cole approached my sleeping position for me to relieve him for guard duty. I reached for my weapon and made my way toward the illuminated watch sitting on top of the radio. It was my first time pulling guard in the field, and I was scared to death.

Sitting on a metal box of ammo, I tried to make myself comfortable. Not knowing what to expect, I placed the safety mechanism on my M-16 on full automatic. Clutching my weapon tightly, I prayed that the hour of guard duty would pass quickly.

Suddenly the field radio squelched, signaling an incoming call.

"7-6 Juliette, 7-6 Juliette, this is 7-6 Hotel, over."

After a brief pause, the radio squelched to life again.

"I say again, 7-6 Juliette, 7-6 Juliette, come in, over."

After hearing the call sign for the second time, I realized the radio transmission was for me and picked up the receiver.

"7-6 Hotel, go ahead, over," I responded.

"What's the matter, 7-6 Juliette, you asleep? Over," replied the main CP.

"No, 7-6 Hotel. It's my first night on guard duty. It won't happen again, over," I responded.

"Okay, 7-6 Juliette, keep me posted if you hear any movement. Out," said the main CP, ending the transmission.

Guard duty passed slowly as my imagination turned shadows into enemy silhouettes and sounds of the jungle into frightening thoughts. Finally, after an agonizing hour, my first watch came to an end. I quickly located my replacement and then returned to my sleeping position, pulling my poncho liner over my head.

***

February 16. Up with first morning light, I was grateful I had made it through the first night. I watched as the soldiers loaded their gear back into their APCs, preparing to move out.

They seemed to be an easy target. I wondered why they were working in the flatlands, patrolling the logging roads.

The experienced grunts were heating up canteens of water and opening C-rations, preparing for breakfast. I packed my rucksack and then rolled up my air mattress, along with my poncho and poncho liner, securing the roll to the bottom of my rucksack.

I opened a can of pound cake and decided to try the cocoa. I stirred a package of cocoa into a canteen cup of water.

"It tastes better if you heat up the water," said Hoskie. "Let me show you."

Hoskie took an empty B2-1 unit (crackers and cheese) C-ration can, punching several holes in it with his can opener.

"Do you have a B-52?" asked Hoskie.

"What's a B-52?" I replied.

"It's a can opener," said Hoskie. "You better get one if you plan on surviving in the jungle. Do you have any C-4?"

"Yeah, the supply sergeant gave each of us a block of it."

"Break off a small piece and roll it up into a ball. Place it under the C-ration can and light it with your Zippo lighter. Put your canteen cup of water on top."

"I don't have a Zippo lighter," I said.

"You better get your shit together. Here, use mine," said Hoskie.

I cautiously ignited the small ball of C-4. Amazingly the water was boiling in less than thirty seconds.

As I was enjoying my first cup of hot cocoa, Sergeant Tomas approached my position. "Grab your things. You're going in, cherry."

"Thank God. I'm finally being taken out of the field for being a soul surviving son?" I replied.

"I don't think so, Garcia. The main CP wants all the beaners in Bravo Company extracted from the field. They're having some kind of Mexican festival on the fire base, and battalion wants you there," said Sergeant Tomas.

"Not because someone finally realized I'm a sole surviving son?" I replied.

"Hell no. You'll be back on log day. Get your shit together. There's a bird coming in to pick you up."

"Aren't you going in? You're Mexican."

"Can't. I'm the platoon leader."

"Why can't I go?" asked John.

"Because you're a fucking Puerto Rican. Now get your squad ready to move out. We have a dead pilot to search for," said the platoon leader. "Okay, shammer, get your shit together. Your ride has landed. Pop smoke, birds inbound!"

"Check you later," I responded as the Huey helicopter sat down on the logging road.

"Where're the others?" shouted the door gunner.

"I'm the only one going in," I replied.

***

Delta Company was setting up the stage when I arrived at the fire base. I found an empty hooch and dropped off my rucksack. The mess hall was still serving breakfast, so I hurried over.

"You're back so soon?" said Sam the Spoon.

"Yeah, I was taken out of the field to see the show today," I replied.

"Anytime you want to pull KP, let me know. I'll make it worth your while," said Sam.

Sam gave me a healthy serving of scrambled eggs and a pile of shit on a shingle. I took a seat next to two Hispanic grunts. Their dark tans and faded boonie hats indicated they had time in-country.

"Were you taken out of the field to attend the show?" I asked.

"Yeah, what company you with?" asked the grunt with a thin mustache.

"Bravo Company, Blackfoot Platoon," I replied.

"We're with Aztec. My name is Mateo and this is Romeo."

Like the other Hispanics on the fire base, they were thrilled to be out of the field.

A Shit Hook (Chinook transport Huey) arrived at the fire base with a group of performers as the troops made their way to the stage. After a quick tune-up of their instruments, the festive performers appeared on stage.

Dressed in traditional bright blue mariachi outfits, the performers played ranchero music. The soldiers drank beer and danced as the Mexican dancers lifted their dresses and twirled.

One of the dancers took my hand and led me to the stage. Infatuated with her grace and beauty, I couldn't resist stealing a kiss.

The return of the Chinook transport meant the end of the show. The mariachis played their final song and packed their instruments.

Taking Hispanic soldiers out of the field to attend a performance by a group of mariachis was a welcome relief, but what would happen if battalion brought in James Brown? Would all the black soldiers be pulled out of the field to attend his show?

Episode Seven

Search and Destroy

February 17. I was scheduled to remain on the fire base until the next log day. I enjoyed a hot breakfast and returned to my hooch. As I wrote letters to family and friends, I sat on top of my hooch, enjoying the warm morning sun. Without a fatigue shirt, I was sure to acquire a nice tan. A dark tan was a symbol of time in-country.

I spent most of the evening with the mess hall cook, Sam the Spoon. Enjoying ice-cold beer, we listened to Sam's only cassette by Marvin Gaye.

***

February 19. Two days on the fire base passed quickly; it was time to return to the field. Log day for Bravo Company meant a three-day supply of food, water, and mail, along with a duffel bag of clean jungle fatigues. For me, log day represented a fearful return to the jungle.

During mail call, I received my first letters from the States: one from Dad and another from a hometown friend. Dad's letter consisted of casual conversation, while my friend's letter entertained me with his sexual encounter with a new girlfriend.

Assigned to the first log bird of the day, I took a seat next to the C-rations and LRPs, along with the two soldiers from Aztec Platoon, Mateo and Romeo. The log bird lifted off the LZ and headed for Bravo Company's current location.

The pilot made contact with the main CP before approaching the LZ. A canister of smoke identified their position below.

"I identify First Cav yellow, over," answered the pilot over his radio.

"That's a solid copy," replied the main CP RTO.

Identifying the color of smoke ensured the pilot was headed for an American-occupied LZ. The enemy was known to pick up US radio frequencies, guiding pilots to enemy-occupied LZs. The enemy used any tactic necessary to level the playing field against the massive firepower of the United States.

The pilot approached the LZ with the nose of the helicopter slightly tilted upward. The LZ was carved out of the mountainside; there wasn't room for error. The pilot landed, bouncing the skids off the hard surface. I stepped off the skid, searching for John.

The door gunner kicked out the C-rations and LRPs, and the pilot slowly lifted off the LZ. Clearing the treetops, the pilot returned to the fire base for another load.

John waved his arms, signaling his location. "Hey, shammer, it's about time you got your ass back in the field."

"If I had it my way, I would never come back," I replied.

"You're lucky you weren't in the field when we found the dead captain."

"Yeah, that must have been a thrill," I replied sarcastically.

"If he hadn't smelled so bad, we would never have found him hanging from a tree."

"How did you get him down?"

"One of the FNGs was ordered to climb the tree. When he reached for the captain's leg, the captain fell to the ground," said John.

"I'm glad I missed all the fun," I replied.

"Have you been resupplied?"

"Yeah, back on the fire base."

"Good. We'll be moving out in thirty mikes. Set up by those rocks until it's time to move out."

I took a position near a large rock outcropping overlooking the valley. A steep vertical incline made it difficult to climb, so I felt fairly safe being out there by myself.

The second log bird arrived with clean clothes and mail. Bravo Company continued to replenish their food and water supply. A few minutes later, the third bird arrived with the rubber water blivet. When everyone was completely resupplied, the backlog bird returned for the discarded C-rations and LRPs, along with a few soldiers going on R & R.

After the CO briefed his platoon leaders, word was given to move out. Aztec and Cheyenne Platoons were ordered to sweep the east side of the valley, while Blackfoot would continue up the mountainside and set up base camp

I slung my heavy rucksack over my shoulder and made my way toward the others. The platoon leader was reviewing his field map. Joe's squad would be first to traverse the steep incline.

"With this rucksack on my back, the climb is going to kick my ass," I said to John.

"I'm not worried about the climb. It's what's on the other side of the mountain that scares the shit out of me," replied John. "Garcia, I want you to take the drag position, and don't forget to keep pace count."

A three-day supply of food and water, along with an air mattress, poncho, and poncho liner, made the climb brutal. An additional two hundred and fifty rounds of M-60 machine gun ammo, claymore, grenades, and M72 LAW (light antitank weapon) would make it nearly impossible.

The first few steps of the climb I struggled to maintain my balance. Knowing there was no one else to protect the squad from behind made the climb more difficult. Not only was I responsible for an accurate pace count, it was my duty to protect the platoon from the rear.

Halfway into the climb, the platoon leader called for a desperately needed break. With aching shoulders and a sore back, I managed to stay up with the rest of the squad. Everyone labored for three hundred meters until it was time for another break. With less than a hundred meters to the ridge, the platoon leader decided to find a suitable position to set up for the night.

"Get your night work out," instructed John.

"What night work?" I asked.

"If you hadn't been goofing off in the rear, you would have learned how to put out your claymore and trip flare with the rest of the cherries. Grab your claymore and trip flare; I'll show you."

John ran my claymore wire to tree ten meters from my sleeping position. He placed the trip flare at the base of the tree, setting the claymore on top and slowly releasing the pin. He placed the blasting cap, attached to the end of the electrical wire, into the detonator well. Then he ran the wire with the clacker (detonator) back to the guard station.

I didn't mind placing my claymore out at night for extra protection. It was being outside the perimeter that frightened me. John allowed us to blow up our air mattresses, but warned us not to fill them to capacity. Unfortunately, we were set up on the hillside, making it difficult to find a level place to sleep.

I located a suitable area along the perimeter, brushing away the leaves and twigs. I rolled out my poncho, poncho liner, and air mattress. John came by, assigning guard times for the night. I would be pulling guard after Cole, beginning at 2:00 a.m.

I settled down for the evening, wondering if I had an appetite. Since Hoskie had taken the time to teach me how to instantly heat water with C-4, I decided I would attempt to prepare a beef and rice LRP. I pinched off a piece of C-4 and rolled it into a small ball. I placed it under a newly made C-ration can stove and ignited the plastic explosive. I watched in amazement as the water quickly came to a boil.

I poured the heated water into the plastic bag of freeze-dried field ration and folded the packet, placing it into the thermal pouch. It was my first hot meal in the jungle. Surprisingly, when you're hungry, an LRP can be a comforting meal.

Jungle life during the day was bad enough, but when day turned to night, the jungle was more intimidating. Knowing the enemy could be planning an attack at any moment made it difficult to get a decent night's rest.

In the dark, vibrant green patches of light radiated from the jungle floor. When I scooped up a handful of the mysterious illumination, I discovered thin veins of fluorescent moss. As time passed, the temperature dropped. Slipping into a wool nightshirt, I attempted to get some sleep before pulling guard.

Early in the morning, I was awakened by footsteps. I wasn't taking any chances, so I reached for my weapon. Placing the safety mechanism on full automatic, I raised my weapon, trying to focus on the body heading in my direction. In a soft-spoken voice, the silhouette called out my name. It was Cole, searching for his replacement.

With the help of the vibrant patches of light, I felt my way to the guard station. Placing my steel pot over my head, I settled in for an hour guard. I kept my M-16 by my side with the safety mechanism on full automatic.

There were two guard positions protecting our position. Claymores extended from the positions, with the clackers set up next to the radio. The two guards on duty were responsible for the entire perimeter.

Clackers within reach and M-16 by my side, I listened for the enemy. Suddenly, a light flashed across my eyes. Within seconds hundreds of lights were hovering above the guard station.

While I was trying to determine the light source, a call came in from the main CP. "7-6 Juliette, 7-6 Juliette, what's your status? Over."

Not familiar with the proper radio etiquette, I responded, "7-6 Hotel, this is 7-6 Juliette. Over."

"7-6 Juliette, what's your current status? Over."

"7-6 Hotel, there's little lights flying around the perimeter. Over."

"7-6 Juliette, you must be one of the new cherries, over."

At the end of my guard duty, I made my way to my replacement.

"Hillbilly, wake up," I whispered.

"Who is it?"

"It's me, Garcia."

"What the hell do you want, cherry?"

"There are bright little lights everywhere," I said.

"They're fireflies. Get used to it, you fucking cherry."

Like the fluorescent moss generating light on the jungle floor, the fireflies were just another unexpected mystery that came to life during the night.

At dawn the platoon leader ordered everyone to wake up and bring in their night work. The platoon leader discussed the day's objective with his team leaders and ordered his point team to continue up the mountain.

With second squad leading the way, our objective was to make it to the ridge by lunch and set up base camp. I fell in behind Hoskie and started up the mountainside.

The weight of my rucksack wasn't any lighter than on the previous day. I struggled up the hill. When the point team reached the ridge, the platoon leader gave the order to form a perimeter and break for lunch. I selected a beef and rice LRP. Hoskie, seated nearby, emptied a bag of Kool-Aid into his canteen.

"Hey, Hoskie, where did you get the Kool-Aid?" I asked.

"My mom sent it to me in a care package."

"Hey, Hillbilly, where did you get that can of RC Cola?" I asked.

"They come out with the rations on log day."

"Here, you owe me," said Hoskie, tossing over a couple bags of grape Kool-Aid.

"Yeah, you owe me too, cherry," said Hillbilly, handing over a can of cola.

Thirsty for a cool drink, I emptied the package of Kool-Aid into my one-quart canteen and shook it vigorously. After taking a long drink, I immediately pulled out a pen and paper to request a care package filled with assorted flavors of Kool-Aid.

After a short lunch break, the platoon leader ordered Joe's squad to run a patrol down to the valley floor.

"Keep your shit together. I don't want to hit the shit again," said Joe as his point team descended.

The platoon leader stayed back with second squad, monitoring the patrol. Halfway down the mountainside, first squad's point team discovered a well-traveled trotter leading into the valley. Not taking any chances, Joe decided to return to base camp for reinforcements.

"I don't like it down there. There's fucking trotters everywhere. The only way I'm going back down is in platoon strength," said Joe frantically.

The platoon leader met with his squad leaders. After a heated discussion, John's squad was selected to lead the way. Everyone picked up their gear, and the point team descended the mountain.

Following Joe's back trotter, John moved cautiously, discovering a stream on the valley floor. Fresh footprints indicated the enemy had recently been in the area. Concerned that the platoon could be attacked at any time, John informed the platoon leader and ascended to the top of the ridge.

"I have a bad feeling about this place," whispered Hoskie as he crossed the stream.

"I know the feeling," Hillbilly replied, fearing another confrontation with the enemy.

This climb was steeper than the previous day's climb. I followed Hoskie up the mountainside. Laboring with every step, the platoon finally reached the ridgeline.

"Garcia, you and the FO (forward observer) set up by those rocks. The rest of you form a perimeter," said John.

Dragging my rucksack along the ground, I followed the FO to the other side of the perimeter. The FO took a position by a large rock, and I took a position on his left. With the base camp located on a ridge and shaded with fairly thick vegetation, the area appeared secure.

Leaning my weapon against the rock, I took a seat. I pulled out the latest issue of *Playboy* and began thumbing through the pages. The FO wiped the lens of his eyeglasses. Suddenly he reached for his weapon and took aim.

The FO was focused on three NVA soldiers heading in our direction. Meticulously aligning his sights, he squeezed the trigger. The FO fired off three rounds before his weapon jammed. The enemy retaliated with a burst of AK-47 fire, scrambling for cover.

I nervously fumbled for my weapon, releasing the safety mechanism. The three enemy soldiers retreated into the jungle. Engaged in my first firefight, I had failed miserably.

John rushed over, curious to know the outcome. "What the hell happened?"

"I fired up thee dinks," replied the FO.

"Did you kill any?"

"My fucking weapon jammed, but I hit the point man in the chest," boasted the FO.

"How about you, Garcia?" asked John.

"I didn't have a clear shot, but I managed to fire a few rounds," I replied.

"Looks like the enemy had a clear shot at you," said John jokingly.

"Why?" asked the platoon leader.

"Look at that rock behind Garcia," said John, pointing to the evidence of six rounds ricocheting off the rock.

"Welcome to Vietnam, Garcia," said the platoon leader sarcastically.

"Yeah, Garcia, maybe next time you won't have your head up your ass. You could have been killed," said John with a hint of anger.

The evidence on the rock was clearly a sign that I was in a killing zone and needed to be prepared to take a life or die.

"Assemble your squad. You're going out to check for bodies," ordered the platoon leader.

Leading the way, John gave the order to move out. John took point, followed by the FO. Leaving the perimeter, I was grateful to be in the rear and not up front. At the top of the incline, John discovered thick, coagulated blood on the jungle floor. He followed the blood trail cautiously, suspecting he might find a body.

John searched the ridge relentlessly until the blood trail disappeared. He was disappointed when he didn't find a body. He desperately wanted to continue the search, but the CO refused and ordered him to return to the base camp.

"I can't believe my weapon jammed," said the FO.

"Believe me, by the amount of blood loss, I guarantee you ruined his day," said John.

He reported the details of the patrol to the platoon leader and was given the order to set up an ambush where the blood trail had been discovered. Machine guns were placed on each end of the trotter, with first and second squads filling in the positions. Everyone set up their night work and, for the remainder of the day, waited for another encounter with the enemy.

With very little daylight available I rolled out my poncho and set up my sleeping area. Removing my jungle boots, I discovered a large, segmented worm attached to my calf. "What the hell is that?" I asked Hoskie.

"Don't worry. It's only a bloodsucking leech. Don't pull it off," replied Hoskie.

"How do I get it off?"

"Burn it off with a cigarette."

The bloodsucker must have attached itself to my leg when I crossed the stream at the bottom of the valley. The size indicated it was filled with my blood. Hoskie lit a cigarette and carefully placed it on the leech. The leech fell to the ground. Blood oozed from its cylindrical mouth.

That evening I was awakened by Hoskie for guard duty. Once again the pockets of vibrant jungle moss made it easier to find my way to the guard station. It was situated a few meters away from a steep incline. A step in the wrong direction, and I could end up tumbling down the hillside.

The following morning the platoon leader met with the CO to plan the day's objective. Second squad was ordered to follow the ridge line in search of the enemy remaining in the area. First squad would remain in ambush position on the ridge.

While on patrol John discovered a well-traveled trotter leading down into the valley. John persuaded the platoon leader to allow his squad to set up an ambush, hoping to surprise the enemy coming up from the valley.

The area was thick with vegetation, making it ideal for an ambush. The squad members quickly secured the perimeter, and everyone put out claymores. I was set up next to John on the opposite side of the trotter.

Due to the previous day's encounter, I had learned that being prepared for an encounter with the enemy could be the difference between life and death. The enemy's only goal was to inflict damage to American troops. There was no option to relax.

Studying the terrain in detail, I waited nervously, fearing another confrontation. The only sounds were chirping birds and an occasional rodent scurrying through the brush. Once in a while, the sun would peek through the thick triple canopy above, creating a climate ideal for dozing.

Suddenly John jumped to his knees, placing his hands on the claymore clackers. "There's something out there."

"I didn't hear a thing," I replied.

"I smell dinks," said John, staring into the jungle.

Without warning, he blew the claymores. He reached for his weapon, firing blindly into the jungle. With my heart racing, I followed with short bursts of M-16 fire. I fired until my clip was empty. Ejecting the empty clip, I inserted another.

The field radio squelched, signaling an incoming call from the platoon leader.

"7-6 Juliette, come in. Over," called the platoon leader.

"7-6 Hotel, I just blew away three dinks. Probably the same three dinks we fired up yesterday, over," answered John.

"7-6 Juliette, do you have a body count? Over," asked the main CP RTO.

"7-6 Hotel, I don't know, but I'm ready to move out, over."

"7-6 Hotel, that's a solid copy, keep us posted. Out," said the platoon leader, ending the transmission.

"All right, guys, pick it up. We're moving out," said John.

With the sling of my M-16 over my shoulder and finger on the trigger, I followed as John lead the way. He held his weapon in firing position as he cautiously headed out the perimeter.

Locating the tree that took the impact of the exploded claymores, John pointed to the bark that had been peeled back by the blast. Looking closer, he discovered several drips of blood on the ground. He turned and smiled, picking up the headset from the radio.

"7-6 Hotel, come in, over," said John.

"Go ahead 7-6 Juliette," replied the main CP.

"7-6 Hotel, I got one of the bastards. He can't go far; he's bleeding heavily. I'm going to continue the search, over."

I was amazed by John's eagerness to encounter the enemy. It made me believe he was looking for revenge for the recent loss of his platoon members.

We followed the blood trail, finding no evidence of a body. A thorough search of the area revealed the enemy had escaped.

Discouraged with the outcome, John ordered the squad back to the base camp.

***

February 26. In the early morning, Blackfoot was packed and ready to begin the day's mission of cutting out an LZ to resupply the company. Since it was first squad's rotation to secure the area, the platoon leader gave Joe the option of setting up an ambush or clearing the LZ. Because of the recent confrontations with the enemy, Joe decided to stay on the ridge and work.

John was eager to have another opportunity to engage the enemy. He led the way, descending the mountain on a well-traveled enemy trotter. Searching for a suitable location for an ambush, he found an ideal position with an excellent view of the terrain above and below.

John and I set up on the high side of the perimeter, Duggy and his M-60 machine gun on the low side. The rest of the squad filled in. The position didn't provide much cover, but given the sound of chainsaws and machetes, we hoped the enemy would avoid the area.

The first three days of the mission had clearly indicated the enemy was not intimidated by our presence. This didn't concern some of the soldiers, who took the opportunity to write a letter, doze off, or stick an earplug in their ears.

I took the initiative to position myself on the high side the mountain. After an hour seated in the same position, I decided to stand. John remained on his back, napping, while the rest of the squad's attention was focused down the mountainside.

It wasn't until the work ceased above that John opened his eyes. He glanced at me for a brief moment before he dozed off again. Realizing that I was the only one concerned about the enemy, I focused my attention on the trotter above.

Once again the sound of chainsaws and machetes indicated the work had resumed above, making it difficult to hear the enemy. John continued to sleep. I caught myself dozing until I heard someone scurrying down the hillside. Fearing it was the enemy, I reached for my weapon.

I took aim, kicking John on the leg. As I focused on the trotter above, a small pocket of enemy soldiers appeared through the brush. The sling of the lead soldier's AK-47 was resting on his shoulder. They quickly approached the perimeter.

John jumped to his feet. "Dinks!" he shouted frantically.

The enemy leader drew his weapon as John and I fired. The leader tumbled down the mountainside, firing a burst of AK-47 rounds into the ground. With no way to avoid a collision with the mortally wounded soldier, I braced for the impact.

The deceased soldier lay at my feet as John and I continued to lay down a suppressive volume of fire. The enemy scrambled up the hill

"Cease fire, cease fire!" John shouted.

The scent of spent ammunition lingered in the air. The enemy's lifeless body lay at my feet.

"Damn, they were on top of our ass and they got away!" cried John.

"Except for this one," I said excitedly, my heart rate accelerating out of control.

"That must have scared the crap out of you," said John.

"I didn't imagine it would be like this."

"Bring up the gun! The rest of you secure the area below!" John shouted, anticipating a possible counterattack.

Standing over the body I watched as John searched it. "This is no fucking VC. He's NVA!"

"How can you tell?" I asked nervously.

"He's wearing an NVA uniform. Look, I shot him between the eyes," John boasted.

I didn't care who had delivered the fatal shot. I was just happy to be alive. John rolled the dead NVA soldier on his stomach, exposing the inside of his skull where the M-16 round had exited his head. John picked up the soldier's weapon, along with a denim pouch strapped around the soldier's neck. He slung the AK-47 over his shoulder and gave the order to head up the mountain.

"What about the body?" Holt asked.

"Don't worry. His buddies will come back for him, if they're alive. Now let's get going," said John.

I assumed we were returning to base camp as John headed up the hill. But John had decided to search for the other two NVA soldiers, without consulting the platoon leader. He had vengeance in his eyes and didn't waste any time. He was determined to get even with the enemy who had killed four of his platoon members.

Glancing at the NVA soldier lying on the ground, I headed up the mountain. I realized I could take a life in order to save mine.

John quickly picked up a blood trail. Coagulated blood indicated one of the enemy soldiers had been severely wounded.

The CO ordered John to abandon the search and return to the base camp. John persuaded the CO to allow him to continue the search. Bravo Company had stopped working on the LZ when they heard shots fired below. They waited anxiously to learn the outcome.

John became frustrated when he lost the blood trail. He wanted to continue searching for the wounded NVA soldiers, but the CO insisted his squad return. John made his way back up the hill and linked up with the rest of the platoon.

"Good work, Garcia," said Joe as I walked by.

Was I now respected by the same person who had wanted nothing to do with me when I first joined the platoon?

"Garcia, grab your weapon and come with me," said the platoon leader.

"Where are we going?" I asked.

"The CO wants to talk with you and John."

John handed the captured AK-47 and documents over to the CO. The CO studied the weapon and was impressed by its condition. The CO shook our hands and commended us for the kill. John explained the details of the ambush. He tried to convince the CO to allow him to continue searching for the two wounded NVA soldiers, but the CO decided John's intentions were personal and not tactical.

Although I regretted taking a life, I was now respected by Joe and the other jungle-wise grunts. John returned to the LZ, where he was met by other members of second squad.

"Where do you want us to set up?" asked Hoskie, studying the landscape.

"On the south side of the perimeter," said John.

"You mean by the cliff?"

"Just find a spot and get your night work out."

The majority of second squad would have to climb over fallen trees to find a suitable location for the night. I didn't blow up my air mattress, fearing I might puncture a hole in it. My position for the night wasn't comfortable, but it was the safest.

Reflecting on the day's events, I reached for a can of spaghetti and meatballs. When I opened the can, the strings of spaghetti resembled the dead soldier's exposed brains. I tossed the spaghetti and meatballs and turned in for the night.

Throughout the night, my thoughts were focused on the deceased soldier lying on the jungle floor. I understood freedom came with a price, but I hadn't realized until then that it meant taking a life.

Episode Eight

A Visit from Our Commander

The following morning, the platoon was informed the battalion commander would be arriving in the field to pick up the captured weapon and documents.

"The general has balls coming out to the bush," said John.

"Why?" I asked.

"The gooks would love the opportunity to take out a high-ranking officer."

The battalion commander arrived in his shiny First Cav helicopter, and John and I were summoned to the main CP. The commander shook our hands and commended us on our performance during the previous day's ambush. Unexpectedly, the general pinned bronze stars on each of our shirt collars.

"Garcia, I understand this is your first mission," said the battalion commander.

"Yes, sir," I replied respectfully.

"I've requested an increase in your pay grade, effective immediately. Consider it a battlefield promotion. Keep up the good work, soldier."

"I just happened to be in wrong place at the right time, sir."

"There will be an awards ceremony when you return to the fire base. I'm also authorizing a three-day in-country R & R for both of you."

John and I saluted the battalion commander and returned to our position.

"I can't believe the battalion commander increased your pay grade. It took me six months to get one. That's bullshit," said John.

"I don't care about the pay grade. When do we go on R & R?" I asked, smiling.

"I don't know about you, but I'm going when I get back to the fire base," said John.

The battalion commander left the mountain, and the first supply bird arrived. Although I didn't receive any mail, I thought about how it would be nice to hear from someone soon. With all three platoons in position, it took an hour to resupply the entire company.

Bravo Company remained in the highlands, avoiding the valley. Aztec Platoon was sent to patrol the east side of the ridge, while Cheyenne Platoon patrolled the south. Blackfoot Platoon remained at the base camp, running patrols during the day and setting up ambushes during the night.

March 5. After a routine morning patrol, the CO ordered Blackfoot to return to the base camp for the remainder of the day. Aztec and Cheyenne Platoons were positioned nearby. The CO and the battalion commander prepared a strategy to return to the valley floor.

Everyone found suitable sleeping positions and put out their night work as usual. The thought on everyone's minds was which platoon would be selected to return to the valley floor. Assigned to the first watch, I made my way to the guard station, hoping for a peaceful night. Ten minutes into my watch, I began to hear voices projecting from the valley floor. I located the platoon leader.

"I can hear the dinks talking down below," I whispered.

"Yeah, it's obvious they want us to know they're down there, but I'm not falling for that bullshit again," he replied.

Concerned about the situation developing down in the valley, Hoskie joined me at the guard station. Hearing enemy voices painfully reminded Hoskie of the February 7 ambush.

"That's the way it started. I hope we don't go down there and hit the shit again. I can't handle another firefight like that," said Hoskie in a concerned voice.

The CO ordered an artillery strike, hoping the enemy would flee the area before he sent a patrol to the valley floor in the morning.

In the early morning, in order to avoid another catastrophe, the CO decided to call in Echo Recon to run a reconnaissance of the area. Echo Recon's objective was to observe the enemy but not make contact. If the seven elite soldiers engaged the enemy, they would immediately pull back and head to the LZ for extraction.

Everyone was ordered to pull in their night work and prepare for the arrival of Echo Recon Platoon. Ordered to secure the assault, Blackfoot Platoon headed for the LZ.

Precisely at 10:00 a.m., a slick delivered the seven members of the Echo Recon team. Their team leader met with the CO to discuss the day's objective, and then proceeded down the mountainside.

The platoon leader took a seat next to the radio, the receiver in his ear, as Echo Recon descended. Thirty minutes later, a call from Echo Recon's team leader indicated they were approaching the valley floor. Echo Recon's platoon leader decided to recon the area with a barrage of ammunition fire before moving forward.

As I listened to the sound of gunfire echo through the valley, I emptied a package of grape Kool-Aid into my canteen.

Assuming the situation below was stable, I sat down to enjoy a drink. Suddenly a loud blast echoed through the valley. A barrage of AK-47 fire confirmed Echo Recon had encountered a determined enemy force. Echo Recon began to return fire as a call came in over the radio.

"Get it on! Echo Recon is pinned down and can't pull back. We're going down!" shouted my platoon leader.

"Damn it, I knew something was going to happen! It was suicide sending Echo Recon down there!" cried Hoskie, slamming his newspaper on the ground.

Everyone hastily packed their rucksacks and followed the point team out of the perimeter. I was rolling up my bedroll when the platoon leader approached my position.

"You better hurry up, Garcia, or we're leaving your ass!"

"Don't worry about me. I'll be ready," I replied, packing my personal belongings back into my rucksack.

I slung my rucksack over my shoulder as the last soldier in the platoon walked out of the perimeter. Uncertain of the danger, I was grateful my position was at the rear. The point team moved swiftly down the mountainside, trying to reach the pinned-down platoon's position.

"Keep your eyes open!" shouted the platoon leader, staying in radio contact with Echo Recon's team leader.

"We have two men down and taking fire from everywhere!" cried the Echo Recon team leader frantically.

"Hold on, we're coming in from the rear! Over!" responded the platoon leader.

The patrol came to a halt when sniper fire shaved the heads of the point team. It was too dangerous to move forward. The point team decided on an alternate route. With the crack and thump of AK-47 fire whistling over our heads, everyone was forced to the ground.

There was a heavy exchange of fire going on below. It was difficult to provide fire support. A B-40 rocket exploded to our right flank. Fortunately, no one was injured by flying shrapnel.

"Get down!" cried John.

The B-40 rocket was only a diversion so the enemy could flee the area. Nervously waiting for word from our platoon leader, I could hear Echo Recon's frantic plea for help. "7-6 Romeo, 7-6 Romeo, come in. Over!"

A few minutes later, the first marking round arrived above the contact area. "Get down! Incoming!" cried John.

I took a position by a nearby tree when the first artillery round whistled over our heads. It exploded nearby. Everyone took cover.

"That's too damn close!" cried Hoskie, hanging on to the base of a tree.

The second artillery shell landed short of our position, sending shrapnel throughout the jungle. A large piece whistled above my head, peeling a chunk of bark off the tree. Everyone was on the ground, anticipating that the next artillery round might land on our position. Pinned down by our own artillery, the platoon leader demanded a ceasefire.

Battalion aborted the fire mission, and once again Echo Recon was under attack. The point team continued to make its way toward the contact area until they safely linked up with Echo Recon. Knowing additional manpower had arrived, the enemy fled.

Once the area was secured, the job of pulling back the dead and wounded began. We were informed that Echo Recon's Kit

Carson scout had been shot in the chest at the beginning of the ambush and killed instantly. Kit Carson scouts were essentially Viet Cong defectors working as intelligence scouts with US troops. Two members of the rifle team had been wounded by AK-47 fire.

I took a position by a tree, pulling guard, as two members of Echo Recon retrieved the Kit Carson scout's body. I assisted in pulling back the wounded to a secure position until the medevac arrived. Echo Recon's team leader popped a can of smoke, and a few minutes later a medevac hovered over the treetops.

The jungle penetrator was lowered. The two wounded soldiers were placed on the stretcher and lifted out. When the medevac returned, I helped place the Kit Carson scout's lifeless body onto the stretcher. Given the small hole in his chest and very little bleeding, it appeared he was asleep. The medic laid the scout's arms across his chest and secured him to the stretcher. Unfortunately, his fight to defeat North Vietnam was over.

Blackfoot and Echo Recon made their way back to the LZ. Blackfoot secured the area as the four remaining members of Echo Recon were extracted from the field.

It was unusual for Echo Recon to be caught off guard, especially with an experienced Kit Carson scout at point. Although the enemy had been determined to hold their ground, they decided to retreat to fight another day.

With the smell of death on everyone's mind, Blackfoot Platoon returned to base camp and set up for the night. Unbelievably, the sound of voices returned to the valley floor. The CO didn't hesitate to call in artillery, along with additional fire support from the rash bird.

The following morning, the battalion commander ordered Bravo Company's CO to send a platoon into the valley. Blackfoot was the CO's choice, with Cheyenne coming in from the rear of the contact area. Aztec would remain nearby for additional support. Knowing the enemy could be planning another ambush, the battalion commander assured the CO that additional fire support would be available if necessary.

"John, your squad is leading the way. Be careful," ordered the platoon leader.

With a determined enemy force possibly in the valley, I feared for my life. The point team moved cautiously down the steep mountainside until we reached the valley floor. Spent ammunition from M-60 machine gun fire marked Echo Recon's position during the previous day's battle.

The point team quickly secured the area where the Kit Carson scout's body had been recovered. With Cheyenne in position, the platoon leader ordered his point team to recon the jungle with a heavy volume of firepower before moving forward.

The platoon leader's decision was to flank the contact area and move along the creek. Following the creek revealed a well-camouflaged bunker complex. It was obvious why the Kit Carson scout had walked into the ambush. It was well hidden.

The bunker complex had the capacity for a large number of enemy soldiers. The surrounding jungle was thick with triple canopy, making the complex difficult to detect from the ground or air. A nearby stream was ideal for survival. You could only wonder how the enemy was capable of creating such an innovative design.

Besides being well camouflaged, the bunkers were built to survive a major airstrike. A sleeping bunker had taken a direct hit from a 105 artillery shell and sustained very little damage. The enemy was well dug in.

Why would the enemy draw attention to a bunker complex this size? Was there a larger number of enemy soldiers in the area than our intelligence had indicated? The center of the bunker complex contained bench seats along with a stage. It appeared the political propaganda scribed on the trees was intended for the American troops.

"Yankee Imperialists go home or die."

"American soldiers are baby killers."

"Soul Brothers, lay down your weapons. This is a White man's war."

"The Vietnamese People's Army will fight until the last Yankee is DEAD."

A caption written under a well-drawn cartoon character of the president read, *"Hey! Hey! LBJ! How many kids did you kill today?"*

The enemy was well educated in our nation's public outcry to end the war and was using it to encourage blacks to believe they were fighting a white man's war.

The point team discovered a bunker filled with sacks of flour and rice. A major enemy stronghold had been exposed. Fortunately the enemy was not willing to protect it.

Given the large number of bunkers in the area, the CO decided to place canisters of concentrated CS gas—a type of tear gas—in all the bunkers. The CS gas would linger for months, preventing the enemy from occupying the complex.

The CO ordered Blackfoot to destroy the contents in the training area, along with the enemy's food supply. Blackfoot and Cheyenne would remain on the valley floor, with Aztec nearby for support.

Everyone put on their gear and followed the point team across the stream. In the stream bed, I noticed a shiny rock resembling a gold nugget.

"Hey, Hoskie you think there's gold in these mountains?" I whispered.

"I don't know about gold, but there sure is a hell of a lot of dinks," he answered.

Hoskie started up the hill, catching his rucksack on a low hanging vine. The annoying vines were referred to as "wait-a-minute vines." They constantly tied up your gear, and it took at least a minute to break away.

Tugging on the vine, Hoskie shook a small emerald snake from the tree. It landed on his rucksack. Hoskie wasn't aware the venomous snake was only inches from his neck.

"Don't move," I whispered, brushing the thin, tapered snake to the jungle floor with the barrel of my M-16.

"What the fuck you doing, Garcia?" cried Hoskie.

"There was a snake on your rucksack," I replied, pointing to the snake.

"Wow, that was close," he said, quickly stepping to the side.

"What if the snake had bitten you in the back of the neck?"

"I'd probably be dead by now."

Hoskie informed me that the small reptile was known as a bamboo pit viper, one of many venomous snakes in Southeast Asia. Commonly called "Two-Step Charlie," the snake was capable of inflicting severe nerve damage and possible death. The saying was, "If he bites you, you'll only be able to take two steps before dying." If the snake had bitten Hoskie, he might never have made it out of the field.

Sergeant Tomas located a position for the night. Everyone quickly put out their night work and returned to the perimeter. Concerned about the number of NVA soldiers in the area, Joe placed an automatic ambush on the trotter leading into the bunker complex.

There wasn't much daylight left because darkness arrived early in the valley. Hoskie and I prepared a cup of hot cocoa and settled down for the evening. John made his way to our position to inform us of the fire mission that was about to take place.

"Keep your head down. The FO is calling in a fire mission on top of the bunker complex."

"Is he crazy? That's less than a hundred meters away!" cried Hoskie.

"Yeah, that's why you better get your head down," said John.

The FO called in his location, bringing in a marking round directly above our heads.

"That's too close. We better find a tree," said Hoskie.

"No shit," I replied, taking a prone position by a nearby tree.

Hoskie and I lay quietly on the jungle floor as the first round whistled over our heads. It exploded on the other side of the stream, and shrapnel careened off trees. The FO immediately called for an adjustment. Hoskie hugged the ground as artillery shells continued whistling over our heads.

"Hold your fire! Hold your fire!" cried the FO over the horn.

"What's wrong?" said Sergeant Tomas.

"One of the rounds landed near Cheyenne's perimeter, wounding the top sergeant!" cried the FO, shaken by the news.

The CO called for a medevac to evacuate the top sergeant. He had been hit by shrapnel. Within thirty minutes and in near darkness, the medevac was hovering over Cheyenne's position. It didn't take long to secure the top sergeant to the metal litter and hoist him into the helicopter.

"Is he going to be all right?" I asked.

"He's one lucky grunt," said John.

"Why?"

"The only thing that saved him from being cut in half was the bandolier strapped around his waist."

Unfortunately, the risk of being wounded or killed by friendly fire was an unnecessary evil of the Vietnam War.

After a restless evening and a sleepless night on the valley floor, Blackfoot headed back up the hill to link up with Cheyenne and Aztec.

For the remainder of the mission, Bravo Company continued working in the valley, patrolling during the day and ambushing known enemy positions during the night. Aztec and Cheyenne encountered small pockets of enemy, but no casualties were reported.

The documentation taken from the dead NVA soldier led to the discovery of a cache of medical supplies, weapons, rice, and flour. With the enemy's supply source cut off, they would have to relocate, temporarily eliminating the threat in the highlands.

Episode Nine

Securing Fire Base Fontaine

March 12. I had completed my first mission. Blackfoot, Aztec, and Cheyenne Platoons were assembled at the pickup zone, awaiting extraction. Blackfoot would be the last platoon for extraction, with second squad being the final group to leave the field.

The previous bird had picked up half the members of second squad, and only five of us remained in the field. There should have been a bird to follow immediately, but we had been stranded. We had very little firepower or leadership. The RTO notified the main CP immediately.

The RTO informed us that the helicopter scheduled to make the final extraction had experienced engine trouble and made an emergency landing at Fire Base Fontaine. We would remain in the field until another bird could return to the pickup zone.

Everyone waited nervously, keeping an eye out for the enemy. An encounter would be a disaster. Finally, the familiar sound of rotor blades could be heard in the distance.

"Pop smoke, birds inbound," shouted the RTO.

The five of us stood at the wood line. The slick appeared over the treetops and touched down. We ran out to the bird and boarded. When the pilot lifted off the LZ, both door gunners fired their M-60 machine guns into the wood line to prevent any ground attack.

As the helicopter rose over the tree line, the door gunner spotted six VC insurgents advancing toward the LZ. The door gunner realigned his M-60 machine gun and fired. Low on fuel, the pilot decided not to pursue the enemy and headed for the fire base. The final extraction took place with no time to spare.

The bird approached the fire base. Standing on the skid, I raised my weapon as the pilot touched down on the LZ.

"What the hell was that?" asked the squad RTO.

"I don't know. I guess I'm just happy to be back on the fire base," I replied.

"Cool to the onion," replied the RTO.

Cool to the onion was an expression of like. As with the other terms and phrases used in Vietnam, I had to learn to talk the language.

I had completed my first mission in one of the hottest areas in the region. I returned educated and alive. I had learned what was needed to survive in the jungle. Although there were scary times in the field, I was no longer considered an FNG.

Like everyone else, I looked forward to my time on the fire base. I located an empty hooch and dropped off my rucksack. Everyone was heading for the big green cooler. Filled with ice-cold beer and sodas, it was a welcome sight.

Out of respect for the grunts with time in-country, I waited my turn.

"Hey, Garcia, catch," said Joe, throwing an me a can of beer.

"Thanks, Joe."

"You earned it," he said with a smile.

Although Blackfoot remained without a leader, Sergeant Tomas provided the leadership for us to remain combat effective. He was respected and well-liked by his men.

Time on the fire base was a never-ending array of new experiences. The FNGs were usually selected to perform work detail, while the rest of the company enjoyed their leisure time out of the field.

Work detail consisted of KP (kitchen patrol), spreading oil over the LZ, stringing wire, filling sandbags, or burning shit from the latrine. Pulling KP was somewhat rewarding, but burning shit was disgusting.

Burning-shit detail required two soldiers to perform the job—one to hold the hatch while the other pulled out the barrel and doused it with diesel fuel. The diesel fuel was ignited, eventually reducing the waste to a cinder.

Knowing there was no way to avoid work detail entirely, I volunteered for KP. Helping the cooks had its advantages. With Sam in control of the mess hall, I didn't have to work very hard, and received extra portions of the best chow.

The soldiers assigned to work detail worked until noon and then were released for the rest of the day. Most of the grunts spent their leisure time in the shade of the grunt hooch. The thatched roof provided protection from the heat while grunts smoked cigarettes, listened to music, wrote letters, or played a game of cards. Some drank beer or napped until the next meal. Occasionally someone would light up a Park Lane (manufactured marijuana cigarette) for a little relaxation from the war.

With the exception of the main CP and platoon leaders, everyone in Bravo Company pulled their share of guard on the fire base. There were no other exceptions. Guard duty was a necessity to protect the fire base from enemy attack during the night. Stories of soldiers falling asleep and having their throats slashed by Charlie encouraged soldiers to stay awake during their watches.

It was best to know where your replacement slept, making it easier to locate him during the night. If not, you would have to search every hooch until you located him.

Personal hygiene was up to the individual but highly encouraged by the soldiers who lived with you. You were provided a toothbrush and toothpaste. It was up to you to brush. Clean clothes were issued every three days. Unfortunately underwear was not included.

Everyone had the opportunity to shower once a day. There were no private showers. Each platoon was provided with a portable shower. A three-gallon canvas water bucket with a showerhead mounted on a metal tripod was located outside the perimeter of the fire base. Standing on top of empty artillery boxes, you had three minutes to lather and rinse.

Unexpected fire missions from artillery and mortars made it difficult to sleep at night. Sharing a hooch with other soldiers had its disadvantages. Their annoying snoring guaranteed a restless night.

***

The next morning I was awakened by the smell of fried bacon, and discovered holes in the tips of my wool socks.

"Hey, look at my socks," I said.

"Mine are like that too. Something was nibbling on our socks last night," said Bart.

"Yeah, rats. Big rats," replied Duggy, lighting his morning cigarette.

"What kind of rats?" I asked.

"The hungry kind that come out at night, eating wool," replied Duggy.

"How do you keep them from eating your socks?" I asked.

"Don't take off your boots," said Duggy, chuckling as he headed for the mess hall for breakfast.

The discovery of wool-eating rats was just another discomfort on the fire base.

After breakfast, John volunteered second squad for mine-sweep duty. John's intention wasn't to impress the CO but to end up at the village with the hookers. It was also an invitation for soldiers to enjoy a cold Tiger 33 beer and indulge in sex and drugs.

John collected the mine-sweep equipment and led his squad out the main entrance. He placed headphones over his ears and meticulously waved the equipment over the dirt road, slowly making his way toward the village. Everyone kept an eye out for the enemy.

The village children surrounded the soldiers with an assortment of dried fruits, souvenirs, and drugs. Drugs were given little priority in the Vietnamese criminal justice system, and flourished as a main source of income for villagers.

Popular drugs among the troops were *consai* (marijuana), opium, hashish, scag (heroin), and an assortment of amphetamines and barbiturates. Some drug users preferred to smoke scag. Others chose to inject it, usually succumbing to its addiction. Blacks referred to scag as "black man's gold." Most of the blacks in the company were interested in smuggling rather than using.

The consai was potent and the scag was pure. Nothing of comparable potency was available then in the States. With all the drug abuse in Vietnam, the military considered drugs "the other enemy."

John couldn't resist the seductive behavior of the attractive village hookers. For five dollars' worth of MPC, an American soldier could enjoy what was referred to in Vietnam as "short time" or "a little boom-boom."

"A little boom-boom, GI?" asked the seductive Vietnamese hooker, running her hand through John's coarse, black hair.

John needed very little persuading and headed for the wood line with the hooker at his side. The hookers were persuasive, but I had no problem resisting their seductive behavior. I had no desire to have sex in a VC-infested jungle.

John didn't stay very long, because battalion forbade fraternizing with villagers. John got his five dollars' worth, and the squad returned to the fire base.

Recently on the logging road leading into the village, our soldiers had encountered a group of VC traveling on foot. The outcome was two dead and two seriously wounded insurgents. Due to the encounter, battalion had ordered the CO to provide a squad to patrol the wood line and set up ambushes during the night.

On our third day on the fire base, Blackfoot was selected to provide a squad to patrol the wood line. The platoon leader selected second squad, and after dinner, John led his men out of the fire base.

A patrol of the wood line revealed no recent enemy activity. John selected a suitable position for the ambush and set up for the night. Setting up ambushes had become familiar to us. The art of a successful ambush consisted of finding a suitable location that provided the element of surprise and adequate cover in case of a counterattack.

Although I was adapting to sleeping in the field, the creatures inhabiting the jungle remained a threat. "Fuck you, fuck you," chanted the fuck-you lizard. "Re-up, re-up," bellowed the re-up frog. The occasional slithering of a snake or migrating animal made for a frightful experience. At the end of a stressful night, second squad returned to the fire base for a welcome breakfast.

If you were fortunate to be on the fire base on Sunday, you had the opportunity to attend the service of your denomination. Sunday morning, Catholic soldiers were informed the bishop would be visiting to say Mass. I decided it was in my best interest to attend, joining Mateo and Romeo for the reading of the holy gospel.

During the homily, everyone listened as the bishop discussed the importance of being prepared for death. I had never been concerned about death until I came to Vietnam. Now I listened to every word.

Knowing the bishop was filled with religious wisdom, I had questions. After the service, I introduced myself to him as he was packing his pontifical garments. "Can I ask you a question?"

"Yes, my son," replied the bishop.

"Does 'thou shalt not kill' apply to war?"

"The tenth commandment applies to everyone, my son."

"Does God approve of killing?"

"Of course not," he answered.

"Then why did God create the Vietnam War?" I asked.

"God didn't create the Vietnam War. God only creates good things. It's man who makes them bad," said the bishop. "Do you have faith in Jesus Christ, our Savior?"

"Sometimes," I answered.

"You should never doubt your faith, my son. That's why we receive the holy sacraments—to strengthen our faith in the Lord."

"Holy sacraments," I said.

"Yes my son. Were you baptized?"

"Yes."

"Did you receive holy Communion?"

"Yes."

"Were you confirmed?"

I hesitated, and then answered, "No."

"Didn't your priest discuss the importance of receiving the sacrament of confirmation before you came to Vietnam?"

"No."

"Why not?" asked the bishop in a stern voice.

"I didn't realize the importance of being confirmed."

"It would be in your best interest. Sit down, my son."

I listened tentatively as the bishop explained why it was necessary to receive the holy sacrament of confirmation. "I'm concerned about you returning to the field without the sacrament. I'm willing to return to the fire base next Sunday to perform the ceremony."

"I'm going back into the field in three days," I said.

The bishop decided stay a little longer and grant me the sacrament before I returned to the field. After a brief ceremony, he placed his hand over my head and chanted the words, "Christ the Lord has confirmed you. Go in peace."

I kissed the bishop's hand and left, knowing that if I was killed, I wasn't going to hell.

I returned to the grunt hooch and joined the others. I pulled a cold beer out of the green cooler, taking a seat on an ammo can.

"Do you ever think about dying?" I asked the platoon leader.

"Nobody thinks about dying, Garcia. It just happens. Why you asking?"

"Nobody ever talks about it."

"Although I live in fear every day, I never entertain the thought. By the way, the higher-ups are having the awards ceremony for you and John tomorrow. Then you lucky bastards are on your way to China Beach for a three-day R & R."

"Why are they having an awards ceremony anyway? Five gooks got away," said John sarcastically.

"Yeah, but three of them are probably dead by now," said the platoon leader.

"Can you prove it?" asked John.

"As much blood as those NVA soldiers lost, there's no way they can still be alive."

***

The following morning, the platoon leader was up early, reminding everyone to clean up for the awards ceremony. The battalion commander was scheduled to arrive at 10:30 a.m. to present citations.

I grabbed a clean pair of fatigues and a five-gallon water can for a quick shower. Then I made my way to the LZ, where I joined the others waiting in the hot sun for the arrival of the battalion commander.

"He's on his way," said Sergeant Tomas.

"Why can't we wait in the shade until he arrives?" I replied.

"Straighten up and don't forget to salute when he arrives, Garcia."

"Why do we have to play in these military games? We're in the middle of a war, not basic training."

"I don't want to be out in the hot sun any more than you do. I would rather be drinking beer. This ceremony is for you, not me, so tuck in your shirt and blouse your pants. The battalion commander will be here any moment!" shouted the platoon leader.

I was the only soldier in formation who was showered and shaven as the battalion commander's shiny, black Huey helicopter approached the LZ. The helicopter touched down, a bright yellow First Cavalry patch painted on the side. The battalion commander stepped out, along with a staff of four.

The platoon leader saluted the battalion commander as he approached the formation. The battalion commander returned the salute, and the platoon was given the order to stand at ease. The commander's assistant made the announcement for John and me to step forward.

Taking two steps forward, the battalion commander pinned Bronze Star medals on our fatigue shirts.

"For heroism against a hostile enemy force in the Republic of Vietnam. These two individuals distinguished themselves by exceptional valorous action on February 26, 1971, when they became engaged with a determined enemy force, with complete disregard for their own safety. Good job, soldiers," said the battalion commander proudly.

"Thank you, sir," replied John.

"And don't forget, I authorized a well-deserved three-day in-country R & R for both of you," said the battalion commander.

The battalion commander spoke briefly with Sergeant Tomas and then returned to his Huey.

"Dismissed!" shouted the platoon leader.

The battalion commander's pilot started up the aircraft's engine and lifted off the LZ. All the members of the platoon returned to the fire base.

"I guess I didn't get that battlefield promotion the battalion commander promised me?" I said to John.

"Don't worry. The CO put you in for specialist 4 anyway," said John.

March 16. In the early morning, I was assigned to KP. The cooks on duty allowed me to eat before serving breakfast on the line. This was one of the advantages of working kitchen patrol. I served myself a heaping spoonful of my favorite dish, shit on a shingle.

After serving breakfast to the company and permanent party, I returned to the field kitchen to help Sam with the preparation of lunch. Sam always had something on his mind. He was obsessed with smuggling scag out of the country. He claimed that he had a fail-safe plan to get it by customs.

After lunch, I joined the guys seated under the thatched-roof hut, waiting for the convoy to arrive with the day's mail. As usual I hoped that the convoy would bring good news.

Eight new faces climbed off the back of the deuce and a half truck. Accompanied by the company clerk, the soldiers were introduced to Sergeant Tomas.

"FNGs," said Bart with a big grin on his face.

"They're not FNGs. They have more time in-country than you," replied the company clerk.

"They're my replacements," said Hillbilly.

"Are you kidding? You're never going home. You love Vietnam," said Sergeant Tomas jokingly.

"Yeah, you're right, I do love Vietnam. It's the lifers I can't stand," said Hillbilly, puffing on his favorite brand of cigarette.

"Listen up, everyone," said the platoon leader. "These are the new members of Blackfoot."

"They're FNGs as far as I'm concerned," said John.

Unfortunately, the new arrivals hadn't had enough time in-country to go back to the States with their original unit, so they were reassigned to Bravo Company. That's when I was introduced to Albert and Charles.

Albert introduced himself as "Sweet Al." Charles was introduced as "Bear." Charles had a thick afro and a speech impediment. He pronounced my last name "Jarcia."

A tall, good-looking soldier was introduced as "Sundance" because of his resemblance to Robert Redford. The new machine gunner was introduced as "Gunner," and his assistant as BJ. A soldier with little height was introduced as Zane and the soldier with the thick lenses was Rodan.

Other arrivals were Pate, Houston, Clint, Bodie, and Trip. Bodie was given the alias "Teeny Bopper," due to his youthful appearance.

Episode Ten

Return to Bien Hoa

March 19. Bravo Company was combat assaulted back into the field for another mission. With battalion's new policy of "Provide battalion a body count and you will be rewarded with a three-day in-country R & R," we had new incentive to seek and kill the enemy.

Anticipating spending three days in China Beach, John and I were on our way to Bien Hoa in the back of a deuce and a half truck. Our first stop was Fire Base Mace. Fire Base Mace was Bravo Company's headquarters.

Upon our arrival, we followed the company clerk to turn in our rucksacks and weapons. We arrived at the helicopter pad in time to catch the final helicopter of the day leaving for Bien Hoa.

John and I boarded the departing helicopter. Although I was happy to be out of the field for three days, I couldn't remove the fear of returning to the field when R & R was over.

The pilot lifted the helicopter in the air and banked to the left to fly around the mountain that overlooked Fire Base Mace. The low-altitude flight revealed the never-ending route along Highway 1. When the slick touched down at Bien Hoa, John headed for the R & R center.

John decided to stop for a drink before checking in. After a couple cold beers, we headed across the compound and entered the First Cav R & R Center. John approached the desk with confidence, saying, "I'm here to check in."

"Okay, what's your destination?" asked the clerk.

"China Beach."

"Can I see your orders?"

"Orders?" replied John, looking confused.

"We weren't issued any orders," I said to the clerk.

"Then you need to go back to your company clerk and have him cut orders for a three-day in-country R & R to China Beach."

"But the battalion commander authorized the R & R," said John.

"Sorry, grunts. No orders, no R & R."

"That's fucking bullshit! I'm not going back to Fire Base Mace to get some fucking orders. Besides, we wouldn't be back until tomorrow, and we have to be back by log day. But being a fucking REMF, you wouldn't know what log day is!" shouted John, storming out of the room.

John had a take-no-nonsense personality, so I tried to calm him down before he did something he would regret.

"No one mentioned we needed any orders to go to China Beach, especially when the general authorized it!" said John, scratching his head in disbelief.

"Hey, look at it this way. We have three days in-country, so let's take the time to enjoy Bien Hoa and party right here," I told him.

"You're right," said John. "I have a friend stationed somewhere around here. I just have to find him. We have three days; let's take advantage of it."

John walked outside the R & R compound, trying to remember the location of his friend's hooch. It would have been easier to locate with transportation, but John insisted on walking. He had a general idea where it was, but unfortunately it was on the other side of the base.

John finally identified a landmark that led us to the place. "I hope he's there," he said as he knocked on the door.

The door opened slowly and a cloud of smoke poured out. John walked in and embraced his friend. I walked in and inhaled the lingering smoke of consai.

"Come in!" said John's friend enthusiastically.

"Man, we've been walking all over this base trying to find you," said John.

"You never could remember anything. Who's your friend?"

"This is Garcia. He's in my squad," replied John. Then he turned to me. "This is Sam the Man, my good buddy from Queens, New York."

"Are you as crazy as John?" I asked.

"Crazier, man," Sammy replied.

"That's no lie." John laughed.

"Come in and make yourself comfortable. I bet you guys could use a cold beer."

"You better believe it," said John.

John envied his friend. Unlike John, Sammy was stationed in the rear, where he was out of harm's way. He pulled out a couple cans of Pabst Blue Ribbon from a small refrigerator located in the corner of his bungalow.

"Thanks," I said. "I really needed this. John had me walking all over looking for you."

Sammy took a shoe box from under his bunk and removed the lid. Out came a hand-carved ivory pipe, along with a plastic bag of consai. He packed the pipe, and then reached in his fatigue shirt pocket for a gram vial of scag. He added the white powder to his pipe and fired it up with his Zippo lighter. Sam inhaled the smoke and handed the pipe to John. "Take a hit of this shit, John. I mixed a little scag in it, just like the old days."

"Yeah, right," replied John, taking a hit off the pipe. He exhaled and started coughing. "That's some good shit, man. Here, take a hit, Garcia. It goes down great with beer."

"Sure, why not," I replied, taking the ivory pipe from John's hand. I inhaled the potent concoction, taking a drink of beer to wash it down. Immediately, I felt the euphoric effect of the powerful narcotic.

"What do you grunts want to do tonight?" Sammy asked.

"We don't care. We have two days to party before going back to the bush," replied John.

Sammy inhaled another deep breath of smoke from his pipe, tilting his head back and filling his lungs. Sammy remained in that position until he expelled the smoke. His eyes rolled back in his head, and I feared he had overdosed. Suddenly, Sammy regained consciousness, opening his eyes.

"Let's party!" said Sammy. "Let's go down to the EM club and enjoy a few drinks on me. Then we can watch the go-go dancers. Tomorrow I'll take you on my run to Saigon."

He put his pipe back in his mouth and inhaled another deep breath of smoke. "Let's go," he said and headed out the door.

John and I followed him to the parking lot, where he climbed into a new deuce and a half truck. When we arrived at the EM club, we were greeted by two attractive Vietnamese girls dressed in hot pants. Both girls grabbed an arm and led Sammy to a table by the stage.

"Sweetheart, how about a round of drinks for my friends," said Sammy, giving the girls a pat on the butt cheek and handing them five dollars in MPC.

Another attractive Vietnamese girl, wearing a long, white, silk dress, strolled over to the table. She sat on Sammy's lap and gave him a kiss on the mouth. "What happened to you last night? You didn't come see me," she said.

"Hey, I want you to meet a couple friends. This is John and his friend."

The attractive girl whispered in Sammy's ear and left the table.

"What was that about?" John asked.

"Oh, let's just say she is one of my girls."

"How about giving us a little piece of the action?" said John jokingly.

"Don't worry. You'll get plenty of action in Saigon tomorrow, but for now leave my girl alone. Now drink up and enjoy the show," said Sammy with a grin on his face.

The two girls who had escorted Sammy to the table were on stage, entertaining the soldiers with a sexy dance as the band played a popular tune.

"Hey look, your girlfriends are go-go dancers," said John.

John and I enjoyed the evening, singing and drinking. At the end of the night, Sammy dropped us off in front of his hooch.

"Where you going?" asked John.

"It's a little too crowded, so I'm going to crash at my girlfriend's hooch. See you in the morning," said Sammy.

"You mean that hot little potato that sat on your lap and gave you a kiss?" asked John.

"No, my other girlfriend. See you in the morning," he said again and then drove off.

John crashed on Sammy's bunk and I ended up on the wood floor. I didn't mind because sleeping on a hard surface was better than the jungle floor anytime.

Early in the morning, Sammy entered his hooch. Nursing well-deserved hangovers, we all headed to the mess hall for breakfast. A Vietnamese boy brought us coffee and took our order.

After a hearty breakfast, the three of us climbed into Sammy's deuce and a half and headed for Saigon. I was feeling a little sick, so John allowed me to take the seat next to the window.

"Let's roll," said Sammy.

Sammy started his truck and drove across the base to a metal building. He backed the truck up to the building, and two soldiers filled the back with dirty laundry bags.

One of the soldiers handed Sammy a package wrapped in brown paper. Sammy placed the package behind the seat and climbed into the cab. I was surprised John didn't question Sammy about the contents in the package.

Sammy drove his deuce and a half through the main gate, where armed guards waved as if they knew him. He accelerated and headed for Highway 1. Although the majority of vehicles were foreign made, occasionally I saw an American car. The only difference was the Vietnamese steering column was located on the right side.

The majority of Vietnamese transportation consisted of bicycles, motorcycles, and Lambrettas (a three-wheel taxi). When it came to their driving skills, Vietnamese drivers didn't demonstrate much etiquette. They drove without regard for other vehicles or pedestrians. Somehow they managed to avoid collisions.

The drive to Saigon revealed a different side of the war. A golf course alongside Highway 1 provided a stress-free round of golf for those who weren't stationed on the front line. Concrete barracks insured a secure living environment for the soldiers stationed in the rear. Not threatened by the war, the individuals were known as REMFs (rear echelon motherfuckers).

Sammy indicated he had to make a stop in Long Binh to deliver the package, so he turned off the highway and headed for a heavily guarded compound. He stopped in front of a gate sign that read *"You Are Unwelcome to Long Binh Jail."*

Sammy drove through gate. Unshaven and desperately in need of haircuts, the prisoners peered through the bars of their confined quarters. The imprisoned soldiers shouted obscenities as we drove by. What crimes could these soldiers have committed to earn them a stay at Vietnam's most undesirable military prison?

"What is this place?" I asked.

"It's known as LBJ. It houses criminals waiting to be shipped back to the States for trial. Their charges range from actual crimes to physiological disorders," said John.

"Why so many blacks?"

"Because the blacks are pissed off about fighting in a white man's war."

"Hell, I'm white, and I'm pissed off about fighting in a white man's war," said Sammy, slowing down the truck.

He parked by a guard tower and climbed out of the cab. Retrieving the package from behind the seat, he walked into the tower without saying a word. John assured me it was only a package of laundry.

A few minutes later, Sammy returned with two bags of laundry plus another package wrapped in butcher paper. He threw the laundry bags in the back of the truck and placed the package behind the seat.

"What's in the package?" asked John.

"Dirty laundry," replied Sammy.

Sammy started up the truck and headed for Saigon.

Saigon was the capital of South Vietnam and second-largest city in the country. It was a thriving metropolis with a population of two million. A network of enemy tunnels lay ten miles away, and there was a good possibility the enemy had infiltrated the city.

Sammy turned into an alley and backed his truck into a laundry factory. Vietnamese laundry workers began unloading the laundry bags.

"Wait here. I have to deliver a package," said Sammy.

John didn't seem to be concerned about Sammy's suspicious packages and awaited his return.

Sammy delivered the package to a Vietnamese woman standing across the alley. They talked for a few minutes, and then the Vietnamese woman handed Sammy an envelope. Sammy returned to the truck and directed us to the bar across the alley, called Little Saigon.

"Mama-san will take care of you. I'll be back in an hour. Have a good time," said Sammy and walked off.

"Where you going?" asked John.

"I got to take care of some personal business. I'll see you in an hour. Enjoy."

Mama-san was a name for a Vietnamese mother. In this case, it defined the Vietnamese woman who owned the bar and controlled the girls working in her establishment.

John and I walked across the alley and up the wooden stairs. Entering the bar, we were greeted by Mama-san, the same Vietnamese woman who received the package from Sammy.

"You Sam friend?" she asked.

"Yes," John answered, smiling at the girls sitting at the bar.

"You like? Sam pay for you," said Mama-san.

"You're kidding," replied John with a devilish grin.

John didn't waste any time. He selected one of Mama-san's best-looking girls and led her upstairs. Again, although prostitution was considered illegal in Vietnam, the exploitation of their women seemed to be tolerated. Vietnamese women were compelled to work for Mama-san as bar hookers because of their few job prospects and economic needs. It became another occupation providing services to American soldiers.

Mama-san took my hand and escorted me to the bar. "You like? Sam pay for you too," she said, gently patting my hand.

Mama-san's girls were attractive, appearing to be around eighteen years of age. Their scent of their perfume was hard to resist.

"First I take bath," I said to Mama-san.

"Okay, GI, then girl take you bath," said Mama-san.

Mama-san handed me a cold Tiger 33 and gestured to two of her girls to escort me upstairs.

"You take bath, and then you have fun with my best girl," said Mama-san.

The girls led me up the stairs and down the hall to a room with a Victorian-shaped tub. The girls filled the tub with warm water as I undressed. One of the girls giggled as I took off my boots. "What's so funny?" I asked.

"Number ten," said the Vietnamese girl, squeezing her nose with her fingers.

"Number one" was defined as the best and "number ten" was defined as the worst of anything.

"I know my feet smell. That's why I want to take a bath," I replied.

The girls giggled as I slipped out of my fatigues. "Okay, now what's so funny?" I asked.

"You crazy, GI! Why you wear no underwear?" asked one of the girls.

"Because the military doesn't give me any underwear," I replied, slipping into the tub of warm water. Resting my head on the back of the tub, I thoroughly enjoyed feeling clean once again. When I opened my eyes, Mama-san was standing over me with a big grin.

"You like bath?" asked Mama-san.

"Yeah, it feels great."

"I clean clothes while you take bath," said Mama-san, gathering my filthy fatigues.

The girls scrubbed my back and washed my feet. Suddenly, the door opened and John burst into the room.

"What the hell are you doing, Garcia? You're supposed to be taking care of business, not taking a bath. I'll be downstairs drinking a cold beer. Hurry up. We have thirty minutes."

After my desperately needed bath, I climbed out of the tub and dried off. Mama-san was waiting with my clean fatigues and shined jungle boots.

"Which girl you like? Both very pretty," said Mama-san.

"Thank you, Mama-san, but I have to go downstairs."

"But Sam already pay for you," she replied.

Although I turned down the opportunity to enjoy one of Mama-san's best-looking girls, taking a warm bath was just as satisfying. I met John downstairs and enjoyed a cold beer while we waited for Sammy to arrive.

"You could have had a little boom-boom, but you wanted to take a bath. I don't know about you guys from California," said John.

He was about to order another cold Tiger 33 when Sammy arrived. "Well, did Mama-san take care of you?" he asked.

"She sure did, but Garcia insisted on a bath," replied John.

"Thanks for the good time," I said to Sammy.

"No problem. What are friends for, right, John? You would have done the same for me. Let's roll, we're burning daylight," said Sammy.

Sammy's truck was washed and loaded with white sacks of clean laundry. We climbed into the cab and headed back to Highway 1.

"Where did you go, Sammy?" asked John.

"I had to take care of some personal business," he repeated.

***

The following morning, Sammy dropped us off at John's favorite steam and cream (massage parlor). The military was aware of its presence but chose to ignore the service it provided. Located on the far side of the base, the parlor was at the highest point, overlooking the Dong Nai River.

"What you looking at?" John asked.

"That's the widest river I've ever seen," I said.

"You haven't seen anything yet. Wait until you see the Mekong Delta. Let's get going. I have more important things to do, like get a massage. One for the road."

"I could use a massage," I said.

"Yeah, a massage with a fringe benefit," replied John, chuckling.

Most single soldiers in Vietnam enjoyed an occasional sexual encounter with a hooker, but John seemed to be obsessed with it. Anytime John was in proximity to a hooker, he didn't hesitate to take advantage of her service.

John was greeted by an attractive Vietnamese girl in a long, white satin dress as we entered the lobby. "No see in long time. Where you been, John?" said the girl, taking John by his arm.

John and I were escorted down a corridor and greeted by ten more attractive Vietnamese girls. Each girl tried to entice me to enter her room. With all the girls being so attractive, it was hard to choose. I decided on the one with the cutest feet.

I was handed a towel. Wrapping the towel around my waist, I climbed onto the massage table. The girl with cute feet spoke English with a heavy Vietnamese accent.

Mama-san collected her money, along with my fatigues. "Where are you going with my fatigues?" I asked.

"I clean for you," replied Mama-san.

"They're clean enough," I said.

"I clean again," said Mama-san, leaving the room.

"What kind of massage you like today, GI?" asked the girl.

"What kind do you give?"

"Good kind. Lie down and be quiet. You talk too much," said the girl.

She vigorously massaged my neck and shoulders. Although the massage therapist was a hooker in disguise, I still enjoyed the massage.

"Now you take steam bath and wait for Mama-san to bring clothes."

"Sure, why not?" I replied.

I jumped off the table and slipped into the steam bath. The girl cranked up the steam, closed the door to the bath, and left the room.

The soothing warmth of the steam was comforting until it became unbearably hot. I tried to open the door, but I couldn't reach the latch. I shouted for help, but no one responded. I was about to kick the door down when the Vietnamese girl returned to the room.

"What matter, GI, too hot?" asked the girl, chuckling.

"No, I love being boiled alive," I replied sarcastically.

"No problem. Lie down on table, I make better," she commanded.

Episode Eleven

Visitor in the Night

March 25. By the time John and I returned to the base, a few of the soldiers injured on February 7 had returned to the field. Pate, one of the new arrivals, had been reassigned as the company clerk. Pate didn't remain in the field very long because his education qualified him for the company clerk position. His new assignment allowed him the privilege of being stationed in the rear. I gave him the alias "Pate the REMF."

Due to VC and NVA forces moving into the province, our mission remained search and destroy. Although large-scale battles were no longer a threat, Bravo Company's objective was to run patrols during the day and ambush trotters during the night.

A typical pattern was to insert a company into the LZ by helicopter, break into three platoon-size patrols, and scout the area. The three platoons would remain close to assist one another if anyone ran into trouble. Every three days, the platoons would link up for resupply.

With the Vietnamization program now in place, ARVNs were slowly taking over the fighting in the northern provinces. The program was developed to equip and train the Army of the Republic of Vietnam to eventually take over the ground defense in the North.

A typical day in the field consisted of waking up at dawn, preparing a light breakfast, pulling in the night work, and repacking our rucksacks. When the order was given to "put it on," the platoon headed into the wood line.

Our point team would lead us through valleys, over mountains, and across streams, searching for the enemy. At the end of the day, the platoon leader found a suitable position for the night and the process started over again in the morning.

The final three days of the mission were shifted to the flatlands. The objective was to patrol a suspected enemy supply route for main-force VC. The point team was able to cover a lot of ground since the area had been stripped of vegetation. There were trees but no leaves; the foliage had fallen to the ground. When it was time to search for a night defensive position, it was difficult to find a suitable location.

The platoon leader settled for a position in a dense growth of shrubbery and small trees. Although there was no greenery, the thicket provided adequate cover. I set up next to the only tree in the area. The others spread out among the thicket. Everyone pulled out their night work and found suitable locations for their claymores and trip flares.

"Why is all the vegetation gone?" I asked.

"I'm not sure, but I think the military sprayed the jungle with an herbicide to kill it," said Sundance.

"Why would the military want to kill the jungle?"

"To make it easier to find the enemy."

"Yeah, and make it easier for the dinks to find us too," said Hillbilly.

Everyone settled in for the night. I prepared a chicken and rice LRP, along with a canteen of grape Kool-Aid. I blew up my air mattress and settled down for the evening. With no moon or fluorescent moss, it was going to be difficult to locate the guard station.

I pulled my poncho liner up to my chest and looked up at the sky. Then I heard something moving along the jungle floor. It appeared to be moving away from the perimeter, so I dozed off.

During the night, I was awakened by the weight of something lying across my body. Placing my hand on top of its scaly skin confirmed my worst fear—it was a snake, a very large snake. Trembling with fear, I could feel every scale as the reptile slithered over my body.

It seemed like eternity waiting for the large reptile to slither into the night. Finally, when the reptile's tail had passed over my body, I low-crawled straight for the guard station.

"Did you hear the big snake crawling through the perimeter?" I whispered to Brother Charles nervously.

"What snake?" he replied.

"The snake that just crawled over my body!"

"All I heard was Bart snoring," replied Brother Charles.

When it was time for Brother Charles to search for his guard replacement, I decided to remain at the guard station.

"Be careful. There's a big snake out there."

"Sure, Jarcia," he muttered.

At the break of dawn, I searched the perimeter for the snake that had nearly given me heart failure. I spotted it lying at the base of a tree. I didn't hesitate to direct everyone's attention to the six-foot-long boa constrictor. "Look! That's the snake that slithered over me last night!"

"Damn, Jarcia, you're lucky that big-ass snake didn't swallow you like a rodent," said Brother Charles, chuckling.

"Don't worry, Garcia, the snake isn't venomous. The only way it could have killed you was by wrapping its body around you and suffocating you. The snakes are bigger in the hills of Virginia," said Hillbilly.

Duggy poked at the snake with a stick until it slithered into the jungle. For some reason, no one believed my story about the encounter with the snake.

March 27. Sergeant Tomas received word that Blackfoot was being extracted for green-line guard at Bien Hoa Air Force Base. Given the recent attacks on the base, additional security was required. The point team led the platoon back to the LZ, and Blackfoot was promptly extracted from the field.

The platoon was flown back to Fire Base Mace and convoyed to Bien Hoa. For the next three days, Blackfoot Platoon would provide base security. Second squad was assigned to green-line guard the first night. Joe and his squad had the night off, enjoying a night's sleep without guard duty.

After dinner, second squad was driven to their assigned guard bunkers on the green line. Brother Charles and I were assigned to bunker number eight. It was the farthest from company headquarters, and we were the last to be dropped off.

Number eight was a fortified bunker, providing protection from incoming, with an opening to view the wood line and a cot for sleeping. Given the hundred meters to the wood line and several rows of concertina wire, the area seemed fairly secure.

Brother Charles decided to spend a little time writing a letter before nightfall. I climbed on top of the bunker to get better reception for my transistor radio. The AFVN (American Forces Vietnam Network) radio station was our only link to the outside world. The station featured America's popular music keeping us up to date on current affairs and sports.

Listening to a popular Top 40 song, I took the opportunity to reminisce about my summer romance with a redhead named Lisa. Interrupting my thoughts, AFVN broadcasted a special news report regarding US negotiations with North Vietnam to pull troops out of South Vietnam.

I listened but didn't expect to hear any good news. Prior negotiations had been a waste of time, meaning the communists would never accept a peaceful settlement with the US government.

Time passed slowly. Fortunately, there were no signs of an enemy attack. When my watch came to an end, I woke Brother Charles and quickly fell asleep.

At dawn's first light, I was awakened by Brother Charles. We boarded a deuce and a half and were driven to the mess hall. Second squad was off for the day, so I decided to head for the PX. I turned in six rolls of 35 mm film to be developed and purchased six more. Sergeant Tomas took the opportunity to purchase two bottles of Early Times Whisky and a Chevrolet Malibu. The PX provided an opportunity to purchase vehicles direct from the manufacturer at a discounted price. His new vehicle would be shipped to a dealership in his hometown.

After dinner, first squad prepared for green-line guard. John and I enjoyed an evening at the EM club. With no early wakeup call, I indulged in the alcohol. John managed to locate a hooker disguised as a hooch maid for a late-night rendezvous.

Blackfoot Platoon provided base security at Bien Hoa Air Force Base for three nights and returned to Fire Base Fontaine to join the rest of the company. The time in the rear was a welcome break from the bush and an opportunity to take care of any personal business.

***

March 30. Blackfoot joined Aztec and Cheyenne on Fire Base Fontaine. The newly assigned platoon leader was awaiting our arrival, along with a soldier known as Son-in-Law. The original members of the platoon were pleased to learn of their new leader but weren't too excited about Son-in-Law's return.

It had taken two months since my arrival to fill Blackfoot's critical leadership role. Sergeant Tomas had taken the position temporarily and provided excellent leadership. He was well respected for it.

The young lieutenant stood in front of the platoon and was introduced. "Attention, everyone," said the lieutenant. "My name is Lieutenant CJ, and I am your new platoon leader. Although I don't know any of you, I will try my best to give you the leadership you expect and deserve. As your new platoon leader, I have the privilege of informing you that every forty-five days, beginning in April, Bravo Company will enjoy a three-day R & R at China Beach. This is a new battalion policy, implemented to improve morale."

The new platoon leader had no field experience and had never commanded a light weapons platoon. Sergeant Tomas was aware his replacement had no field experience but was relieved that Blackfoot platoon had a new leader.

Sergeant Tomas and his squad leaders spent the rest of the day preparing Lieutenant CJ for his leadership role. When it was time to return to the field, Lieutenant CJ would have to depend on Sergeant Tomas and his team leaders.

***

March 31. Another month came to an end, and the company prepared for another mission. Everyone in Blackfoot was concerned about returning to the field with an inexperienced platoon leader. Like the rest of us, Lieutenant CJ would have to prove himself before gaining the respect of his men.

***

April 1. During the first day of the mission, Lieutenant CJ unexpectedly led his platoon into an enemy bunker complex. Fortunately, the complex had been abandoned.

"I didn't see those bunkers," he said.

"Everyone makes mistakes, but in the field, mistakes get you killed," replied Sergeant Tomas.

Lieutenant CJ realized he had a lot to learn and needed to rely on his team leaders until he became jungle-wise.

***

April 3. In preparation for log day, Blackfoot linked up with Aztec and Cheyenne. I received several letters from Dad and a few others from friends. Although I didn't receive letters from any female acquaintances, it was good to hear from someone.

The backlog bird returned to the LZ, and the remaining supplies were placed on the helicopter. Everyone prepared to move out with a new objective. For the next three days,

Bravo Company would run a sweep through suspected enemy territory, and set up platoon-size ambushes during the night.

With the help of experienced team leaders, Lieutenant CJ was becoming a jungle-wise leader. After a night in ambush position, everyone brought in their night work. Lieutenant CJ gave the point man an azimuth and gave the order to move out.

By day's end, the platoon covered one thousand meters of jungle. When the order was given to set up for the night, everyone was exhausted but relieved. Humping long distances wasn't good for the platoon's morale, especially when the First Cavalry Division was considered air mobile. Fortunately, the point team didn't have to break through thick brush, making decent time.

***

April 4. It was the beginning of another stressful day. Triple canopy made it difficult to move through the jungle but provided excellent cover. The order was given early in the day to set up for the night.

Some took the opportunity to enjoy a short nap or write a letter. John took the opportunity to read *The New York Times*. Ever since my first encounter with the enemy, I had never allowed myself the privilege of relaxing. If I had the opportunity to engage the enemy before they engaged me, I had the advantage of coming home alive.

"How can you read the paper, knowing there's dinks out there?" I said to my squad leader.

"It's easy when I know you're looking out for me. Don't you know how to relax?" asked John.

"Not in the jungle," I replied.

"If the higher-ups took care of business like Lieutenant Calley, this war would have been over a long time ago," said John, holding up the headlines printed on the front page dated April 1, 1971. *Lt. Calley Convicted of Premeditated Murder,* read the headlines.

"What could Lieutenant Calley possibly have done to get convicted of murder?" I asked.

"You mean you haven't heard about Calley?"

"No, but I'm curious to know."

"His platoon killed a bunch of gooks under his command," said John.

"Isn't that why we're in Vietnam?"

"Not the way Lieutenant Calley did it," said John and went back to reading his paper.

What I learned was that Lieutenant Calley had been accused of ordering and participating in the killing of innocent civilians in a small hamlet near My Lai, including women, children, and infants. Calley's defense was that his commanding officer claimed everyone in the hamlet was considered Viet Cong.

The bloody atrocity could only be considered premeditated murder. Unfortunately, for a nation that already had an attitude of coldness and indifference regarding the Vietnam War, this was just another reason to shun returning American soldiers.

April 5. Once again Blackfoot was on the move, searching for the enemy. When the point team came upon an abandoned bunker complex, the patrol came to a halt. Footprints indicated a platoon of NVA soldiers had recently been in the area.

Curious to know what was going on, John headed for the front of the patrol, joining Joe and Lieutenant CJ. "What's going on?"

"There's a fucking platoon of dinks nearby," said Joe.

"What do you want to do, Lieutenant?" asked Sergeant Tomas.

"The CO wants the platoon to ambush the bunker complex," replied Lieutenant CJ.

"We should set up outside the bunker complex," said Sergeant Tomas.

"Yeah, Lieutenant, this is fucking ridiculous. We can't set up inside the bunker complex with a fucking platoon of dinks in the area," said Joe.

"It's suicide," said John.

"The order came from the CO, not me. Now tell your platoon to get their shit out, Sergeant Tomas," said Lieutenant CJ.

"If we're setting up inside the bunker complex, I'm putting out an Alpha, Alpha, and you're coming with me," said Joe.

Joe was the only team leader with experience in setting up an automatic ambush. No one else wanted the responsibility. Joe collected the equipment and headed out of the perimeter. Following close behind was Lieutenant CJ and a few selected men to stand guard.

Joe located a position on the trotter and set out six claymores. He daisy-chained the claymores with detonation cord and strung the trip wire across the trotter. He connected to the battery and slowly stepped back. With the automatic ambush in place, Joe signaled for Lieutenant CJ and the others to head back to the perimeter.

Joe put himself in danger every time he set up an automatic ambush. If it accidently went off, he would be killed instantly. This was the price to pay for additional security during the night.

Fortunately, no one in Bravo Company had ever been injured or killed setting up or dismantling an automatic ambush.

Joe and Lieutenant CJ returned to the NDP as everyone was settling in for the night. With the threat of the enemy returning to the bunker complex, we were grateful for the automatic ambush being in place. I set the safety mechanism of my M-16 on full automatic and placed my weapon within arm's reach.

Sleeping in ten- to fifteen-minute increments, I made it through the night. The following morning, everyone pulled in their night work in anticipation of moving out of the area. Unfortunately, the order was given to continue the search for the enemy in the area.

A thorough search revealed the enemy had vacated the area. The CO called off the search and ordered Lieutenant CJ to set up for the night.

April 6. Lieutenant CJ, having become familiar with his new platoon, decided to be part of the point team and lead the way. The patrol came to a halt when the point team discovered two bunkers. Well hidden, the bunkers served as an outpost for a larger bunker complex.

A nearby campfire indicated a small group of enemy soldiers had spent the night. I took off my rucksack and sat down as Lieutenant CJ met with his team leaders. Due to lack of sleep, I closed my eyelids and fell asleep. When I opened my eyes, there were two enemy soldiers standing by a nearby stream. Without hesitation, I reached for my weapon and took aim.

Duggy, sitting nearby, realized I had seen something and swung his gun around. He started to shoot, but his M-60 machine gun jammed. "Damn it!" he shouted.

I didn't have a clear shot, but I fired off three rounds as the enemy scurried across the creek and up the hill. The M-16 rounds ricocheted off the trees. The enemy soldiers disappeared into the jungle. Duggy cleared the gun and started firing, but the enemy was out of range.

Duggy was outraged that his gun had jammed. I was relieved I hadn't taken another life. Lieutenant CJ made his way to the rear of the platoon, demanding to know why shots were fired. "Who fired the shots?"

"Garcia did. My gun jammed," said Duggy.

"How many were there?"

"Two VC," I replied.

"Should we prepare for a counterattack?"

"Don't worry, they're just a couple strays," Duggy replied.

Lieutenant CJ sent Joe's squad to patrol the immediate area. A quick search across the creek revealed the enemy had fled. Joe returned to the perimeter, and the platoon continued the mission.

As we suspected, we discovered a bunker complex. Besides a number of sleeping bunkers, there was a mess hall with showers nearby. The bunker complex appeared to be a recreational center. Vegetation was growing over the top bunkers. The CO decided the complex posed no threat and ordered Blackfoot to move beyond the bunkers and set up for the night.

April 7. The morning started out like any other morning in the field. The platoon brought in their night work and moved out in search of the enemy. Bravo Company's mission was still in the flatlands, with Cheyenne and Aztec working nearby for support. Working in the flatlands made it easier to navigate through the jungle. At the same time, the enemy's presence was becoming more apparent.

Team leaders John and Joe having left the platoon, I was assigned slack position and Cartwright was assigned point position. We were now the new point team.

Fearing for my life, I tried to convince Lieutenant CJ to allow me to remain in the rear, but John convinced Lieutenant CJ that our experience was needed up front. I saw it as an invitation to be killed. Cartwright had a different attitude about his new position and embraced it.

"I never intended to be in this position," I said to John.

"Did you think you would never be part of my point team?" John asked.

"There are other soldiers in the platoon with more experience, so why me?" I asked.

"Joe and I both agree. You and Cartwright are the best choices for these positions. Now do your job," he said.

"If you want the best grunt for the job, then why don't you and Joe take over point?" I said sarcastically.

"Oh, hell no, we're too short," said Joe, chuckling.

I placed my weapon on full automatic and followed Cartwright out of the perimeter. John and the squad RTO followed.

"I'm depending on you to watch my back," said Cartwright.

"I'll try my best. I want to go home just as bad as you do," I answered.

My new position demanded I learn a new set of rules. My job was not only to be the second set of eyes for Cartwright, but to assist in breaking brush. Cartwright and I were now in control of the platoon's destiny, and I wasn't sure if I was the right man for the job.

The jungle gave way to a clear path, allowing Cartwright to move at a steady pace. The pace count was at two hundred meters when Lieutenant CJ and the others fell behind. I stood under the shade of a tree as I waited for them.

Lieutenant CJ was the first to arrive, and then the others slowly appeared. When Cartwright came to an area with thick vegetation, he began chopping his way though. Unfortunately, he chopped through a gigantic hornets' nest.

"Hornets!" cried Cartwright, running to avoid the painful stings.

Amid a swarm of angry hornets, my only choice was to follow Cartwright. Lieutenant CJ, Sergeant Tomas, and the RTO followed, with the remaining members of the platoon retreating in the opposite direction.

I tried to outrun the hornets, but the angry insects managed to crawl under my boonie hat, delivering painful stings. Cartwright and I eluded more of the hornets by diving into the creek. Lieutenant CJ, Sergeant Tomas, and the squad RTO followed headfirst.

With our heads above water, we waited for the rest of the platoon to arrive.

"I must have been stung at least a dozen times," said Cartwright, walking with his head slightly above the waterline.

"Are you all right, Cartwright?" asked Lieutenant CJ

"Do I look all right? I just been stung by angry hornets, and I'm soaked from head to toe," complained Cartwright.

"How about you, Garcia?"

"Hell no," I replied.

The four of us waded across the creek and climbed onto the bank. Soaking wet, I proceeded to lay everything out to dry. Cartwright and I were the only members of the platoon who had been severely stung. The hornets were no longer a threat, so Lieutenant CJ began the task of locating the remainder of his platoon.

Although both parties had radio communication, the only way to guide the others to our location was to bang steel pots. Sergeant Tomas ordered the first squad RTO to bang two steel pots together. When we heard their response, we determined the others were farther away than anticipated.

"How far away do you think they are?" asked Lieutenant CJ

"As far as it takes to get away from painful hornet stings," replied Cartwright.

Lieutenant CJ continued to bang the steel pots together until the remainder of the platoon reached the edge of the creek.

"How do we get across the creek?" called John, grinning.

"Swim like we did," said Cartwright.

Lieutenant CJ decided to set up next to the creek for the night. After putting out my night work I located the field medic for an injection of morphine.

"Your face is swollen. How do you feel?" asked the medic.

"I feel like crap, and I have an unbelievable migraine."

"I'm going to have you medevaced," said the medic.

I accompanied him to Lieutenant CJ's position in the center of the perimeter.

"Garcia needs to be taken out of the field," said the medic.

"What for?" he said.

"He's having a serious reaction to the hornet stings."

"For a few bee stings? Can't do it," said Lieutenant CJ.

"Are you kidding? He needs medical attention."

"Can't you give him something?" the lieutenant said, looking at me. He continued to refuse to have me taken out of the field.

Discouraged and in severe pain, I made my way back to my sleeping position. The field medic gave me another injection of morphine to help with the pain.

During the night, I was awakened by someone who sounded like he was in agony. Concerned that the noise would give our position away, I made my way to Cartwright. "What the hell is going on?"

"Son-in-Law is overdosing on heroin," replied Cartwright.

"Why doesn't the medic do something to shut him up?"

"If the bastard doesn't shut up soon, I'm going to put him out of his misery," said Cartwright angrily.

"The lieutenant is on the horn, calling for a medevac," whispered Sergeant Tomas.

"You have to be kidding. If anyone needed a medevac, it was me," I said, unable to hide the anger in my voice.

Son-in-Law had recently rejoined Blackfoot. He had been disciplined for heroin use on the fire base, and now he was using in the field.

"That's bullshit," I said to Sergeant Tomas.

"I agree, but I don't call the shots anymore," replied the sergeant.

The enemy was probably aligning their mortar tubes to our position as the platoon waited in the dark for the medevac. Frustrated and in pain, I made my way back to my sleeping area. I should have moaned during the night. Maybe that would have taken me out of the field.

The medic guided the medevac pilot to our position with a device that flashed a beam of light easily detected from above. Once the pilot confirmed our position, he hovered over the treetops and lowered a jungle penetrator with a metal litter. Son-in-Law was quickly secured to the litter and lifted into the medevac. Lieutenant CJ, along with everyone else in the platoon, wanted the hell-raiser out of the field at any cost, even if it called for an emergency night medical evacuation.

Episode Twelve

China Beach

April 10. Blackfoot made it through the night medical evacuation without incident. I survived the painful swelling of the hornet stings and was able to wear a steel pot again. Son-in-Law survived the heroin overdose and was on the fire base, dealing with his addiction. Unfortunately, he would return to the field once he was released for duty.

Bravo Company was extracted to Fire Base Fontaine and convoyed to Fire Base Mace to prepare for our first trip to China Beach. Bravo Company would spend the night on the base and fly to China Beach in the morning. Knowing the company would return to Fire Base Fontaine to pull base security duty made the trip to China Beach even more enjoyable.

Morale was high. Everyone was excited to have an opportunity to enjoy life once again. We met at the big green cooler, drinking beer and soda, waiting for the convoy to arrive. There were even smiles on the faces of the survivors of the February 7 ambush.

The convoy arrived and everyone was eager to climb aboard. The trip down Highway 1 was becoming familiar to me. I recognized villages and even a face or two. I definitely knew how many water buffalo roamed the countryside.

The convoy arrived at Fire Base Mace late in the afternoon. After a comforting meal and hot shower, I joined the brothers in a game of spades. Spades was a popular card game among the brothers. Two-card guts was the popular game among whites. If you liked to gamble, two-card guts was the game for you.

After a few games of spades, Brother Charles and I went to see the movie *Airport* being projected onto the barracks wall. The movie reminded me of the time Jet, Little Joey, and I spent a day together walking across Fort Ord in the rain to see the new release.

Movies featured on the fire base were the latest releases. Most of the time the projector was louder than the sound, and there wasn't any popcorn or candy. After the movie, I headed to the barracks to relax and listen to a little music.

The batteries powering my cassette player needed replacement. No regular batteries were available. I discovered a unique way to create my own. A discarded Prick 25 field radio battery made an excellent alternative.

Removing the cardboard backing from the case, I separated the cylindrical cells. The energy in two electrical cells was equivalent to an A-size battery. The radio battery could no longer power a field radio but provided enough power for my cassette player.

April 11. After a 7:00 a.m. wake-up call, everyone was up preparing for the flight to China Beach. I took a cold shower, put on a pair of clean fatigues, and headed for the mess hall. I had a light breakfast, fearing the flight might upset my stomach.

The platoon leader assembled Blackfoot in front of the supply room, and everyone boarded the waiting convoy. The convoy rolled through the local village. Children ran alongside, begging for food and money. The platoon was driven to a nearby landing strip, where villagers were awaiting our arrival.

Villagers and their children surrounded the soldiers as they climbed off the trucks. Although Americans were discouraged from fraternizing with the locals, we saw no harm in it. The children peddled souvenirs, sunglasses, jewelry, watches, wallets, knives, playing cards, beer, sodas, drugs, drug paraphernalia, and pornography.

Drugs were plentiful and impossible to control. The drug problem was an extension of the Vietnam War. Grunts were doing it to take the edge off everyday stress. Others were doing it because they were addicted. The only authority controlling the drug problem was the soldiers themselves.

The blistering-hot red clay caused everyone to migrate to the shade of a nearby tree. Some of the grunts climbed over a barbed-wire fence, away from view of the platoon leaders, where they purchased consai and scag.

Trip, one of the recent arrivals, was addicted to scag. In dire need, he purchased a vial from a Vietnamese peddler. With a KOOL filtered cigarette in hand, Trip packed the tip with the white powder. Placing the scag-laced cigarette in his mouth, he inhaled the smoke.

"Do you want a hit?" he asked.

Having tried the narcotic once before, I refused, knowing the drug created a feeling of euphoria that could lead to a powerful addiction. "No, go ahead, knock yourself out."

Scag smokers preferred the white powder over marijuana because it was odorless and went undetected. According to scag smokers, the high was an incredible feeling of euphoria. I called it addiction.

Several soldiers climbed over the low barbed-wire fence to drink Tiger 33 beer and share a Park Lane—a manufactured marijuana cigarette, popular among pot smokers.

"Here comes the C-140 transport plane!" shouted Sundance.

Everyone cheered when the transport touched down on the red clay runway. It taxied to the end and stopped, engines idling. The ramp was lowered, and the load master, wearing an olive drab flight helmet, waved us aboard.

Blackfoot filed in and took seats as the load master raised the ramp. The pilot revved up the engines and taxied down the runway. The pilot went full throttle and lifted the plane.

Twenty minutes into the flight, I was awakened by the nauseating odor of vomit. Trip had vomited on himself and on my fatigue pants. With nowhere else to go, I had no choice but to remain seated, inhaling the disgusting smell.

Fortunately, the pilot was soon making his descent into Vung Tau Airport. The C-140 transport safely landed and taxied over to the terminal. I couldn't get out fast enough for a breath of fresh air.

Expecting a modern airport, I walked into a waiting area that had been built by army engineers. It had a metal canopy and wood benches in the waiting area. A sign mounted on the roof read, *Welcome to Vung Tau Airport.*

Everyone boarded the buses waiting to transport us to the China Beach R & R center. A soldier dressed in nicely tailored fatigues boarded the bus and addressed the group of enthusiastic soldiers. "Welcome to China Beach. On our way to the R & R center, we will be driving through Vung Tau Village to give you an idea what it has to offer."

The drive through the village revealed nightclubs, bars, and restaurants. Bar hookers waved as street vendors worked the streets.

"Can we spend the night in the village?" shouted Bart, seated at the back of the bus.

"You can spend the night in the village as long as you're off the streets by eleven o'clock," said the nicely dressed soldier.

The driver turned onto the street that fronted the South China Sea beaches. Everyone looked out the windows, enjoying the view of an attractive Vietnamese girl in a red bikini. The bus entered the R & R compound, parking in front of the special services center.

Everyone was instructed to lay down their rucksacks and stack their weapons military style. When the remainder of Bravo Company arrived, the orientation officer addressed the entire company.

"Good afternoon, gentlemen. My name is Lieutenant Green. Welcome to the First Cav R & R Center in China Beach. Before I let you go, there are a few things I need to address.

"First of all, you can stay at the R & R center or the village. If you decide to stay at the R & R center, we have clean barracks, a mess hall, showers, and a night club with live music. It's all free. If you decide to stay in Vung Tau Village, you will have to pay for a hotel room. Every afternoon we have a great barbecue. If you want to go swimming in the ocean, see Mama-san and she'll give you a pair of cutoff khakis, but remember to return them.

"When you visit the village, don't forget to exchange your MPC for piastres. Do not, I repeat, do not exchange your money in the village. The cowboys (teenage Vietnamese thugs) will cheat you every time. The MPC you exchange in the village just might buy the weapons used against you in the field. We strongly recommend you stay within the limits of the business area and don't wander into the locals' part of the village.

"There is an enforced 11:00 p.m. curfew. You better obey it unless you want to spend the night in the brig. Are there any questions?"

"What about the hookers?" shouted BJ, standing in the back of the formation.

"Don't worry, there's plenty of hookers. Just be a little selective unless you want to visit the medic when you return to the fire base."

"What did he mean by being selective?" asked Holt.

"He's talking about the shrimp boat, dummy," replied Brother Al.

"What shrimp boat?" Holt asked.

"Your shrimp boat that stays out in the ocean forever because there's no cure for the black syph," explained Brother Al, referring to a myth about an incurable venereal disease.

"You're joking, right?" asked Bart.

Lieutenant Green smiled, dismissing the company. I immediately set out to search for a hooch maid. I located Mama-san standing in front of the barracks, rolling a cigarette. She smiled, exposing all of her betel-nut-stained teeth. Older Vietnamese women enjoyed the mild stimulant. Unfortunately, chewing the seeds stained their teeth.

"Mama-san, can you clean my fatigues? I'll pay."

"You smell number ten. Take off, I wash for you," said Mama-san. She handed me a pair of cutoff khakis in exchange for my fatigues and boots. "You go beach now. I have clean when you come back," said Mama-san.

I was drawn to music coming from the Beachcomber Club. Several members of Blackfoot were at the bar, enjoying a cool alcoholic drink. Others were outside enjoying a Vietnamese rock and roll band.

I headed for the beach, where Teeny Bopper and Son-in-Law were entertaining a couple of attractive Vietnamese hookers. Peter Gun was taking photographs of all the Vietnamese girls on the beach.

I managed to take a few photographs of my own. With my 35 mm camera, I focused on members of Blackfoot wading in the sandy waters of the South China Sea. I hoped the photos would convince Mom I wasn't always in harm's way.

A warm southerly stream of air blew over the surface of the water. Whitecap waves and rain-bearing clouds meant the beginning of the monsoon season. With the force of the wind increasing, I decided to return for my fatigues.

Mama-san was waiting in front the barracks with a clean pair of fatigues and shined jungle boots in hand. I handed her five dollars MPC for her service and extended my hand in gratitude. "Thanks for cleaning my fatigues, Mama San."

"Now you smell number one," she said.

After showering, I returned to the Beachcomber Club to enjoy the band's last set. I drank a few beers and decided to visit the village. I stopped at the exchange shack to convert MPC to piastres, and saw a sign that read: *The current exchange rate is at 200 piastres to one US dollar.* The cashier handed over 18,000 piastres in exchange for $90 MPC. Placing the piastres in my fatigue pocket, I boarded a waiting Lambretta.

"Vung Tau village, please," I said to the driver.

"GI like to have fun?" he asked.

"I sure do."

"Many girl in village for you, GI," he said, accelerating.

Racing down the bumpy, two-lane paved road, the driver didn't hesitate getting me to the village. As I hung on with one hand and held my boonie hat with the other, my first Lambretta ride proved to be equivalent of an E-ticket ride at the Disneyland amusement park.

The driver entered the village, stopping in front of the Grand Hotel. A circular courtyard and giant white pillars marked the entrance to the high-rise. Built by the French, it was one of the tallest buildings in the village.

Around the corner was a hotel named the Palace, another high-rise towering over the structures in the village. With this number of sleeping establishments, restaurants, and nightclubs, I was determined to enjoy my first night.

Unfamiliar with the layout, I decided to visit all the hotels and nightclubs. My first stop was the Mi Lien Hotel. Grunts staying at the hotel were easy to identify—they were the soldiers with the faded jungle fatigues and worn-down jungle boots.

The military was the only source of income for the villagers, who provided all the services and entertainment to satisfy a soldier's needs. Street vendors peddled food and drink, and attractive Vietnamese hookers enticed soldiers to enter their bars. Every drinking establishment provided an assortment of hookers wanting to have sex with anyone willing to pay the price.

I couldn't resist a sandwich from one of the street vendors. Not knowing if the food was safe to eat, I dared to take a chance. The elderly Vietnamese vendor smiled, exposing his missing upper front tooth as he diligently prepared my meal. Adding a few chili peppers, he wrapped the sandwich in butcher paper.

The roll of bread tasted freshly baked, and the Peking chili peppers added a spicy flavor. The vendor smiled as he watched me enjoy the sandwich. I washed it down with a Vietnamese orange drink to soothe the burning sensation of the chilies.

After the better-than-expected sandwich, I was eager to visit the rest of the village. Wandering through the streets, I noticed a strong influence of French architecture, stemming from when the French occupied Vietnam.

I returned to the rooftop bar at the Mi Lien for a drink. Walking up several flights of concrete stairs, I entered the nightclub. After a few cocktails and a conversation with Mama-san, I was convinced that I would return for the evening entertainment.

On my way to the next club, I was swarmed by a group of Vietnamese children. None were more than five years of age. The children insisted on placing a string of flowers around my neck. There was no avoiding their persistent generosity. When the children scurried away, I realized their generosity was only a distraction to take the piastres from my fatigue shirt pocket. The cute children proved to be well-trained little thieves.

Amused by their speed and agility, I watched as they hustled inebriated soldiers walking down the street. I followed them until they led me to the part of the village where they lived. The locals pedaled their bicycles and children played in the streets.

Villagers glared as I walked through their neighborhood. Tropical gardens surrounded small family homes, with chickens running through the streets and ducks swimming in ponds. Animal carcasses hung in the store windows.

I was approached by a young Vietnamese boy. "Hey GI, where you going?" he asked.

"Where did you learn to speak English?" I asked.

"From you, GI!"

"Where can I get a little chop-chop?" I asked.

"No chop-chop in village for you, GI."

"Why not?"

"Vietnamese restaurant no serve you. They think you number ten," said the boy with a frown on his face.

"It's getting late anyway. I better get back," I said.

"Where you sleep tonight, GI?"

"I'll probably stay at the Mi Lien Hotel."

"You pay too much money to stay there. I take you to number one place. Follow me, GI."

"Wait a minute. Where we going?" I said.

"You want girl, right?"

"You mean hooker?"

"Not hooker, girlfriend," replied the boy.

I decided to check out what he had to offer and followed him into a courtyard lined with palm trees and tropical plants. The boy walked past a blind papa-san playing the harmonica. He headed for a mama-san standing in the center of the courtyard.

One-bedroom bungalows made of adobe surrounded the tropical garden and waterfall. I recognized a soldier from Bravo Company escorting his attractive date into a bungalow. I was convinced this was a safe place to stay.

"How much for the night?" I asked the Vietnamese boy.

"For you, ten dollar, GI."

"What do I get for ten dollars?"

"No sweat, girl come with bungalow," replied the boy.

I handed the boy ten dollars in piastres. He snatched the money from my hand and handed it to Mama-san. The boy took my hand and escorted me to my bungalow.

The one-room bungalow came with a bed, a toilet, and an attractive Vietnamese girl seated on a couch. Twisting her hair and chewing gum, the girl was thoroughly involved in a comic book. She looked up and smiled. Then she continued to enjoy her comic book.

The boy returned with two buckets of water. "Do you like?" he asked, raising his eyebrows several times.

"Yes, she's very pretty, but why two buckets of water?" I replied.

"For shower, one for you and one for her. No sweat, GI, I see you tomorrow," he said, heading for the door.

"Hey, wait a minute! What's your name?"

"They call me Easy Money."

"Thanks, Easy Money," I said, handing over five dollars MPC.

"Hey, GI, you number one, no matter what village people say," said the boy, running out the room and clutching his money tightly.

I pushed aside the curtain of beads that separated the room from the toilet. In the corner was a hole chiseled through the concrete that led to the sewer. The room didn't provide the luxuries of American hotels, but it provided the necessities. Paying ten dollars for a room and an attractive girl was worth it.

"What's your name?" I asked the Vietnamese girl.

The girl lowered the comic book, placing her mouth by my ear. "My name is Kim," she said in a soft voice.

"Kim, that's a nice name."

"What your name?" she asked, speaking with a Vietnamese accent.

"Ricky," I answered.

"You want boom-boom, Ricky?"

"There will be plenty of time later. I want to get to know you," I replied.

Kim listened as I told her stories about family and friends, along with a description of my hometown. I even told her about Disneyland. I continued my conversation until a strong whiff of consai entered the room.

"GI next door smoke boo-koo (from the French *beaucoup*, a lot) consai," said Kim.

Knowing it was the grunt from Bravo Company, I decided to visit. The soldier was seated on the floor, smoking a hand-rolled marijuana cigarette the size of a cigar.

"What's going on?" I asked.

"Just smoking a hooter, trying to forget the war. You want a hit?"

"What platoon you with?" I asked.

"Aztec Platoon. Who you with?"

"Blackfoot."

"Oh yeah. You're the renegade who fired up those dinks the other day. Hey, I'm Stash from Jersey," said the stoned soldier.

I gave Stash the peace sign and returned to my room. Once again, Kim was thoroughly involved in her comic book. I took off my boots and relaxed on the bed. A few minutes later, Stash and his girlfriend entered the room.

Stash placed a plastic bag filled with ice and a few Tiger 33 beers on the floor and got comfortable.

"Hey man, this is my girl, Binh," said Stash, his eyes half closed.

"Hi, Binh. That's a nice name. What does it mean?"

"Peace," she replied.

"Like a piece of ass," said Stash, laughing hysterically.

Stash was a hippie who abused drugs and ended up in Vietnam. He was annoying from the time he entered the room. I wanted him to leave, but he kept drinking and smoking Park Lanes.

"Does anyone want a little chop-chop?" asked Stash.

The girls smiled and nodded. Stash reached into his fatigue shirt pocket and pulled out a handful of piastres. He threw the money on the floor, and the girls scrambled to pick it up.

"Buy some chop-chop and Tiger beer, and I'll love you forever," said Stash.

The girls ran out of the room with handfuls of money, giggling. Stash reached into his plastic bag for another beer and realized it was empty. He pulled a pack of Park Lanes from his shirt pocket instead. He fired one up with his Zippo lighter and took a hit. He exhaled the smoke and then handed it over to me.

I took a hit and handed it back. I began feeling nauseated and wondered if Stash laced his cigarettes with scag. After a few hits, Stash passed out, the cigarette burning between his fingers. He drew his hand back when the flame burned down to his fingers. "What the hell happened?" he asked.

"You passed out," I answered.

"Wow! That shit is dangerous, man. If I keep smoking, I'm not going home next week," said Stash, slurring his words.

"How long have you been in Vietnam?" I asked.

"Six months too long."

"Are you going home for good?"

"Hell no, I'm going home for two weeks, but I'm not coming back."

"You have to come back or you'll be charged with treason."

"I don't care what they do to me. I'm never coming back to this fucked-up place!"

Stash continued to ramble until the girls entered the room with two large sacks. They had purchased dried meat, bread, noodles, and several bottles of Tiger 33 beer. The dried meat tasted like leather and the bread was hard. Since there were very few dogs and cats around the village, I wondered if the meat had come from a domestic animal.

Stash managed to drink a couple more Tiger 33 beers before passing out. The girls helped me get him into his bed, and then I was finally alone with my date. The only problem was getting Kim to put down her comic book.

The following morning, I was up at the break of dawn. Kim was asleep, her comic book lying next to her ear. I left her two thousand piasters, neatly folded in her comic book, and headed for the door.

Ready for another day in the village, I left the bungalow. For Kim, it had been just another day of work. For me, it was one less day in-country. Waiting in the courtyard was the Vietnamese boy who called himself Easy Money.

"Hey GI, you have good time last night?" he asked.

"Yes, thanks for the recommendation," I replied.

"You come back later. I get you better price and different girl."

"Thanks for the invitation, but I think I'll stay at the R & R center tonight."

Well rested, I drew a deep breath of fresh morning air and made my way to the Mi Lien. Although I was a considerable distance from the hotel, I enjoyed the morning walk.

Waiting in the lobby were Brother Al and Brother Charles.

"Where you been, Jarcia?" asked Brother Charles.

"I spent the night with a good-looking girl over on the west side of the village," I said.

"Officer Green said to stay away from that part of the village," said Brother Al.

"It was safe," I replied.

"You better stay out of that area or you might get your throat cut," said Brother Charles.

"What did you guys do last night?" I asked.

"We found this bar where the brothers are loved by all the girls, and Mama-san entertained us with sweet soul music," said Brother Al with a grin on his face.

"Yeah? What's it called?"

"The Soul Bar," answered Brother Charles.

"Sounds great, but right now I'm hungry. How about breakfast?" I suggested.

"Are you buying?" asked Brother Al.

"Yeah, I'm taking you to the Grand Hotel outdoor café," I said.

Eager for breakfast, we headed for the Grand Hotel. We were greeted at the entrance and promptly seated. Hanging on the walls were pictures of the original hotel, built by the French.

Sharing a conversation with Brother Al and Brother Charles was a good way to start the day. I learned a lot about the two brothers, who remained friends throughout their tour in Vietnam. I explained that I had been separated from two friends at the beginning and hadn't heard from them since.

After breakfast, we made our way back to the Mi Lien, where a crowd was gathering. Everyone's attention was focused on the third floor. A drunken soldier had climbed out of a window and was threatening to jump. His friends were trying desperately to convince him to return to the room.

Just as it appeared the soldier would take the advice of his friends and start toward the room, he stumbled. The crowd watched as he fell, potentially to his death. Unexpectedly, he landed on communication wire, which absorbed the force of his fall. When he rolled to the ground, everyone rushed over.

Fortunately, the drunken soldier escaped with a fractured ankle, broken collarbone, and trip back to the world. It was a miracle he survived the fall and was not on his way home in a body bag.

It wasn't clear if the soldier really had attempted to commit suicide or just had an unnecessary, drunken accident. Soldiers not able to cope with the war had been known to take their own lives. It was just another ugly side of the war.

The injured soldier was taken to the field hospital at China Beach, and the crowd dispersed. Brother Al and Brother Charles caught a Lambretta ride to the Soul Bar, and I decided to stay in the area and check out the Hong Kong Club.

I entered the club, looking for a familiar face. The club was busy with soldiers from different branches of the military, but I didn't recognize anyone from Blackfoot. I fixed my eyes on an attractive Vietnamese girl seated at the end of the bar. I was drawn to her shiny dark hair and a shapely backside, so I decided to join her. "What's your name, sweetheart?" I asked.

"My name is Qui," said the girl.

"That's a nice name. What does it mean?"

"My name means *turtle*," she said. She leaned over and whispered in my ear, "If you want to talk, you have to buy me tea."

That's when I discovered "tea" was a drink soldiers had to buy from Mama-san to have a conversation with one of her girls. It was just another way to make money from the American troops. Nothing was free in Vietnam. Not even the conversation.

Tea cost a dollar and didn't come with any liquor. Usually, it was a small glass of mint- or orange-flavored drink. I ordered tea for Qui and a rum and Coke for me. It was well worth a few dollars to have a conversation with the attractive girl.

Infatuated with Qui's beauty and the fragrance of her perfume, I continued to purchase tea from Mama-san. The conversation wasn't about anything meaningful; it was just a way to pass the time. I spent the afternoon talking with Qui and didn't notice the clock. With curfew only a few hours away I needed to make arrangements for the night.

"How much do I have to pay Mama-san to be with you tonight?" I asked.

"Where you stay, GI?" Qui asked.

"I haven't decided."

"No sweat, GI. Pay Mama-san twenty dollars MPC, and I stay with you tonight."

Qui took my hand and led us over to Mama-san. Without negotiating, I paid Mama-san five thousand piastres, equivalent to twenty dollars MPC. Mama-san patted Qui on the head.

"Where are we going?" I asked.

"No sweat, follow me," she said.

It was near curfew. Qui started walking and I followed. At an intersection, Qui turned right and headed for a masonry-block building. In the lobby was an elevator shaft but no elevator, so we headed for the stairwell.

Two adolescent girls giggled as they ran down the stairs. They seem to know why I was there. Qui climbed four flights until she reached an apartment door. Reaching into her bra, she pulled out a key and quietly opened the door.

We entered a modest apartment and headed to the back room. She pushed aside a bedsheet and waved to an elderly man and woman lying in hammocks. Papa-san nodded and returned to his television program on a small black-and-white console.

"Who's that?" I whispered.

"Mama-san and Papa-san," she answered.

Her parents waved, ignoring the fact that I was there to spend the night with their daughter. It was difficult to understand Vietnamese culture, especially when their country was engulfed in war.

Qui led me to her bed in the living room, situated next to a tall banana plant. Not sure if I could spend the night with a girl whose parents were in the next room, I watched as Qui undressed. I admired her milky skin and slim body as she stood before me totally nude.

"I can't believe your parents would allow you to bring a stranger into their home," I said.

"They understand. It's my job," said Qui, slipping into bed.

This was the price she paid for America's involvement in the war. Although prostitution was illegal, it was considered legitimate work among the Vietnamese. Sitting on the edge of her bed, I unlaced my boot strings and took off my boots. By the time I removed my fatigue pants, Qui was fast asleep. She must have been exhausted.

The following morning, I was awakened by a kiss as Qui quietly lay on top of me.

"You come see me at Hong Kong Club when you come back," said Qui.

"Only if you promise to be with me," I said.

"No problem, GI, I promise," she replied.

I kissed her on the forehead and left twenty dollars MPC on her pillow.

Leaving the building, I took a deep breath of morning air. I was thrilled that I had spent the night with Qui. I felt that I had developed a relationship that I could continue when I returned.

I returned to the Mi Lien Hotel and joined Brother Al and Brother Charles.

"How come you didn't join us at the Soul Bar last night, Jarcia?" asked Brother Charles.

"Let's just say I met a girl I could fall in love with," I said with a big grin.

"What you do, Jarcia, fall in love with a hooker?" asked Brother Charles.

Everyone laughed and climbed into a Lambretta. Not only did my first trip to Vung Tau Village prove to be a well-deserved rest, it became a sanctuary from the war I despised.

Episode Thirteen

Fire Base Donna

April 13. Bravo Company returned to Fire Base Fontaine to pull base security for four days. Soldiers who had the misfortune of having symptoms of venereal disease went to the medic's hooch for an injection of penicillin.

Lieutenant CJ informed the platoon that Bravo Company was occupying Fire Base Fontaine for the last time. The fire base that had become our home had served its strategic purpose and would be moved to provide fire support for battalion's new area of operation. Four days passed quickly, and then it was time to prepare for another mission.

***

April 17. Bravo Company was inserted back into the field as a blocking force at the base of a nearby mountain range. Although battalion had controlled most of the enemy activity in the highlands, small pockets of main-force Viet Cong and NVA remained in the region. With skills I learned from leadership, fear became an emotion I could control. After three months in-country, I had learned that knowing your enemy was the key element to survival.

***

April 20. This was the first log day of the mission. Blackfoot linked up with Aztec and Cheyenne Platoons and waited for the log birds to arrive. When mail was issued, I received a care package from home, along with an official envelope from my congressman. Was this the news I had been waiting for? Was I about to be released from combat and taken out of the field? Staring at the letter, I prayed it contained the news I desperately wanted to hear. Taking a deep breath, I slowly opened the letter.

The congressman's letter said, "*I would like to commend you for your valiant effort in the participation in the Vietnam War. But with regrets my office is unable to help with your request. The Sole Survivor Policy only applies if your family has already suffered a combat-related death.*" It was stamped with the congressman's official seal, and a certificate of appreciation was included.

The answer was not what I expected. I felt that I had been dismissed with no effort. I wondered if the congressman had actually read my letter. From the time I was inducted into the army, I had claimed to be a sole survivor. The sole survivor policy had been reinstated since 1964. No one had taken me seriously. Though I was upset with the news, I was not discouraged.

I set the letter on fire and tossed it on the ground. I decided I would continue to write the congressman, just to be a pain in his ass. I accepted the fact that I would remain in the field until the end of my tour.

I opened my care package and found a sixteen-ounce premium canned ham, canned tortillas, canned jalapeno peppers, Tabasco sauce, A1 steak sauce, Heinz 57 steak sauce, and assorted packets of Kool-Aid. At the bottom of the box, wrapped in the local newspaper, was a bush knife in a leather case. It had an eight-inch cutting edge and would be useful in the field.

The condiments would spice up my meals. Normally C-rations and LRPs were not very appetizing, but with a variety of sauces, I would be able to prepare a zesty meal.

The newspaper wrapped around the bush knife revealed a bit of interesting news. Lieutenant Calley had been sentenced to life for the My Lai Massacre. I wasn't sure if Dad intentionally wanted me to read the news or just included this newspaper by coincidence.

***

April 22. The mission came to an end. Bravo Company humped to the designated pickup zone and was extracted from the field. With Fire Base Fontaine completely torn down, all that remained were memories of a strategic piece of ground that once provided fire support for the Second of the Eighth, First Cavalry Division.

Bravo Company was flown to the newly built battalion fire base. Everything was in operation. Everyone enjoyed a hot mess-hall lunch and settled around the green cooler for ice-cold beer.

I was just about to finish my first beer when a call came in from battalion. By the look on Lieutenant CJ's face, it wasn't good. "Get your shit on!" he cried. "Delta Company hit the shit, and Blackfoot is going in first."

The unit closest to the point of contact was assembled as the QRF (quick reaction force). It was decided Blackfoot would provide the support, with Aztec as backup. Cheyenne would remain on the fire base and pull base security.

"I don't know how long we're going to be in the field, so you better pack a three-day log," said Lieutenant CJ. The supply sergeant brought out cases of C-rations and LRPs, along with boxes of M-16 and M-60 ammo.

"We just left the field; now we're going back," I said angrily.

"That's just the way it is, Garcia. Now get your shit together and get out to the LZ!" hollered Lieutenant CJ.

Within five minutes, everyone was packed and headed for the LZ. I could only pray Delta Company had stabilized their situation before we hit the ground. Battalion dispatched a gaggle of five birds to insert Blackfoot into the field. Fear was on everyone's face. Blackfoot was in the air, heading toward the killing zone.

The first bird touched down, and the first five soldiers on the ground headed for the wood line. Lieutenant CJ met with his point team and issued Cartwright an azimuth. Sporadic machine gun and small arms fire echoed through the jungle. When the last team member arrived, Lieutenant CJ didn't hesitate to give the word to move out.

Cartwright, followed by the point team, entered the wood line and advanced toward the contact area. Delta Company's second platoon advanced on the rear of the enemy's position. Third platoon waited in ambush. Lieutenant CJ's instructions for Cartwright were to head in the direction of the contact.

Positioned at slack, I was ready to fire at anything that moved. I despised my assigned position, especially when going into a hot AO. I desperately wanted to be back at drag position. John was confident my jungle-wise skills were needed up front, but I saw it as a guarantee to be killed.

Cartwright cautiously approached the battle. The sound of M-16 and AK-47 fire meant Delta Company remained engaged in a firefight. Although Cartwright was moving at a steady pace, he remained cautious, not to be caught off guard by enemy fleeing the contact area.

Lieutenant CJ halted the patrol to notify Delta Company of our position. We were nearing the rear of the contact area and didn't want to be mistaken for the enemy. After verifying our location, Cartwright linked up with the last man in Delta Company.

The enemy began fleeing the area when Blackfoot arrived with additional fire support. Blackfoot secured the perimeter so Delta Company could pull back the wounded. The wounded were treated by Delta Company's field medic and transported back to the LZ.

Blackfoot escorted Delta Company to the LZ as the wounded were medevaced out of the field. Delta Company then continued their mission, and Blackfoot and Aztec remained in the field to assist.

April 25. The search for the enemy continued until Peter Gun suffered a serious malaria attack and Scotty severely cut his finger. Both soldiers needed immediate medical attention. Lieutenant CJ ordered the platoon back to the LZ to have both soldiers medevaced out of the field.

By the time the platoon arrived at the pickup zone, Peter Gun was delirious and had to be restrained. Scotty had lost a large amount of blood, but was stable. Blackfoot quickly secured the LZ, and Lieutenant CJ pulled the pin from a canister of yellow smoke.

Within five minutes, the medevac bird touched down. Peter Gun and Scotty were lifted in. Blackfoot moved back into the wood line and located a position for the night.

April 27. Everyone pulled in their night work and prepared to move out. After discussing the day's objective, Lieutenant CJ called his two team leaders together. John returned with good news. Blackfoot was being extracted from the field to pull security for Fire Support Base Donna.

Lieutenant CJ studied his topographical map, searching for the shortest route to the LZ. He gave Cartwright an azimuth. The order was given, and everyone put on their rucksacks.

I was relieved when John assigned me to the drag position. Although I was responsible for the rear, the position was safer than being on the point team. This was the position I had become familiar with, and I was comfortable working there.

We searched for the LZ for an hour, finally determining that Lieutenant CJ had given Cartwright an incorrect azimuth. Lieutenant CJ ordered a fifteen-minute break as he consulted his team leaders. With no guidance from the air, the lieutenant would have to search for the LZ on his own.

Getting lost meant waiting until leadership figure out where we were. Sometimes the team leaders spent more time figuring out where we were than getting us there. Regardless of their navigational ability, we always seemed to get where we were going.

Not knowing how long we would have to wait, I decided to take off my rucksack. The sun peering through the trees made it difficult to see, so I shielded my eyes. I had dozed off when something bounced off my head. "Okay, who's wise guy?" I remarked.

"What you talking about, Jarcia?" replied Brother Charles, sitting across the trotter.

A few minutes later, something struck me in the chest.

158

"Which one of you is joking around?" I demanded.

"Not me," said Brother Al, shaking his head.

Curious to know who the perpetrator was, I stood up to investigate.

Brother Al pointed to the trees above. Focusing through the branches, I noticed a gray-haired monkey tossing a ball of mud. When the ball of mud landed on the ground, I discovered it was monkey manure. I don't know why the gray-haired monkey had selected me as his target, but the cute little animal was amused by it. He continued his mischievous behavior until it was time to leave.

The platoon leader gave Cartwright a new azimuth and ordered the platoon to move out. Cartwright located the LZ, and the platoon secured the area.

Blackfoot was transported to Fire Support Base Donna. Located near Highway 1, the base housed a battery of 155 mm howitzers. Its only purpose was to provide fire support for units working within a nine-mile radius of the base.

The company clerk was waiting with clean clothes, mail, and a green cooler filled with beer and sodas. I picked up my mail, along with a couple cans of beer, and claimed a hooch.

"Don't get too comfortable, Garcia," ordered Lieutenant CJ.

"What now?" I replied.

"You're going to Fire Base Mace to pull green-line guard."

"Why do I have to go? Ask one of the new guys to volunteer."

"I thought you would appreciate the break," said Lieutenant CJ.

Green-line guard had its privileges, but I would rather have stayed on the fire base and enjoyed my time out of the field. With no choice in the matter, I packed a clean pair of fatigues

159

and accompanied the company clerk on the returning convoy to Fire Base Mace.

It was dinnertime when we arrived. I dropped off my weapon and rucksack at headquarters and headed for the mess hall. Hot chow was one of the privileges of green-line guard. Fire Base Mace was battalion headquarters, so the chow was better than the mess halls in the field.

After a comforting meal and desperately needed shower, I put on a clean pair of fatigues and prepared for guard duty. Assigned to green-line guard bunker number eight, I grabbed my weapon and headed for the west perimeter. Guard duty was divided between two soldiers per bunker, with first guard ending at midnight and second at the break of dawn. There hadn't been any recent attacks on the fire base, so I thought the duty should be safe.

Stepping inside the bunker, I noticed the silhouette of a soldier sitting in the guard chair. I introduced myself, but the soldier failed to acknowledge me. I assumed he was napping, so I went to sleep.

I fell into a deep sleep and was awakened by an illumination round exploding above the bunker. Glancing at my illuminated watch I noticed it was four in the morning. The soldier on guard must have fallen asleep.

I tapped the soldier on the shoulder, and he rolled over and fell to the ground. My first thought was that he had been killed by the enemy. I felt for a pulse as his body lay lifeless on the bunker floor. I feared the worst and ran for the medic.

After I had knocked several times, the medic finally answered the door. "What's wrong?" he said, slipping into his fatigue shirt.

"A soldier in green line bunker number eight is dead."

The medic grabbed his field medical bag and followed me back to the bunker. The medic entered the bunker and shone his flashlight into the soldier's eyes. He placed his hand on the soldier's neck, searching for pulse, and pulled back the eyelids.

Rolling back the soldier's sleeves the medic discovered signs of heroin injection. The medic pulled a hypodermic needle out of his medical bag and slammed it into the soldier's chest. The revival attempt failed.

This overdose was nothing new to the medic. Overdoses were just another tragedy of the Vietnam War. Unable to cope with the everyday stress of war, soldiers intentionally or unintentionally overdosed, taking the easy way out.

The medic pronounced the soldier dead and returned to the field hospital for a body bag. When the medic returned, we gently lifted the deceased soldier into the bag. He appeared to be sleeping as the medic zipped the bag over his head. We removed the body from the bunker and carried it back to the field hospital.

Unfortunately, the parents of the deceased soldier would have to be notified. How would his parents react, learning their son's death was due to a heroin overdose?

By the time the medic arranged to have the body sent to the rear, it was first morning light. The smell of breakfast wafted in the air. I retrieved my weapon and went to the mess hall for an early morning cup of coffee.

***

April 28. I prepared for another day of life or death. I was back on a convoy, returning to Fire Support Base Donna. I joined the platoon and told the story of the soldier who overdosed on heroin. Brother Charles shook his head and walked away.

That evening I experienced the wrath of the 155 mm howitzers. Five minutes after midnight, I was awakened by a blast that lifted me off my air mattress. The blast signaled the beginning of a fire mission, and 155 projectiles whistled over the bunker.

"Oh, I forgot to warn you about the 155s," said Brother Al.

"How many times does it happen?" I asked.

"Only three," he replied.

Although we were awakened three times a night by the howitzers, everyone enjoyed their time out of the field. In a fairly secure environment, there were three hot meals, a cool shower, and light duty every day.

It was the beginning of monsoon season. Everyone was in for half a year of wet weather. When it started, it never stopped.

Blackfoot remained on Fire Base Donna for another five days. On the final day, Lieutenant CJ informed the platoon that Bravo Company would return to China Beach on May 28. Knowing there was another trip scheduled made my life in Vietnam a little more tolerable.

***

May 1. With anticipation of returning to the field, everyone was resupplied and loaded with ammo. After lunch, everyone migrated to the shade of the grunt hooch. With nothing to do, I decided to impersonate our leader, Lieutenant CJ. Impersonating officers was a talent I had developed during basic training. I was fairly good at it and enjoyed making everyone laugh. The only person who wasn't impressed was Lieutenant CJ, who, unknown to me, was standing behind me.

"Since you have nothing to do but impersonate me, I'm looking for two volunteers," he said.

"Give us a break, Lieutenant! We're going into the field tomorrow," I said.

"Sounds like you just volunteered, Garcia."

Bart laughed hysterically.

"Bart, you just volunteered to help Garcia," said Lieutenant CJ.

Lieutenant CJ sent us out to the LZ to spread oil over the landing area. The oil eliminated the dust when Hueys came in for a landing. Lieutenant CJ thought it was punishment, but Bart and I saw it as an opportunity to pass the time away.

I jumped into the three-quarter-ton truck and surveyed the job. Bart thought it best to punch holes in the tops of the barrels and allow the oil to spill onto the LZ as I drove around.

The reflection off the oil increased the temperature on the LZ. There had to be faster way to get the job done. I decided to add another barrel of oil spilling onto the ground.

Now that we were spreading a larger amount of oil, I climbed into the cab and started the motor. Wheels turned to the right, I placed the truck in gear. I drove around the LZ, spreading the oil in a circular pattern. Bart decided to nap and fell asleep shortly after.

Lieutenant CJ came out to check on us, only to discover we were both asleep. "What the hell are you guys doing? Can't you do anything without screwing up?" he screamed.

"I thought I would speed up the process. It's hot out there," I explained.

"Get back to work, and do it right this time," ordered Lieutenant CJ. He told us not to return to the fire base until the entire LZ was covered with oil. Bart and I jumped onto the bed of the truck and began hammering holes in the three remaining barrels.

Attempting to help Bart lay the first barrel down, I lost my footing. I landed on the ground under the flow of oil. My hair was saturated with oil. I decided this detail was over.

"The lieutenant is going to shit when he sees you," said Bart with a smirk on his face.

"Right now my only concern is getting this oil out of my hair."

I jumped onto the running board as Bart drove back to the fire base. Soldiers who witnessed the incident rushed for their cameras. Saturated with oil, I posed for photographs as we drove by.

"What the hell happened, Garcia?" the lieutenant demanded. "I should have known not to send you and Bart to do the job. Now get the hell out of my site and get cleaned up."

***

May 12–28. Bravo Company successful completed two back-to-back missions and witnessed the birth of a new fire base. We tore down Fire Base Donna and started building Fire Base Hall. This was the third fire base battalion I'd worked out of since being assigned to Bravo Company.

Aztec and Cheyenne were combat assaulted into the field. Blackfoot was convoyed to the site of the new fire base and remained in the wood line while Delta Company assisted in the construction.

The construction of a new fire base was an interesting process. The Army Corps of Engineers removed trees and brush, leveling the land with bulldozers. They cleared a pad for the LZ and graded a dirt berm around the fire base. Artillery, mortars, supply, and mess hall were responsible for setting up their own equipment and sleeping hooches. Delta Company was responsible for the communication bunkers, officers' quarters, and grunt hooches along the perimeter.

Blackfoot remained in the wood line, pulling security. A grass-covered mound provided a comfortable place to rest while I prepared lunch. Waiting for my canteen cup of water to come to a boil, I pulled out my machete. When I struck the grass-covered mound, a metallic sound indicated there was something buried. Curious to know what it was, I cleared away the grass and dirt.

"What are you doing, Garcia?" asked Bart.

"Help me clear away the dirt; there's something buried," I said.

Bart and I cleared away the dirt, exposing a metal object. The only person with authority at the time was Sundance. Lieutenant CJ had returned to the rear, and both squad leaders were on R & R. The RTO located Sundance and informed him of our discovery.

"What's the matter?" asked Sundance, returning to our position in the wood line.

I pointed to the partially exposed metal object. Sundance kneeled down and brushed away the dirt, exposing markings.

"This is a five-hundred-pound daisy-cutter," said Sundance.

"And I was banging on it with a machete," I said.

"It could have exploded?" said Bart.

"Yeah, and we would all be dead," said Sundance.

The military's use of daisy-cutters in Vietnam was primarily for bombing campaigns. Capable of inflicting major damage, the high explosives were designed to detonate above an impact area. Daisy-cutters were dropped in the dense jungles to create landing zones.

A demolition team was brought out to the fire base to determine if the bomb was armed. After a thorough investigation, the experts disarmed the daisy-cutter, and everyone returned to their positions.

Episode Fourteen

Discrimination in Vietnam

In the few months I had been with Blackfoot Platoon, I spent the majority of my time with the blacks in the platoon. I had gained the confidence of the brothers from the South and been accepted into their brotherhood.

The black power movement was alive and well throughout Vietnam. The brotherhood provided strong unity during a time when blacks were bitter about fighting in a "white man's war." Being compelled to fight for a nation where blacks were not viewed as equal created tension between whites and blacks. Because of the high percentage of blacks serving, blacks tended to view a tour in Vietnam as a way to be accepted by whites.

Most Hispanics ignored the politics and generally had good relations with blacks and whites, but eventually there was resentment among Hispanics and whites about taking sides with the blacks.

Needless to say, sharing frightening experiences in the battlefield created strong bonds among black and white soldiers. When forced to face danger and the threat of death together, they tended to band together for protection.

Brother Al and Brother Charles emphasized their disrespect for whites due to extreme racial injustice in their hometowns. It was hard to imagine being treated with hatred because of the color of one's skin. Raised in a racially diverse community, I never had an opportunity to witness such an act. Although there were signs of discrimination, it wasn't violent as that suffered by blacks in the South.

During my adolescence, I attended schools composed primarily of black students. Although there were racial differences, everyone seemed to get along. Even the few whites who attended didn't have any trouble.

It wasn't until the Watts riots in Los Angeles that racial tension between blacks and whites separated my community. Neighbors harbored weapons, and riots broke out in community high schools. Only at the end of the riots did our neighborhood return to normal.

The only time discrimination affected me personally was during my senior year. Introduced to an attractive sophomore, I became infatuated by her beauty. Betty's flawless complexion and beautiful long hair were inherited from a white father and Japanese mother.

Although Betty cared for me, she only allowed me to spend time with her at school. Wanting to be with her, I agreed to her terms. Finally, during the Thanksgiving break, I was invited to Betty's birthday party to meet her parents.

I worked two weekends in the grape fields to buy her a nice gift. It was the perfect opportunity to give her a friendship ring. I made a special trip to get a haircut and purchase a new outfit. I had recently been issued a California driver's license, and Dad offered me the use of his 1964 Dodge Dart.

Unfamiliar with Betty's neighborhood, I went in search for her home. I followed her instructions and eventually located her residence. I could only dream of having a home like hers.

There was no parking nearby, so I parked down the street. A quick look into the rearview mirror and a touch-up of the hair, and I headed for the party. Betty had given me specific instructions not to knock on the front door but to enter by the side gate. I walked into the backyard, where friends and family were enjoying a brisk autumn day. Betty was nowhere to be found, so I took a seat at the picnic table, next to her birthday gifts.

Some of the guests glared, obviously wondering who I was. They made me feel uncomfortable, but I was here to see Betty. When Betty stepped out the back door, she smiled, knowing I had arrived. She headed in my direction and embraced me.

"You smell great," I said.

"It's a birthday present, Chanel No. 5," Betty responded proudly.

"Happy birthday, Betty," I said, handing her a small, neatly wrapped box.

"Thank you. Would you like some punch?" she asked.

"Punch is fine," I replied.

She brought me a plastic cup of punch and took a seat next to me. She seemed a little anxious; after all, she was about to introduce me to her parents. "I'm going to tell my parents you're here," she said and went back into the house.

I waited nervously as I sipped my punch. I had always felt Betty was too good for me, but since she had invited me to her home, I thought this was an indication that she truly cared for me.

A few minutes later, the back door opened and a tall, slender, middle-aged white male stood in the doorway. Scanning the backyard, he fixed his eyes on me and then stepped inside.

Betty returned with a somber look on her face. She took me aside and placed the gift in my hand. "I can't accept your gift," she said.

"It's your birthday present. Open it," I replied.

"I can't. I have something to tell you." She took my hand and led me through the side gate.

"What's wrong?"

I waited nervously as she looked into my eyes, tears in hers.

"I'm sorry, Rick, but when my father saw who you were, he refused to meet you. He wants you to leave and doesn't want me to see you anymore." She brushed her tears away.

"Why? What did I do?"

"Nothing. It's just the way my father is."

"I don't understand. Why can't I see you anymore?" I asked sadly.

"Because my father doesn't want me dating—uh," said Betty, unable to complete her sentence.

"Dating what, a Mexican?" I demanded angrily.

"I'm sorry."

"But I thought you liked me."

"I do like you. That's what makes it hard to tell you this," she said.

"I guess I'll see you in school."

"It's best if we don't see each other anymore," said Betty, walking away.

"If you really like me, then why do you care how your father feels?"

"I don't want to hurt my father," said Betty, sobbing as she returned to her party.

"I understand, but what about my feelings?"

I left Betty's home, never to speak to her again. At first I was hurt and confused, but I realized it was her father's decision and not Betty's. It was difficult to understand why I wasn't allowed to date the daughter of an interracial couple due to the color of my skin.

Although I had been excluded from Betty's life, I was able to cope with the rejection and move on, unlike many blacks who bore the emotional scars of years of racial injustice.

Blacks serving in Vietnam strengthened their unity by the creation of symbols like the black power sign, bracelets, and the handshake known throughout Vietnam as the *dap*. The black power sign consisted of a clenched fist. The bracelets were woven out of boot shoestrings with M-60 machine gun rounds attached to the ends. The dap was a greeting consisting of a series of clapping, tapping, snapping, and slapping movements, ending with an embrace. There were variations of the dap depending on the region where you were stationed.

Like the blacks, the whites had their own symbol of unity. It was the *peace sign*. As simple as it was, it represented the times and brotherhood. Because the peace sign resembled the floppy ears of a rabbit, blacks referred to whites as "*Brother Rabs*." Blacks never used the peace sign, and whites never performed the dap.

Episode Fifteen

Return to China Beach

May 29. Another month had come to an end. Blackfoot continued to provide security until Delta Company completed the new fire base. When Delta Company returned to the field and Alpha Company returned to the fire base, it was time for Bravo Company to return to China Beach for a little rest and relaxation.

Four months had passed and there was still no sign of me getting out of the field. I continued to write my congressman with no response. In a recent letter, Dad indicated that Jet and Little Joey had written to my parents. Now that I had their addresses, I could write to the two friends I hadn't seen since January.

Headquarters had recently moved from Fire Base Mace to Bien Hoa Air Force Base. Although the distance increased from the field to the rear, supplies were still convoyed to the fire base. The finance officer arrived on the convoy with combat pay for the month.

I collected forty-five dollars MPC, placing it in my wallet along with the fifty dollars I had won playing two-card guts. It was more than enough to celebrate Brother Al's upcoming twenty-first birthday.

Directed to the LZ, everyone waited eagerly for transportation to arrive.

"Pop smoke, birds inbound!" shouted Lieutenant CJ.

Within minutes, a Chinook transport helicopter touched down on Highway 1. Blackfoot promptly filed in and took their seats.

Blackfoot arrived at Vung Tau Airport and boarded the buses to the R & R center. The drive was familiar, since we had previously visited China Beach. Greeted by the familiar face of the orientation officer, we received the same orientation as before. Everyone listened except for BJ, who enjoyed mimicking Officer Green. When Officer Green completed his orientation, the company was free to enjoy China Beach.

I searched for the familiar face of the mama-san who had helped me before. When I found her, she recognized me and smiled. I handed her a pair of tailored fatigues to starch, along with my jungle boots. Mama-san's hooch maids spit-shined my boots, while Mama-san went off to starch my fatigues.

Within thirty minutes, Mama-san returned with my nicely starched fatigues. Dressed and ready for a visit with my girlfriend, Qui, I headed for the exchange shack to convert MPC to piastres. The exchange rate was 250 piastres to one US dollar, so I was given 23,750 piastres.

Brother Al and Brother Charles joined me and took a seat on the bus headed for Vung Tau Village.

The driver made his way down the familiar two-lane paved road, making his first stop in front of the Grand Hotel.

"It's your birthday. Where do you want to stay?" I asked Brother Al.

"The Palace," replied Brother Al, pointing in the direction of the modern high-rise.

"The Palace it is my friend," I said, and we headed for the hotel.

Brother Al and I strolled into the lobby and were greeted by a cute Vietnamese receptionist working behind the desk.

Brother Al admired the hand-painted ceramic floor tile as I registered.

"I would like a suite, please," I said to the receptionist.

"I have a two-bedroom suite overlooking the bay," she replied.

"Perfect," I said, as Brother Al continued to view the decor on the walls.

"Enjoy your stay," said the cute Vietnamese girl.

Brother Al was eager to see his suite, and I was eager to visit my girlfriend. When Brother Al entered the suite, he was surprised to see a well-furnished living room along with the two bedrooms, especially when he stepped onto the balcony with a spectacular view of the South China Sea.

"Enjoy your suite, Brother Al. I'll meet you later at the Soul Bar."

"Where you going?" asked Brother Al.

"I'm going to the Hong Kong Club to see my girlfriend, Qui," I replied.

"Man, that woman ain't waiting for you," he said in a sarcastic tone.

"Qui will be there. She promised."

"That's what she says to all the guys she sleeps with. She's a bar hooker," said Brother Al, flopping down on the couch and placing his jungle-worn boots on the coffee table.

"Qui's different. She cares for me," I said.

"Okay, but don't say I didn't warn you," said Brother Al, chuckling.

Rushing down to the lobby, I flagged down one of the three-wheeled Lambrettas passing by. Only a few blocks away, the driver dropped me off in front of the Hong Kong Club. I handed the driver five hundred piastres and entered the smoke-filled club.

I had envisioned Qui embracing me with a hug and a kiss. There was no sign of her anywhere. I sought out Mama-san.

"Have you seen Qui?" I asked.

"Qui busy. Come back later," replied Mama-san.

"I'm not leaving until I see Qui." I took a seat and ordered a drink.

Thirty minutes later, Qui entered the club, escorted by an air force captain. The couple sat down at a table and ordered tea.

Qui was wearing a traditional red Vietnamese dress. She was gorgeous sipping her tea. Growing impatient, I decided to interrupt her conversation with the captain.

"Remember me? You promised to be with me when I returned to the village," I said.

"I remember, but busy now, come back later," said Qui.

"Move along grunt. She's with me," said the tall captain.

Discouraged, I returned to the bar and ordered another drink.

"Why you look so sad?" asked Mama-san.

"I thought Qui liked me," I replied.

"Why you want Qui? All my girl number-one at Hong Kong Club," boasted Mama-san.

I continued to look at Qui as she sipped her tea.

"Hey GI, buy me tea," said an attractive hooker, tapping me on the shoulder.

The girl was very pretty, so I accepted her invitation, thinking it might make Qui jealous.

I purchased tea for the hooker and a drink for me. After a few drinks, I realized any one of Mama-san's girls could provide the companionship I had experienced with Qui.

Unexpectedly, Qui placed her hand on my shoulder.

"Why you no wait for me? I thought I was your girlfriend," she said, sounding a little upset.

"Because you were with the captain," I said.

"No sweat. I be with you later."

"Why can't you be with me now?"

"Not now. Captain pay boo-koo piastre for short time. Sorry. I come back later," said Qui, looking over her shoulder at the captain.

Although Qui was just a hooker, I had developed feelings for her anyway. After all, she was my first one. Knowing I couldn't spend the night with Qui, I turned to my date.

"Mama-san was right: all girls are number one at the Hong Kong Club, Let's have some fun." I handed Mama-san five dollars MPC, and the attractive hooker escorted me upstairs to her room.

***

After a brief stay, I left the Hong Kong Club to enjoy the remainder of the day. Searching for another bar, I heard the familiar sound of Creedence Clearwater Revival. When I entered the dark, smoke-filled club, I noticed a Vietnamese band playing to an enthusiastic crowd of soldiers. When my eyes adjusted to the light, I recognized Lieutenant CJ, along with four members of the platoon.

The Vietnamese musicians produced a decent imitation of the popular rock and roll band. Everyone stood up, singing along. Lieutenant CJ ordered a round of beer and shots of tequila for everyone in the group.

The band played another popular number. It was one of my favorites, and I jumped onstage and started singing along.

"Show'm how it's done, Garcia!" shouted Rider.

The lead singer handed me the microphone, and everyone in the audience joined in. Lieutenant CJ applauded my performance as he sang along.

The lead singer invited me to come back and sing another song. I took a sip of my beer, downed the tequila, and jumped back onstage. I accidently backed into a cymbal, landing on the keyboard player. Upset with my drunken clumsiness, the lead guitarist grabbed the microphone from my hand and shoved me off the stage. As I was preparing to punch the lead singer, Lieutenant CJ quickly jumped in, stabilizing the situation.

"It's all right, I'll take care of him," he said, escorting me outside.

"I'm sorry, Lieutenant CJ," I said apologetically.

"I think it's time to find another bar, Garcia," he replied.

Embarrassed by my disruptive behavior, I climbed aboard a Lambretta and gave instructions to return to the Palace Hotel. It was Brother Al's birthday, and I wanted to surprise him with a gift. I told the driver to stop at the bar across from the hotel.

I entered the bar, searching for two of Mama-san's best-looking girls to accompany me back to the hotel. I was immediately surrounded by Mama-san's girls. It was going to be difficult to make a selection.

"You want number one girl?" asked Mama-san, standing behind the bar, smoking a cigarette.

"I want two number one girls. How much piastres for all night?"

"You crazy, GI. Why you want two number one girl? One number one girl too much for you," replied Mama-san sarcastically.

"The girls are a birthday present for my friend," I said.

"Where you stay?" asked one of the hookers.

"Across the street at the Palace," I replied.

All the girls pleaded with Mama-san to be the ones selected to go with me.

"Okay, you pay seventy-five hundred piastre and you take two girls," said Mama-san.

For thirty-five dollars MPC, I believe I got the best deal. I counted out the piastres and laid them out on the bar. I selected two girls and escorted them across the street.

JC and Stanney were standing in the lobby as we headed for the elevator.

"Hey, lover boy, one girl isn't good enough for you?" said Stanney.

"The girls are a birthday present for Brother Al," I replied.

"Wish him a happy birthday for us," said JC.

Giggling as we entered the elevator, the girls were excited to be spending the night. I brought them to the room and knocked on the door. I was eager to see Brother Al's expression when he saw the girls.

Brother Al slowly opened door.

"Surprise! I brought you a birthday present."

"No can do. Soul brother boo-koo big," said one of the girls when she realized her date was black.

The following morning, I was awakened by the sun peering through the window and two girls lying next to me. I climbed out of bed, looking for my roommate, but Brother Al had already showered and left.

"Where's my friend?" I asked.

Brother Al's date sat up in bed, removing the sleep from her eyes. "Your friend boo-koo horny, he want boom-boom all night, no can do. He no let me sleep, so I come sleep with you."

"Where did he go?" I asked.

"I don't know and I don't care," said the girl, shrugging her shoulders.

After a quick shave and shower, I set out to find my friends. I accompanied the girls down to the lobby, where I found Bart and Peter Gun drinking Tiger 33.

"Have you seen Brother Al?" I asked.

"Not this morning," replied Bart.

"Hey Garcia, let's get a tattoo?" asked Peter Gun.

"I don't think so," I replied

"Everyone in Vietnam gets a tattoo," he said.

"Not this soldier."

I left the hotel to search for Brother Al. I checked out the brothers' favorite hangouts, but they were nowhere to be found.

Later that afternoon, I joined Peter Gun and Bart for a drink. "We're on our way to get a tattoo. You want to join us," said Peter Gun.

"Come on, Garcia, let's get a tattoo," said Bart.

After a few drinks, I agreed to accompany them but refused to get a tattoo. Peter Gun located a tattoo parlor and stepped inside. The Vietnamese tattoo artist was sitting in his chair, taking a nap.

"How much for tattoo?" Peter Gun asked.

The tattoo artist slowly opened his eyes, stretched his arms, and yawned. "Two thousand piastre."

"For the three of us?" asked Peter Gun.

"No, for one."

"That's a lot of money for one tattoo."

"What you mean? You pay more for girl."

The tattoo artist provided a photo album of his work. Peter Gun and Bart searched for the perfect tattoo.

"Who first?" asked the tattoo artist, dusting off his chair.

"I am," boasted Peter Gun, taking off his fatigue shirt.

"You need drink before I start?"

"Sure, why not. What do you have?"

"Beer, tequila," said the artist.

"How about a round of Tiger 33 and a shot of tequila?" ordered Peter Gun.

The artist went into the back room, dusted off a bottle of white tequila, and filled three shot glasses. He grabbed three Tiger 33 beers from an old Pepsi cooler and returned.

Then he pulled out his needles and went to work. He worked on Peter Gun's upper arm with intense concentration. When he completed his work, Peter Gun proudly showed off his new tattoo.

"What is it?" I said, trying to focus on his chest.

"Who next?" said the tattoo artist.

"I am!" shouted Bart, jumping into the chair.

"Another round of drinks for everyone!" shouted Peter Gun, stumbling over the chair.

The artist served another round of alcohol and went to work on Bart's arm. I managed to keep the tequila down but dozed off in the chair.

I was awakened by the strong odor of tequila as Bart waved his glass under my nose. "What do you think of my tattoo?" he asked.

"What tattoo?" I answered drunkenly.

"It's your turn, Garcia. The tattoo artist is waiting. What kind of tattoo are you getting?" asked Peter Gun.

"I told you, I'm not getting a tattoo. Now get out of my way," I said, pushing Bart aside and rushing for the door.

"I guess your friend no get tattoo today," said the artist.

I didn't regret not getting ink embedded in my skin that day, but I did regret drinking the tequila. After throwing up my guts, I managed to get into a Lambretta and head to the Palace Hotel.

Staggering into the lobby, I focused on Brother Al and Brother Charles entertaining two attractive Vietnamese girls.

"You don't look so good, Jarcia," said Brother Charles with a girl in his lap.

"Where did you find these two good-looking girls?" I asked.

"The Soul Bar," said Brother Al.

"Yeah, Jarcia, all of Mama-san's girls at the Soul Bar are good-looking. You have to join us next time we're in Vung Tau Village," said Brother Charles

"Mama-san has number one girl for you," said the girl sitting on Brother Al's lap.

"Sure, I'll check it out the next time I'm in the village, but right now I'm going to my room," I said.

"You want a drink?" asked Brother Al.

"Yeah, Jarcia, how about a little hair of the dog that bit you?" said Brother Charles.

"Hell no," I replied.

Episode Sixteen

Australian Sweep

June 1. Another trip to Vung Tau Village came to an end. Bravo Company returned to the fire base to replace Charlie Company, who were beginning a new mission. Once again the unlucky ones visited the base medic for an injection of penicillin.

Now that a half a year had passed, I was counting down the days. I was looking forward to becoming "a two-digit midget." The CO gave me a recommendation to transfer to Echo Recon Platoon. It was considered a privilege to be part of the elite seven-member team. I saw it as an invitation to get killed.

After spending a day with Echo Recon, I determined I wasn't suited for the assignment. The group was a little too enthusiastic about killing. Besides, I didn't want to leave my friends in the platoon.

I was also offered an opportunity to attend sniper school. Although the training would take me out of the field for two months, I didn't care to work alone. Neither assignment would have pulled me out of the battlefield. They would only put me in greater danger. Though I was grateful for the CO's recommendations, I decided to remain in the field with Blackfoot.

I made use of the remaining time on the fire base as best I could. I received mail every day, and I wrote everyone back home several times. The company clerk provided us with plenty of beer and sodas, along with a supplement package filled with toothbrushes, toothpaste, pens, writing paper, candy, and cigarettes—items we couldn't get in the field.

Battalion provided a movie every night at eight, followed by a late-night snack. Occasionally, the "Flying PX" would land at the fire base, bringing desperately needed items not supplied in the supplement package. If you were fortunate to be at the front of the line, you had access to a decent selection of what the PX had to sell that day.

June 5. The evening prior to the next mission, everyone was logged and prepared for combat assault in the morning. After an early guard-duty assignment, I returned to my hooch and prepared a chicken and rice LRP. Rodan smelled the aroma.

"What you making, Garcia?" he asked.

"Mexican food."

"Oh, I love Mexican food," he said, walking by my hooch.

I tossed a couple jalapeno peppers and sliced onions into my chicken and rice as it simmered on the stove. Rodan returned, hoping I would offer a taste.

"What you making, Garcia?" he asked again.

"I told you, Mexican food."

"I love Mexican food."

The curious soldier wouldn't go away unless I offered a taste. So I gave him a heaping spoonful, along with a whole jalapeno pepper. I watched as he chewed the pepper, savoring the flavor.

"Wow, that's hot, Garcia!"

He reached for his throat with eyes open wide open. His face turned beet red gasping for air. "Water, I need water!" he pleaded.

"What's the matter, Rodan? I thought you loved Mexican food?"

"Yeah, but not this hot! Water!"

"Here, drink this," I said, handing him a can of warm beer.

Rodan guzzled the warm beer, trying to relieve the burning sensation. I could only laugh as he stormed away. Biting into a spicy jalapeno pepper can be a painful experience, especially the really hot ones.

June 6. After an early breakfast, Bravo Company was ordered to the LZ. With a three-day supply of food, water, and ammo, we waited for the gaggle of birds to take us to our new area of operation. Lieutenant CJ would not lead the platoon on this mission because he was headed for a well-deserved R & R.

"Everyone, listen up," he cried out. "I will join you on the fire base when you return. Joe will be your acting platoon leader. He's familiar with the leadership role, so you will be in good hands. Good luck, gentlemen. I'll see you when you return. Pop smoke, birds inbound!"

The gaggle of birds delivered Aztec into the field and returned to the fire base for Blackfoot. When the first bird arrived, the five of us assigned to the first bird climbed aboard with Joe, the acting platoon leader. The rest of the platoon would follow.

"Where we headed?" I asked.

"All I know is we're going to be working in company size," replied Joe.

The pilot followed a path along Highway 1, headed for a man-made landing strip.

"Why are we being dropped off in the middle of nowhere?" demanded Sundance as the bird touched down.

"You'll find out when I find out," said Joe sarcastically.

Sundance just shook his head and stepped off the bird. The five of us joined Aztec Platoon and waited for the remainder of Blackfoot to arrive.

"Wait here," said Joe and walked over to meet with the CO.

"I hope Delta Company didn't hit the shit again," I said.

"No, something's up, and I don't like it," replied Sundance.

I dropped my rucksack and waited alongside the others. When Cheyenne arrived, their platoon leader assembled his platoon and joined the meeting.

After a lengthy discussion, the CO addressed the entire company. "Listen up, everyone. I have just been informed of a change of mission. We have been dropped off at this location to allow the Australians to position their armored personnel carriers to assist us with our mission. There's been a recent discovery of a massive tunnel complex, and intelligence has confirmed the area is being used by the enemy as a major route into Saigon. Our new objective is to set up in squad size while the Australian personnel carriers sweep any hostiles into our ambushes.

"You can set up hooches as long as they are low to the ground, but you will not be allowed to inflate your air mattresses. There will be no automatic ambushes, so you need to remain alert at all times. Good luck, gentlemen."

Any time there was a change in mission, the outcome was never good for Blackfoot. With a bad feeling, I pulled out a recent letter, hoping to draw strength from Mom's comforting words. Zane flopped down next to me and started reading a letter from his wife.

"Read this, Garcia," he said, offering the letter to me.

"Why?" I asked.

"Just read it, please."

I took the letter and read a few lines. It was obvious Zane's wife was asking for a divorce. Zane was devastated by his wife's betrayal, because she was leaving him for his best friend. Why couldn't his wife have waited until he returned to ask for a divorce?

"What am I going to do?" said Zane, holding back the tears.

"You're going to show the CO the letter and ask him if you can go home on emergency leave and kill the bastard who's trying to steal your wife," I replied.

Zane showed the CO his letter. After reading the entire letter, the CO handed it back and placed his arms around Zane's shoulders to comfort him. Zane talked with the CO for a few minutes longer, and then returned.

"Thank you for the advice, Garcia. The CO is sending me home," he said, shaking my hand.

The monsoon clouds blew in from the southwest, and it started to rain. It was the beginning of monsoon season, and we were in for a wet mission. After two hours of agonizing waiting, the time came to begin the assault.

"Pop smoke, birds inbound!" cried Joe, pulling the pin from a canister of yellow smoke and releasing it to the ground.

A gaggle of slicks appeared overhead, banking to the left to approach the pickup zone. Aztec would be the first to be inserted into the field, Cheyenne would follow. Blackfoot would bring up the rear.

"Guide the birds in, Garcia!" shouted Joe.

I picked up my weapon and ran out to the center of the landing zone. When the first bird approached, I raised my weapon with both arms fully extended. All five birds landed softly on the LZ. When Aztec Platoon was safely aboard, I raised my weapon, signaling all five birds off the LZ.

The five-bird gaggle returned to the LZ for Cheyenne Platoon. When all of the members of the platoon were safely aboard, the lead pilot lifted off the LZ.

The monsoon rain had subsided when the gaggle of helicopters returned. Everyone in Blackfoot quickly boarded the slicks and lifted off. All the door gunners opened fire into the wood line.

The monsoon rain began to fall again as the pilot circled the drop-off zone. The lead pilot entered the zone as the last man in Cheyenne entered the wood line. With everyone safely on the ground, Joe ordered first squad to follow the path of Cheyenne Platoon.

The gaggle of helicopters disappeared, and I knew it was time to go to work. The labor of breaking through thick triple canopy had been done by the lead platoon. This was only the benefit of being the last to enter the wood line. We were able to move freely through the jungle.

Thirty minutes into the wood line, Joe asked for a pace count.

"Two hundred meters, pass it up," I said.

"Let me know when we hit three hundred meters," said Joe.

I remembered when I hadn't known Joe very well and he didn't seem very likable. Working with the take-no-nonsense squad leader had shown me he was squared away, and his only concern was the safety of his men.

Joe ordered first squad to hump another fifty meters and set up an ambush. Joe would remain with second squad, setting up the final ambush in a string of ambushes. The thick canopy provided an excellent location. He ordered everyone to put out their night work and stay alert because of the Australian LPCs pushing our way.

It was late in the afternoon, so everyone hurried to put out their night work before the second monsoon rain of the day arrived. I ran my claymore out to a tree in front of my location. It was pointed in the direction of an opening leading out of the wood line.

I placed my clacker alongside the others and returned to my sleeping position. Since we were unable to set up an automatic ambush, the claymores were our only defense if the enemy walked into our NDP during the night.

The rain started coming down, so I quickly set up my hooch. I placed my weapon on full automatic, leaning the barrel against a tree. With the Australians sweeping the enemy in our direction, I didn't want to be caught off guard.

The cool, damp weather called for a cup of hot cocoa. Cartwright was on my left and Duggy was on my right. Cartwright was writing a letter and Duggy had dozed off. While I heated up a canteen cup of water, I did a thorough scan of the jungle.

The water came to a boil. I poured the package of cocoa into my canteen cup. Slowly stirring, I listened to the pitter-patter of the rain falling on my poncho.

In this brief window of security, I took the opportunity to reach for a pen and paper and began writing a letter. The cup of cocoa didn't agree with my stomach, so I rushed out of the perimeter. Toilet paper in hand, I alerted Cartwright. Duggy remained asleep and wasn't aware I had left.

I never went farther than the claymores allowed me. As a courtesy, I dug a hole and covered it when I was done. If you ever had the misfortune of forgetting the toilet paper, it could end up being a painful experience.

The only time I forgot my toilet paper, I had to substitute leaves from a nearby plant. By the time I returned to the perimeter, the irritation was so painful I needed to seek the attention of the platoon's field medic.

I pleaded with the medic to give me something for the discomfort, as he investigated the reddish lesions. He was curious to know what had caused the rash. I led him to the plant. He laughed when he identified it.

"What the hell is so funny?" I asked.

"You wiped your ass with poison ivy," said the medic, laughing hysterically.

I didn't think wiping my ass with poison ivy was humorous, because the discomfort was unbearable. The medic gave me an ointment, and the discomfort eventually went away.

Returning after the current, properly supplied occasion, I realized I had left my weapon back at the perimeter. What had I been thinking? What if the enemy had caught me with my pants down? With only toilet paper in hand, my shit would literally have been blown away.

Once again I settled under my hooch and prepared another cup of cocoa. A twig snapping caught my attention. When I looked up there stood an NVA soldier twenty meters away. I was afraid someone was about to die.

The fierce look on the soldiers face revealed he was ready for battle. With a green bandanna wrapped around his forehead, clenching the blade of a knife with his teeth, he started for the perimeter. I reached for my weapon and took aim.

With no time to warn the others, I was forced to make a decision. Duggy remained asleep and not aware the NVA soldier was heading in his direction. Cartwright was writing a letter, facing the opposite direction.

I started to squeeze the trigger when I noticed three NVA soldiers advancing on the perimeter. When their point man lifted his weapon and took aim at Duggy I fired three rounds into his chest.

He fell to his knees, then went facedown on the jungle floor. The others scrambled for cover as I laid down a heavy volume of fire. My heart rate accelerated as I nervously ejected the empty magazine, replacing it with another. Awakened from a deep sleep, Duggy jumped to his knees and blindly fired his M-60 machine gun into the jungle. The assistant machine gunner rushed to his side with more ammo.

Duggy reloaded and continued to fire. Joe, along with of the remainder of the squad, moved forward to the heaviest point of contact. With everyone laying down a heavy volume of fire, Joe detonated claymores, preventing the enemy from returning fire.

After a massive amount of firepower had been dispensed into the jungle, Joe gave the order to cease firing. "Hold your fire! Hold your fire, damn it!"

The familiar smell of spent ammunition lingered in the cool, damp air as rain continued to fall.

"How many dinks did you fire up, Garcia?" asked Joe excitedly.

"One is down and three are still out there," I replied.

"Get ready to move out. We're going to check out the body."

"Are you crazy? The enemy is still out there!" shouted Cartwright.

"No one could survive the massive amount of firepower we just fired," said Duggy.

"All right, but I'm taking my time," said Cartwright, fearing a counterattack.

"Don't worry, I'm right behind you," said Joe.

Cartwright advanced slowly toward the slain NVA soldier. Everyone scanned the jungle thoroughly until Cartwright reached the body. Standing over it, Joe placed the muzzle of his M-16 into the chest. Confirming that the enemy soldier was dead, Joe searched him. I stared at the enemy lying on the ground. It was difficult to guess his age.

Joe handed me the AK-47 and removed the knife from the soldier's teeth. Next, he untied a plastic bag on the soldier's belt, emptying the contents onto the ground. He discovered several documents among the personal belongings.

Joe ordered a quick sweep of the wood line, searching for additional bodies. Brother Charles noticed a claymore wire had been cut. This meant the enemy knew of our presence.

A heavy blood trail revealed the enemy soldiers were headed for an opening in the wood line. The rest of us followed until the blood trail was lost.

"At least one of the NVA soldiers is seriously wounded. That was a thick blood trail. Unless he gets medical attention soon, he's going to die," said Joe.

"Unfortunately, we'll never know," said Cartwright.

Joe ordered the squad back to the perimeter and began investigating the enemy documents. The documents had been issued in Vietnamese, requiring a Kit Carson scout to translate.

Besides the AK-47 and a bush knife, the slain soldier's personal belongings included a military citation, an American soldier's dog tag, and two communist flags, neatly folded. A picture of a young, attractive Vietnamese girl indicated he had a girlfriend or was married.

Joe unfolded the red cloth flags. One was a North Vietnamese Thirty-Third Regiment flag, the other a Soviet Union flag with a yellow hammer and sickle.

"The flags and the knife belong to you, but I have to turn them in to intelligence first, along with the weapon and documents," Joe said to me.

After reviewing all the documentation, the Kit Carson scout revealed the NVA soldier was a high-ranking officer in the People's Army of Vietnam, delivering orders to organize troops in the south. The citation awarded to the officer was for outstanding performance against hostile American forces. Attached to the citation was a dog tag stamped with the American soldier's name, blood type, religion, and social security number.

The citation led Joe to believe that the enemy officer was responsible for killing the American whose name was inscribed on the dog tag: Anthony J.

The documentation also revealed that the soldier was a member of the Thirty-Third Regiment. Once known as one of North Vietnam's fiercest fighting unit, they were supposedly wiped out during the 1968 Tet Offensive.

"If the Thirty-Third has regrouped, this means bad news for American troops in the Long Binh Province. Let's get the hell out of here!" cried Joe.

It would be dark soon, and with a dead NVA soldier lying twenty meters away, Joe was concerned the enemy would return for the body. He decided it was best to search for a new location before dark and gave the order to move out.

With only minutes of daylight remaining, everyone packed hastily and slung on their rucksacks, following Joe out of the perimeter.

As I made my way out, I glanced at the slain soldier "What are we going to do with the body?" I asked Joe.

"What do you want to do, Garcia? Give him a funeral? It's not my problem. There are dinks out there and it's getting dark fast, so let's get going."

Being responsible for the death of another enemy soldier only engraved one more horrific memory I would have to live with the rest of my life.

Joe humped through the jungle, searching for a new location. With no time to link up with first squad, he continued his search until it was too dark to see. We had to settle for our new position, not knowing if the area provided adequate cover. Everyone dropped their rucksacks and quickly set up a tight defensive perimeter.

I found a clearing on the jungle floor and laid out my air mattress, collapsing from exhaustion. At the end of the day, I realized my life had been spared once again. The outcome could have been different if the enemy had spotted me first, but once again I was in the wrong place at the right time.

As I lay on the wet jungle floor, I could hear the squad RTO calling in our coordinates. Rider, the newly assigned main CP RTO, returned the call, requesting the name of the person responsible for the kill. The radio squelched and the squad RTO quietly gave my name.

"7-6 Hotel, 7-6 Hotel, come in. Over."

"Go ahead, 7-6 Juliette."

"7-6 Hotel, his last name is spelled Golf, Alpha, Romeo, Charlie, India, Alpha. Over."

"7-6 Juliette, that's a solid copy. Tell 'One Shot' congratulations, and it looks like CO is putting him in for a Silver Star recommendation. Over."

From that time on, I was known as One Shot.

That evening, the entire squad remained on high alert. Exhausted from the day's activities, I managed to fall asleep. Just before midnight I was awakened by the sound of a 60 mm mortar round leaving the mortar tube. I placed my steel pot over my head and waited.

The mortar round exploded in the area where we had engaged the enemy earlier. Another mortar was fired, and once again I braced for the explosion.

"Keep your head down," whispered Joe.

With no fire support and very little ammo, second squad lay on the jungle floor defenseless. Anticipating another mortar, all we could do was stay down and take cover.

Awake at the break of dawn, everyone wanted to hear from the main CP. We were damp from the night's monsoon rain and without any breakfast. Joe gave the word to move out of the perimeter.

Orders for the day were to find a suitable position to clear an area and replenish our ammo. Joe humped a safe distance away from the previous night's position and located an opening in the jungle. To maintain the element of surprise, a helicopter would have to hover above the tree line and lower the ammo.

A canister of yellow smoke marked our position. The pilot verified our location and hovered over the opening. The door gunner lowered a cargo net filled with ammo and retrieved the documents and weapons taken from the NVA soldier.

Replacing two bandoliers, I realized I had expended practically all my ammo. We were told to conserve food and water because we wouldn't be supplied again for another three days. Battalion ordered Blackfoot Platoon to remain in squad-size ambushes until the Australians completed their mission.

On the fourth morning of the mission, the only ration remaining in my rucksack was a can of spaghetti and meatballs. With very little water, I desperately needed to replenish my supply.

That evening, I managed to capture enough rainwater dripping from my poncho to fill a two-quart. The rainwater was clean, and enough to satisfy my thirst.

The following morning, Joe was ordered to link up with first squad and search for an opening to be resupplied. When the point team crossed the path of several fallen trees, the position was selected as the drop-off point. But the opening was too small for a landing zone. The helicopters would have to hover over the jungle.

The canister of yellow smoke identified our position, and the first resupply bird arrived. The door gunner lowered a cargo net filled with C-rations and LRPs. Moments later, a second bird arrived with the rubber blivet of fresh water. There would be no mail delivery until we returned to the fire base.

Thirty minutes after delivery of the final supplies, a helicopter returned for the backlog. The door gunner lowered the cargo net, and several members of the platoon placed the discarded C-rations, LRPs and water blivet in it. The door gunner lifted it, and the helicopter headed back to the fire base.

Blackfoot's orders were to remain in platoon size and continue searching for insurgents moving into Saigon. Everyone was mentally and physically exhausted, anticipating another confrontation with the enemy. Dense vegetation made it difficult to move. The point team struggled to break brush. Joe was determined to find an easier path through the jungle. When the point team came across an abandoned logging road, he chose to take the easier path of travel.

The point team made good time until Cartwright discovered a shiny object lying beneath the ground cover. Joe carefully brushed away the grass and exposed the top of an old land mine.

"Stand back, it's a Bouncing Betty," warned Joe. "We're lucky no one stepped on it."

Bouncing Betty was the name of a sophisticated communist land mine. Once activated, the explosive popped out of the ground, exploding at eye level. Joe made sure no one disturbed it, and the platoon moved on.

Knowing there could be other booby traps in the area, Cartwright proceeded with extreme caution. Traveling along the edge of the logging road, the patrol came to a halt when a call came in for Joe. Everyone took the opportunity to remove their newly resupplied rucksacks and enjoy a break.

Brother Kelly pulled out a Pall Mall cigarette and took a couple hits. He flicked the cigarette on the ground. It landed near a suspicious wire. Old and rusty, the wire was well hidden beneath the grass. I followed it across the logging road to the base of a tree. Housed in a rusty C-ration can was one of our own M-33 grenades.

"It's another fucking booby trap," said Brother Theo.

"What should we do with it?" Brother Kelly asked.

"The booby trap is so old, there's no safety pin attached to the firing mechanism," I replied.

"We need to get the hell off this logging road," said Brother Theo.

After we informed Joe of the booby trap, he made the decision to head back into the wood line. He gave his point team a new azimuth. For some reason, not everyone got the message.

Cartwright located an opening and entered the wood line. Teeny Bopper and the rest of the squad didn't notice Brother Kelly entering the wood line; they continued to follow the logging road. Brother Kelly was twenty meters into the wood line when he discovered Teeny Bopper and the remainder of the squad weren't behind him.

"One Shot, tell the others to wait," said Brother Kelly in an angry tone.

"What's wrong now?" I asked.

"I have to look for dumb-ass Teeny Bopper and the rest of the squad."

"Where'd they go?"

"They're probably lost. Watch my back. I'm going back to the logging road. I'm too fucking short for this bullshit."

I alerted the rest of the squad to halt, and followed Brother Kelly. I could justify his anger. "Too short" meant he was getting close to going home. It would be a tragedy for him to be wounded or killed so near the end of his tour.

Brother Kelly eventually located Teeny Bopper and the remaining members of Blackfoot, leading them back to the platoon. If Teeny Bopper had traveled any farther, the group would have been difficult to locate. Teeny Bopper followed Brother Kelly into the wood line.

"You better pay attention, dumb ass," said Brother Kelly, unable to hide his anger.

"Don't worry about it," replied Teeny Bopper.

"You better get your head out of your ass, or you're going to get your shit blown away."

"I'll think about it," replied Teeny Bopper.

That was the wrong thing to say to Kelly Hicks. He slung his rucksack on the ground and slammed Teeny Bopper into a thicket.

Joe noticed the heated discussion and addressed the two. "What the fuck is going on? Every dink in the jungle can hear you! Come on, we're on the same side. Get your shit together and let's get the hell out of here!"

"I don't know about you, but I'd like to go home alive," said Brother Kelly with a crazed look on his face.

"Let's get going," said Joe.

Brother Kelly picked up his rucksack and weapon and fell in behind Brother Theo. "You deal with him, One Shot. I'm too short for this bullshit."

Teeny Bopper kept his distance from Brother Kelly for the rest of the mission, never realizing his carelessness could have put the platoon in danger.

Bravo Company continued to work with the Australians. Blackfoot was fortunate not to have any further contact with the enemy. Aztec and Cheyenne weren't so lucky. Both platoons engaged the enemy on two different occasions.

During that time, we were resupplied but never received any mail. I normally wrote Mom and Dad every other day. Not hearing from me in ten days must have been hard.

***

June 17. We were scheduled for resupply. The CO received word from battalion to assemble all three platoons at a nearby pickup zone. Joe gave the order to pull in our night work and link up with Aztec and Cheyenne. Originally scheduled for a sixteen-day mission, Bravo Company was being extracted from the field.

The company's new orders were for Aztec and Cheyenne to be extracted to Fire Base Hall, with Blackfoot being extracted to a remote fire support base located south of Highway 1. Aztec would be the first platoon to leave the field, followed by Cheyenne and Blackfoot.

After Cheyenne was extracted, Joe received a call informing him that one of the birds returning to Fire Base Hall had drawn enemy fire and had to return to Fire Base Mace. Joe was furious, knowing the final pickup would be delayed.

Usually the platoon leader was the last to leave field, but as acting platoon leader, Joe decided he would be extracted with the first five members of the squad. With only thirty days remaining in-country, he didn't want to take any unnecessary chances.

After thirty minutes of waiting, a bird returned to pick up Joe and the first five members of the squad. A second bird would follow to pick up the remaining members. Assigned to the last bird, I was grouped with Brother Al, Brother Charles, Bart, and Cole, the squad RTO. We had to wait for one of the birds to return from the mini fire support base.

Bart panicked when he realized we were the only soldiers on the ground. Brother Al tried to keep him occupied while the rest of us kept an eye on the wood line. When the final helicopter arrived, we didn't hesitate to rush to the bird. The pilot lifted off the LZ, and the door gunners gave the signal to fire up the wood line.

After ten days without clean fatigues, hot chow, or mail, the mission that had started with the Australians finally came to an end.

Episode Seventeen

The Death

June 17. Brother Al and I stepped off the bird and entered the fire base. Claiming a hooch near a guard bunker, I unloaded my equipment and waited for clean clothes and mail. Hot chow wouldn't be served for another two hours.

I began peeling the thick red clay from my worn jungle boots. Monsoon season was the worst season of the year, ideal for jungle rot and other infectious diseases. It rained three times a day. We lived in damp clothing, day and night.

Sundance arrived with a duffel bag of clean clothes and two welcome red sacks of mail. No one cared about the clean clothes, just their mail. There were ten days of news and care packages in those red sacks. I looked forward to reading every letter.

We all waited eagerly to hear our names as Sundance passed out the mail. "One Shot, get your ass up here! You have a care package," he hollered.

I had received letters from everyone, including Little Joey. Never having heard before from the friend left behind at the Tan Son Nhut Processing Center, I was eager to read his letter.

I usually opened Dad's letters first, but this time I opened Joey's. As I unfolded the letter, a photograph fell on ground. It was a picture of Little Joey lying on his back, holding a bouquet of flowers. With his arms crossed and eyes closed, he appeared to be sleeping.

"*Rest in peace*" read the caption on the back of the photograph.

Not understanding his humor, I began reading his letter. "I'm writing this letter as I wait to be combat assaulted into the field. I volunteered for point man last mission, and I like it. What do you think of my picture? Ha ha!"

The letter went on to explain that he had remained at the Tan Son Nhut Processing Center for two more weeks until he was assigned to the 101st Airborne Division. His unit was currently working out of a fire base near Thua Thien Province. Now that he had my address, he promised to write, hoping I would do the same.

Now eager to hear from Dad, I opened his earliest-dated letter. "I hate giving you tragic news, but Little Joey was killed June 3."

Stunned, I read the first line again in disbelief. Praying it wasn't true, I read Little Joey's, letter searching for a date. Coincidentally, his letter had been written June 3.

I had just read his letter, and now I was being informed he had been killed on the day he had written it. Little Joey had been killed thirteen days ago, and I was just learning of his death. Had he suffered, or was he killed instantly? I suspected he gave his all until he drew his last breath.

I believe Little Joey would still be alive today if he had remained with Jet and me. Unfortunately, there is no way to control anyone's destiny, especially when serving on the front line in Vietnam.

My memories of Little Joey temporarily outweighed the tragedy of his death. There had been many humorous moments in the short time I had known Joey, but the one memory that was engraved in my heart occurred during our thirty-day leave. After a night of celebration, Little Joey entered my bedroom early in the morning. My dog, DI (the abbreviation for drill instructor), barked as they both jumped up and down on my bed. With a major league hangover, I refused to get out of bed. Little Joey wasn't going to let me sleep, and neither was DI.

Once I was out of bed, Little Joey and I set out to enjoy another day of our leave. He wasn't much of a drinker, but he was well liked by my friends. I could only imagine the pain his family suffered when notified of his death.

There was never a pleasant way for the military to notify parents of a son's death. Although there were an overwhelming number of death notifications during the Vietnam War, the job was never easy for the personnel sent to notify the family. My dad grieved Little Joey's death too, fearing the military might pay him a visit someday with the same death notification.

The news of Little Joey's death left me with anger. I just wanted to kill the bastards who had killed my friend. The war the government conveniently labeled a "conflict" had taken another life. We were fighting with a lack of support from the Americans back home, and I had six more months to deal with it.

Hearing about the death made me realize how fortunate I was to still be alive. Filled with grief, I headed for the guard bunker to be alone. With death on my mind, my thoughts were focused on Jet. Was he all right? Was he on the front line or somewhere in the rear? He probably wasn't even aware Little Joey had been killed.

Curious to know why I was alone, Brother Al took the time to come by. "What's wrong, brother? You look like you lost your best friend."

"I did," I said sadly, handing Brother Al Dad's letter. He read the first few lines and replied sympathetically, "I'm sorry about your friend, One Shot. Come on, they're serving hot chow. Let's get something to eat."

The following morning, my thoughts remained focused on the death. Joe came by and informed me of a ceremony that battalion was planning on my behalf. "One Shot, you better get ready. The battalion commander is on his way to present you with another citation."

"I don't care about any citations," I said.

"The CO put you in for a Silver Star for saving Duggy and the rest of the squad, but because there wasn't a higher body count, battalion reduced your Silver Star to a Bronze Star for valor."

"I don't want any more medals for killing people. I just want to go home."

"Sorry, One Shot. That's just the way it is out here. By the way, the documents the NVA soldier was carrying led intelligence to an enemy field hospital. Great job. You did it again," said Joe.

"Once again, I happened to be in the wrong place at the right time. Besides, receiving a Bronze Star for same war that killed my friend is senseless."

Joe went on to say that the NVA soldiers I had encountered were from the North, organizing troops in the South. Their objective was to prepare for the new lunar year offensive. The discovery of one of their caches was just a temporary setback. History had proven the communist forces were determined to defeat the Americans at any cost.

The battalion commander arrived at the fire base as usual in his shiny First Cav helicopter. He was met by acting platoon leader Joe Braden as the platoon assembled on the LZ. The commander stepped out of his Huey, along with a staff of four, and headed for the formation. Referencing the contact with the hostile enemy force on June 6, the commander addressed the platoon.

"For heroism in connection with military operations against hostile enemy forces in the Republic of Vietnam, I hereby award the second Bronze Star to Specialist Garcia, who distinguished himself by exceptionally valorous action on June 6, 1971, when his unit became engaged with a determined enemy force. With complete disregard for his own safety, he exposed himself to intense hostile enemy fire as he moved forward to the point of heaviest contact and began placing a heavy volume of suppressive fire upon enemy insurgent forces. His actions are an inspiration to other members of his unit and were instrumental for a successful completion of the mission. His display of personal bravery and devotion to duty is in keeping with the highest traditions of the military service and reflects great credit upon himself, his unit, and the United States Army. Not only did Specialist Garcia singlehandedly save his squad from a determined hostile enemy attack, he also eliminated the threat. I might add that the documents captured on June 6 led us to a major discovery, creating another setback for the enemy. Keep up the good work, gentlemen. It's soldiers like you who give us the advantage in winning this war," stated the battalion commander proudly.

The battalion commander pinned a bronze star with *V* device on my fatigue shirt. He also awarded additional citations to Joe, Cartwright, and Brother Charles for their support on June 6.

The battalion commander personally thanked me, returning the NVA soldier's bush knife, two communist flags, and dog tag. The captured flags would make an interesting conversation piece with friends and family back home. The captured AK-47 was probably taken by a high-ranking official as a war souvenir.

In my opinion, the performance of the AK-47 was better than the M-16. Somewhat bulky, its distinctive sound was intimidating. When fired, the flash suppressor forced the muzzle downward, following its kill to the ground, as opposed to the M-16 that rose rapidly upward. Because of its slightly larger casing, the AK-47 was capable of firing M-16 ammo, whereas the M-16 could not fire AK-47 ammo.

After the completion of the ceremony, the battalion commander requested that the other citation recipients and I join him in a tour of the fire base.

"How's morale on the fire base, Garcia?" asked the battalion commander.

"I'm not the person you should be asking that question, sir," I replied.

"Why not, Garcia?"

"Being an only son, I shouldn't be in the field in the first place, sir."

"You're an only son? How did you end up on the front line?"

"Yeah, that's something I'd like to know. There isn't a day I don't think about it."

"You need to speak to your congressman about that, soldier. I'm sure there's something he can do for you."

"I've been trying for the last six months with no response, sir," I said.

"You're a valuable asset to the battalion. Without soldiers like you, we can't win this war."

"The outcome of this war has nothing to do with me, sir. I just want to go home."

"I understand, but so does everyone else participating in this war. Keep up the good work. It will pay off someday."

The commander returned to his shiny helicopter and left for the safety of his quarters in the rear. Curious to see my captured communist flags, everyone wanted a picture. The story around the fire base was I that I had singlehandedly prevented the Thirty-Third Regiment from overrunning second squad's perimeter.

Episode Eighteen

Revenge

June 20. Bravo Company was inserted into the field to begin another mission. The length was uncertain, but I was allowed to return to Bien Hoa for an emergency dental visit. The pain from the loss of a filling had become unbearable.

The trip to the rear was a welcome relief from the field. I located battalion's military dentist and was taken in immediately. Casual conversation revealed the doctor had been drafted after graduation from dental school at the age of twenty-five. The dentist replaced the filling, relieving the pain, and I was off to enjoy a few days out of the field.

I came across a soldier who had attended my advanced infantry unit at Fort Ord, California. A brief conversation revealed McKeon had originally been assigned to a light weapons infantry unit until he was reassigned to the army military police.

***

June 24. I returned to the field on log day and received my first letter from Jet. After six months, I heard from the friend left behind at First Team Academy. His letter stated he was on his way to Hawaii to spend time with his wife. Jet hadn't seen his newly wedded wife in six months, so it was going to be a happy reunion.

***

July 2. After a twelve-day mission denying sanctuary to NVA and main-force Viet Cong, Bravo Company assembled at the pickup zone for extraction. Although a strong presence of NVA and main-force Viet Cong remained in the lowlands, the enemy was beginning to avoid large-scale battles with American troops. This created false hope among the soldiers because it appeared we had turned back the enemy. In reality, the enemy was just waiting for us to turn over the fighting to the South Vietnamese Army.

Bravo Company was extracted without incident and flown to Fire Base Fanning. Lieutenant CJ returned to duty and was awaiting our arrival.

Due to my two Bronze Stars, I was the company commander's choice to spend the day with the battalion commander. Battalion believed the "Grunt for the Day" program would be good for morale. I was grateful to be considered one of the best to represent Bravo Company, but after twelve days in the field, all I wanted to do was rest. Lieutenant CJ said I had no choice in the matter. I was ordered to grab my weapon and a canister of yellow smoke.

"Pop smoke, the battalion commander's bird is inbound!" shouted Lieutenant CJ. The battalion commander's Huey touched down, and the door gunner waved me aboard. I was greeted with a handshake and a smile by the battalion commander. He was a large man and was wearing a .45 caliber pistol strapped to his side.

The commander's pilot lifted off the LZ and headed for Charlie Company's location in the field.

"I identify First Cav yellow," said the commander's pilot as he began his descent into the LZ.

The Huey touched down while Charlie Company was being resupplied. The commander unbuckled his seat belt and insisted I join him. I grabbed my weapon and followed him into the wood line.

"Are you lock and loaded, soldier?" he asked.

"Always, sir," I responded.

"I hope you don't have to use it," he joked.

"Yeah, for your sake, I hope not," I said, shaking my head as I walked away.

The CO escorted us to an area where Charlie Company had engaged the enemy, killing one and capturing another. The engagement revealed a large bunker complex. The number of bunkers could have easily housed a company of VC insurgents.

After a brief visit, the battalion commander was back in the air, flying to Delta Company's location a click (one thousand meters) away. The pilot identified yellow smoke and made his descent into the LZ. The Huey touched down, and we were off to see Delta Company's CO.

"Come with me, sir. We have something to show you," said Delta Company's CO.

We followed the CO into the wood line until we came to a mound of dirt piled to the side of a trotter. Delta Company had uncovered an underground storage system.

"One of our soldiers discovered a bamboo vent sticking out of the jungle floor. He started digging and found an underground bunker that led to a food cache filled with flour and rice. A tunnel system led to another underground bunker that revealed an assortment of medical supplies. What was interesting was the medical supplies were US military issue," explained the CO.

After touring the underground storage system, we were back aboard the helicopter and heading for Alpha Company's current location. They were farthest away from the fire base.

The battalion commander took the time to inform me that Alpha Company had recently captured an NVA soldier, whose interrogation led the company to an NVA base camp.

By the time we arrived, Alpha Company had secured the base camp and was awaiting our arrival. The battalion commander toured the bunker complex with the CO. Following close behind, I listened as the two leaders discuss their options to dismantle the camp.

Although I despised spending the day with my commander, I turned it into an opportunity to get to know the one person who could pull me out of the field. What I learned that day was the commander was well acquainted with my performance in the field and had specifically requested I be the first to spend the day with him.

"All right, Garcia, you ready to head back to the fire base?" he asked.

"We're not there yet," I replied jokingly.

"I enjoyed your company today. Keep up the good work, soldier."

The battalion commander shook my hand, and I stepped off the skid and returned to the fire base. I arrived in time to take on Aztec in a game of softball. Accompanied by Mateo and Romeo, I headed down to the helicopter pad with a plastic bag filled with beer.

"How was your day with the battalion commander?" asked Mateo with sarcasm.

"Although I would have preferred drinking beer with you, I believe the time spent with the commander might turn out to be beneficial to me someday," I said.

"Right, Garcia," said Romeo, chuckling as we made our way to the LZ.

The softball game provided a stress-free opportunity to enjoy the afternoon. Between innings, both teams enjoyed a refreshing cold beer. The game tied 6-6 when the last out had been made after six innings of play. Aztec was taking the field when Lieutenant CJ ran out to the LZ with disturbing news.

"Charlie Company has hit the shit, and Blackfoot has been selected to help stabilize the situation. Get your shit together and get back to the LZ, ASAP. The birds are on their way. Now move it!"

Everyone ran back to the fire base and loaded their rucksacks with food and ammo. I collected two bandoliers of M-16 ammo, six grenades, 250 rounds of M-60 ammo, and a LAW (light antitank weapon). Not knowing how long we would be out there, I stuffed a few LRPs in my rucksack and filled my five-quart with water. I slung my rucksack over my shoulder and ran down to the LZ as the first bird approached.

"One Shot, Sundance, Al, Charles, Cole, you're with me on the first bird. Let's get it on and remember to keep your shit together. We're going into a hot fucking LZ," said Lieutenant CJ with a hint of fear in his voice.

He briefed us on Charlie Company's grave situation as our bird lifted off the LZ. I could read the fear on everyone's faces as we flew toward the contact area. I embraced the opportunity to kill the bastards who had killed Little Joey.

Charlie Company's demise began when their point team entered the wood line. As when a black widow spider waits for her prey to become entangled in her web, the point team had wandered into a well-camouflaged bunker complex where the enemy lurked.

Leading the way was the dog handler, who must have been instantly killed. Several others in the lead squad were lying wounded on the jungle floor. Under a barrage of heavy AK-47 fire, the remaining squad members had managed to pull back their wounded to safety. Sniper fire prevented the remaining members of the platoon from retrieving the deceased dog handler and his dog.

The first medevac arrived to pick up the wounded, only to be shot down by a direct hit from an enemy B-40 rocket. The pilot didn't realize he had flown over the enemy's position. The pilot managed to crash land his Huey helicopter off to one side of the LZ, saving himself and his crew. The crew evacuated the helicopter as it burned to a cinder.

Lieutenant CJ pointed to the burning wreckage as our pilot circled the LZ. A second medevac was determined to maneuver around the burning wreckage to pick up the wounded.

My hands were damp, and beads of sweat dripped from my forehead. My heart accelerated as the pilot approached the LZ. Without warning, a B-40 rocket flashed by. The pilot tilted the Huey's nose slightly upward, determined to deliver his passengers. Flames from the burning wreckage prevented him from touching down. The door gunner signaled for us to jump as the helicopter hovered. Lieutenant CJ stepped onto the skid and took the first plunge. I followed along with the others.

I landed in tall, muddy grass. Struck on the head with my own claymore, I fell to the ground. Slightly dazed, I managed to get to my feet and follow Lieutenant CJ into the wood line. Sundance, Brother Al, Brother Charles, and the squad RTO followed close behind. Now that I was on the ground, my concern was for the rest of the platoon to be safely combat assaulted into the field without casualty.

The smell of burning magnesium and ammunition lingered in the air as we waited for the remainder of the platoon to arrive. The sound of sporadic AK-47 fire and an occasional B-40 rocket explosion indicated the enemy was determined to hold their ground.

I was determined to get even. I moved forward, hoping for a clear shot at the enemy who had killed my friend.

"One Shot, what the hell are you doing?" shouted Lieutenant CJ.

"I saw something move," I replied.

"Wait until the rest of the platoon is on the ground. Now get back here!"

At this point, I had no regard for my own life. I just wanted to kill the enemy.

When everyone in the platoon was safely on the ground, Blackfoot secured the LZ and waited for word to move out.

The enemy realized reinforcements had arrived and began to withdraw. A sniper or two remained in the area, preventing Charlie Company from pulling back the dog handler. They pulled back to the LZ instead.

It was late in the afternoon when Lieutenant CJ ordered Blackfoot to set up on the opposite side of the contact area, linking to Charlie Company. We were instructed to remain on high alert and be prepared to engage the enemy fleeing the area. Everyone quickly located sleeping positions and put out their night work. With claymore and trip flare in hand, I headed out of the perimeter.

"One Shot, be careful. There's dinks out there," whispered Sundance.

"I know, I can smell the bastards," I replied.

"Get your night work out and return to the perimeter."

"Go on. I'll follow you." I searched for a suitable location to set up my claymore. I could hear the enemy shuffling through the jungle in the distance. Not sure if they were fleeing the area or repositioning for a counterattack, I dropped to one knee. I would wait for a clear shot; I was going to get even right here and now. That didn't happen.

Disappointed that I didn't get a chance to engage the enemy, I inserted the blasting cap into the detonator well and returned to the perimeter. From my position, I could see an expensive piece of American machinery burned to a cinder. When night fell, everyone settled in, with anticipation of moving out in the morning to help Charlie Company retrieve the dead dog handler and his dog.

During the night, we could hear the enemy shuffling through the jungle. Besides sleeping in enemy-infested jungles, there was nothing more intimidating than the jungle itself. There was a saying in Vietnam: "If the enemy didn't get you, the jungle would."

The jungle was a never-ending succession of life-threatening experiences. Besides being burdened with the constant fear of death, grunts had to endure a host of miseries: firefights, incoming, body bags, boredom, moaning, groaning, and never enough to eat or drink.

Humping a weapon through steamy-hot jungles and wearing a heavy rucksack containing C-rations, LRPs, water, claymore, M-60 ammo, grenades, and a LAW was no party. Not to mention enduring torrential monsoon rain, boot-sucking red clay mud, intense humidity, dehydration, heat exhaustion, sunburn, malaria, dysentery, jungle rot, and the endless battle with obnoxious wait-a-minute vines—plus a host of bloodsucking leeches, poisonous spiders, poisonous centipedes, malaria-ridden mosquitoes, fireflies, bush snakes, bamboo pit vipers, scorpions, rats, fire ants, fuck-you lizards, re-up frogs, and a thousand other discomforts.

I truly believed a prisoner serving a life sentence for murder lived a better life than the grunts serving in Vietnam. Unfortunately, the life of the grunt went unnoticed by the average American civilian. But among other grunts fighting the battle, he was well respected and honored.

***

July 3. In the early morning hours, I was awakened by Brother Charles for final watch. He indicated movement during the night. It appeared the enemy had waited until early morning to completely retreat from the area. I made my way to the guard station and settled in. Listening relentlessly, I hoped to blow a claymore on enemy soldiers wandering into our perimeter.

When my watch ended at the break of dawn, I returned to my sleeping position and began packing. I was eager to help Charlie Company retrieve the deceased dog handler. I rolled up my air mattress, poncho, and poncho liner. I was blousing my fatigue pants when I felt a painful sting near my groin. Before I could get my fatigue pants below my knees, I received another painful sting.

"What's wrong, Jarcia?" said Brother Charles.

"I think I've been attacked by a hornet," I said. Struggling to get out of my fatigue pants, I fell to the ground. With two painful welts in my groin, I lay on the ground in agony.

"One Shot, are you all right?" Brother Charles asked.

"No! I can't move."

You don't look so good. I'm going to get the medic."

Brother Charles returned with the medic, who asked, "What's the trouble, One Shot?"

"I think a hornet stung the crap out of me."

"Let's take a look."

The medic determined the welts were not from the stinger of a hornet. He stuck his thermometer in my mouth, and took my pulse. "You have an accelerated heart rate, and your temperature is well above normal. Whatever got you is definitely causing some serious symptoms."

"What do think it was, Doc?" I asked.

"I'm not positive, but it could have been that scorpion lying by your boots."

"Oh, crap, am I going to die?"

"Fortunately, scorpion bites aren't fatal, but if I don't get you out of the field soon, you might suffer some nerve damage. Try to relax, One Shot. There's a medevac coming to pick up the dog handler."

The medic convinced Lieutenant CJ to place me on the incoming medevac for immediate medical treatment. The lieutenant agreed and prepared to move his platoon across the LZ. "Hang on, One Shot. The medevac is on its way," he said encouragingly.

By that time the medevac arrived I was blinded by a migraine headache, along with spasms in the back of my neck. I was lifted into the medevac and placed next to the dog handler.

The medevac lifted off and headed to the field hospital located at Fire Base Mace. I could only pray that I would survive. Unfortunately, the dog handler lying lifeless beside me had not.

The medevac touched down at the medical evacuation center. The dog handler and I were lifted off and carried into the field surgery room. I was placed on a cold medical table, and again the dog handler was placed beside me.

Placing his stethoscope to the dog handler's chest, the field surgeon confirmed he was dead on arrival. The chaplain was called into the surgery room to administer last rites.

The field surgeon pulled back my eyelids and peered into my eyes with a medical flashlight as the chaplain prayed. "So we were bitten by a scorpion," said the field surgeon, studying my wounds. "The good news is no one has ever died from a scorpion attack on my watch, so you're going to live."

"Why do I feel like I'm dying?" I replied.

"The bad news is you're going to experience a hell of a hangover," said the field surgeon jokingly. "Looks like he got you several times. Any closer and he would have gotten the family jewels. Can you describe the pain from one to ten?"

"Yeah, twenty."

"Okay, I'm going to put you on an IV drip and give you something for the pain. The medication will make you drowsy but will take care of the pain. You should be ready for duty in a few days. It will take a few minutes for the medication to take effect. Try to relax. You're going to be all right," said the field surgeon.

The chaplain held my hand as he offered a few encouraging words. "How are you feeling, soldier?

"Like crap."

"I bet, but at least you're going to survive, unlike your brother lying on the table next to you."

The chaplain reached for the deceased dog handler's hand and started reciting the Lord's Prayer. Unexpectedly, the dog handler squeezed the chaplain's hand.

"I think he's still alive!" said the chaplain, looking startled.

"Nonsense. He was brought in as a line one (deceased)," said the field surgeon, placing his stethoscope on the dog handler's chest. "Oh my God, he *is* alive!"

"You're damn right I'm still alive," moaned the dog handler.

I thought I was hallucinating. I sat upright to witness the miracle for myself. The dog handler had been pronounced dead, and now he was alive.

Immediately, the field surgeon positioned the dog handler on his stomach and began attending to his wounds. Trying to recall the events that led up to the ambush, the soldier struggled to speak.

"The only thing I remember was moving into the wood line with my dog, Skip. When Skip refused to move, I should have known something was wrong. Twenty meters in, I hesitated when I heard movement. Suddenly, a loud blast knocked me off my feet. With shrapnel piercing my back and two broken legs, I managed to crawl underneath two palms. Enemy machine gun fire scraped the area. All I could do was pray the enemy didn't finish me off.

"I could hear the LT shouting out my name, but I couldn't answer. I didn't want to give my position away. I frantically felt around the ground for Skip, who was trained to lie beside me in that situation. But he wasn't so lucky. The bastards killed my dog," said the dog handler, now weeping.

"The last thing I remember was a loud explosion. It knocked me unconscious. When I opened my eyes, it was dark. I didn't know what time it was, but I knew I was in trouble when I couldn't feel my legs. I had been left in the jungle to die. Although Skip was lying dead a few meters away, I felt he was still protecting me as he was trained to do.

"I lost a tremendous amount of blood, making it difficult to stay conscious. I lay quietly in agonizing pain as the enemy searched for me in the dark. They were only steps away when they called off the search.

"In the morning, I could hear voices as I lay in a catatonic state. I tried to respond, but I didn't have the strength. The point man discovered my jungle boots under the palms. 'He must have been killed instantly,' he said. They thought I was dead."

I was taken to the recovery room as the field surgeons prepared the dog handler for surgery. The surgical team removed the shrapnel and closed his wounds. They set his broken legs and prepared him for the recovery room. The dog handler had gone through a horrific ordeal and would have one hell of a story to tell when he returned from the war.

I slept the remainder of the day and throughout the night.

***

July 4. I woke up with a severe migraine but was able to move my leg. I managed to sit up and remove the IV drip from my arm. The dog handler was asleep on the bunk beside me. It was nearing lunch, so I decided to head for the mess hall.

My boonie hat and a pair of fatigue pants were hanging on the bed frame, but I couldn't locate a fatigue shirt. Stepping outside the recovery room, I was blinded by the bright sunlight and intense heat. I was ready for a meal. I located the mess hall and fell in behind the others.

"The cooks won't serve you without a fatigue shirt," said the soldier standing at the end of the line.

Frustrated, I returned to the recovery room. The field surgeon was attending to the dog handler when I entered the room.

"Where have you been?" asked the field surgeon.

"I went to the mess hall, but they wouldn't serve me without a shirt," I replied angrily.

"How you feeling?" he continued.

"I'm hungry."

The field surgeon sent me to the supply room for a fatigue shirt and suggested I remain in recovery another day. But since it was Fourth of July, I decided to return to the fire base on the next convoy.

"Where's my rucksack and weapon?" I asked the supply sergeant.

"Your things are in the back with the dog handler's. You better hurry. The convoy is leaving in five minutes," said the supply sergeant.

I located my rucksack but couldn't find my weapon. I searched through all the weapons mounted on the wall of the supply room, and my weapon was nowhere to be found. I relied on that weapon; it had protected me for six months. Its ability to fire on demand was the difference between life and death.

To a grunt, his weapon was his best friend, and he never went anywhere without it.

"Where's my weapon?" I asked the supply sergeant. I could feel myself getting angry.

"If it isn't on the rack, take a new one and get on the convoy. The trucks are ready to roll," he answered.

Hastily, I reached for a new weapon and climbed aboard the convoy.

Episode Nineteen

Two-Click Confrontation

July 4. Seated on the back of a deuce and a quarter truck, I was headed back to battalion's current fire base. I had been lucky to find my rucksack, but wasn't thrilled about breaking in a new M-16. Blackfoot Platoon had just returned to the fire base and would remain on the fire base until July 7. We were scheduled to start a new mission on my birthday. It meant I wouldn't be able to celebrate until we returned from the fire base.

For the Fourth of July celebration, mess hall spoons grilled New York steaks, accompanied by potato salad, chili beans, corn on the cob, and plenty of ice-cold beer. After the feast, Aztec and Blackfoot organized another game of softball.

Mateo gathered the softball equipment and headed down to the LZ. Each platoon assembled its team, with Aztec taking the field. Using a single bat, a ball, and four fielders' gloves, the first pitch was thrown. The third baseman was handling ground balls without a glove, and the center fielder was catching high fly balls with his bare hands. Despite the lack of the equipment, everyone enjoyed the game.

Hoskie had brought a plastic bag filled with beer. In between innings, our team enjoyed cold refreshment as Aztec Platoon returned to the field.

"Pop smoke, birds inbound! Delta Company just hit the shit!" cried out Mateo.

"You have to be joking!" shouted Sundance.

"Just kidding," said Mateo.

"That's not funny," said Sundance, returning to the field.

The game was tied 7-7 in the ninth inning. Aztec scored two runs in the top of the ninth, making the score 9-7. In the bottom of the ninth, Blackfoot loaded the bases but wasn't able to score.

Despite the loss, everyone in Blackfoot spent the rest of the day enjoying the Fourth of July celebration. Mateo and Romeo celebrated my birthday with me a few days early, since Bravo Company would be combat assaulted into the field on July 7.

***

July 7. Everyone wished me happy birthday as we prepared for the new mission. The platoon headed for the LZ and waited the arrival of the five-bird gaggle. Lieutenant CJ informed us that Bravo Company would return to the area where they had assisted Charlie Company on the previous mission. Upon completion of the six-day mission, we would return to the fire base and be transported to China Beach for a three-day R & R.

Our area of operation remained a main-force VC stronghold. Delta Company had encountered the enemy in the same area a few days before. Although air and artillery strikes pounded enemy positions, the enemy refused to leave the area.

I was assigned to the second bird, along with five others. The six of us climbed aboard the slick and lifted off the LZ. Lieutenant CJ and the remaining members of the platoon followed.

The charred remains of the downed medevac were another symbol of defeat as the pilot circled the contact area. My thoughts were focused on the dog handler and his dog Skip. It was a miracle the dog handler had survived the ordeal.

The first bird touched down, dropping us off. The second bird was close behind. I stepped off the skid and headed for the wood line. Once the entire platoon was on the ground, the point team was given the order to head across the LZ in the direction of the contact area.

The entrance to the bunker complex displayed the scars of the enemy's fire superiority. The bunker complex was massive. If fully occupied, it could have inflicted major damage to Charlie Company. For some tactical reason, the enemy had decided to avoid a large-scale battle.

Blackfoot swept the entire enemy base camp, discovering a second bunker complex a hundred meters away. The number of bunkers in the area only confirmed the size of the enemy force that once occupied the region.

Blackfoot moved beyond the bunkers in search of a suitable location for the night. Aztec was working to the west and Cheyenne was running a sweep of the area to the east.

Former squad leaders John, Joe, and Sergeant Tomas were no longer with the platoon. Lieutenant CJ was rebuilding team leadership. Sundance had taken over second squad, and Houston had taken over first squad.

Lieutenant CJ halted the patrol to review his topographical map, along with his newly assigned team leaders. The remainder of the platoon waited for word to move out. The sound of enemy soldiers breaking brush alerted everyone to scramble for cover. Everyone feared a firefight as the enemy marched toward our position.

With an accelerated heart rate, I waited to take the first shot. When I fixed my sight on a soldier's chest, I discovered it was an American.

Shots were prematurely fired. No one realized American troops had accidentally wandered into our perimeter.

"Hold your fire! Hold your fire! It's Delta Company!" shouted Lieutenant CJ.

"What the hell is Delta Company doing this far off course?" shouted Sundance.

"Are there any casualties?" asked Lieutenant CJ.

The main CP contacted Delta Company's CO to avoid any further confusion. Both Bravo and Delta Company avoided a catastrophe that day. Luckily, no one was wounded or killed. As I mentioned before, friendly fire was just another element of the war that couldn't be prevented.

***

July 13. Blackfoot returned to the abandoned bunker complex to gas the bunkers. After gassing the entire complex, Blackfoot pulled out of the area in search of a position for the night. Given an overwhelming presence of enemy forces, Lieutenant CJ insisted on automatic ambushes.

Blackfoot continued to sweep the area of operation without casualty. When the mission came to an end, Lieutenant CJ led his platoon to the pickup zone and awaited extraction in the morning.

***

July 14. The following morning, everyone was up early, in anticipation of going back to the fire base. Lieutenant CJ ordered the platoon to pull in their night work and be ready to move out in five mikes. Unexpectedly, a call came in from the main CP.

After a lengthy radio conversation with the CO, Lieutenant CJ called his squad leaders together for a brief meeting. Everyone in the platoon waited eagerly for the outcome. When Sundance returned with a grim look on his face, we knew the outcome wasn't good.

"There's been a change in mission," said Sundance, looking very troubled.

"We're still going in, right?" I asked, unable to hide the concern in my voice.

"It doesn't look like it," replied Sundance.

"That's bullshit! We're scheduled for China Beach tomorrow," I said.

"Hold down the noise and prepare to move out," ordered Lieutenant CJ.

Everyone had been looking forward to China Beach, and now we didn't know what to expect. Lieutenant CJ gave the order to move out, and we headed for the LZ to link up with Aztec and Cheyenne.

"What's going on, LT?" asked Cartwright.

"You'll find out when we get there," replied Lieutenant CJ.

Cartwright located the LZ. Blackfoot quickly secured the area and waited for Aztec and Cheyenne to arrive.

"What the hell is going on, Sundance?" I asked nervously.

"I'm not sure, but it's not Vung Tau Village."

Aztec arrived with the main CP. When Cheyenne arrived, the CO called his platoon leaders together. After a heated discussion, Lieutenant CJ returned with our new objective.

"The CO has informed me that a low-observation Huey has spotted a company of NVA two clicks away. Since Bravo Company is nearest, we've been chosen to patrol the area. The bad news is if battalion can't find transportation, we're going to hump two clicks."

"Let me get this straight, LT. If battalion can't find any slicks to transport us, we're going to hump two thousand meters to encounter a company of NVA soldiers? Hell, we'll be too damn exhausted to defend ourselves," said Sundance.

"I don't call the shots," said Lieutenant CJ

"What happened to the First Cavalry being air mobile?" I asked. No one answered.

Everyone waited with concern for word from the CO. Then the call came in over the horn.

"Put it on, gentlemen. We're moving out in ten mikes," said Lieutenant CJ.

"You have to be kidding!" cried Sundance.

"Who's leading the way?" asked Cartwright.

"Blackfoot will be the lead platoon. Cartwright, head in a thirty-degree alpha-zulu (compass bearing azimuth). Keep your shit together, gentlemen. We have a long way to go."

Although we were about to hump two thousand meters, I felt confident Cartwright would get us there in respectable time. Cartwright adjusted his rucksack, glanced at his compass, and headed into the wood line.

The main CP fell in behind second squad with Mateo, the new main CP RTO, leading the way. It wasn't the rear job Mateo had expected to get, but the position provided additional security in the field.

Cartwright humped hard for the first five hundred meters. He let the slack man be his eyes and ears as he chopped his way through thick triple canopy. It would be a while before we could break for lunch. I just hoped Cartwright would be able to maintain a steady azimuth. One degree off in a thousand meters could mean a hundred meters off course at the end.

At the seven-hundred-meter pace count, the jungle gave way to an easier path. Though occasionally hung up on a wait-a-minute vine, Cartwright managed to make decent time.

"What's the pace count, One Shot?" asked Lieutenant CJ.

"Thousand meters, Lieutenant," I answered.

At 12:45 p.m., we hit the thousand-meter mark. Determined to get to our objective before dusk, the CO ordered a fifteen-minute lunch break. Everyone dropped their rucksacks and prepared a quick lunch.

"I'm starving," said Mateo.

"So am I," I said.

"Let me call in our location." Mateo called in the company's location, and then pulled out a can of El Paso brand tortillas, along with two cans of boned turkey. I sliced up two jalapeño peppers, boiled some water, and prepared a beef and rice LRP. Mateo and I enjoyed a hot lunch and a casual conversation.

"How do you like working for the new CO?" I asked.

"He's not jungle-wise like you, but he'll learn," said Mateo.

Mateo looked up to me and regarded me as some kind of hero. I never considered myself a hero or came close to resembling one. I just wanted to make it home alive, like everyone else. I explained to Mateo that I was someone who happened to be in the right place at the wrong time.

I enjoyed the conversation as we ate lunch. He was a good listener, or maybe I was a good storyteller. Nonetheless, Mateo always had encouraging things to say.

After lunch, the CO gave the word to pick it up and move out. With a thousand meters remaining, the point team headed toward our objective. They moved swiftly but cautiously until Cartwright came across a recently traveled trotter. Upon the discovery of a fresh discharge of human waste, Cartwright slowed the pace.

At this point, we were ready to blast anything that moved. When we reached the fifteen-hundred-meter mark, word was passed back to take a short break. Cartwright had come upon an abandoned bunker complex. The CO determined the bunkers had been abandoned for some time and ordered the patrol to continue.

As Mateo and I moved through the jungle at a steady pace, unexpectedly, a fawn darted out from under the foliage. Startled by the sudden movement, I practically unloaded my thirty-round clip of ammo. The fawn disappeared into the jungle.

"I wonder if anyone has ever died of fright?" asked Mateo.

"I don't know, but you better check your pants, because that scared the crap out of me," I replied.

Pace count indicated we were only a hundred meters from our objective. Knowing a company of NVA soldiers was in the area, everyone remained cautious.

The CO ordered a short break so he could meet with his platoon leaders. I leaned over, trying to relieve my back pain.

"Keep pushing; we're almost there, One Shot," said Mateo, giving me an encouraging word.

"I can't go any farther. My back is killing me," I replied.

"The LZ can't be very far away."

The CO grabbed the horn and called the battalion commander circling overhead. Lieutenant CJ popped a canister of yellow smoke, and the battalion commander gave us a direction to the LZ.

"Damn it, the LZ is a hundred meters to the south," cried Lieutenant CJ.

"I don't understand. I've never been this far off course," said Cartwright in disbelief.

"Yeah, but we never had to hump two thousand meters in one day," replied Lieutenant CJ.

Cartwright headed in the new direction and located the LZ. Exhausted, I took off my rucksack and slammed it on the ground. Lieutenant CJ met with the CO to decide where his platoon was going to set up for the night.

After a brief meeting, Lieutenant CJ returned with a discouraged look on his face. "Aztec and Cheyenne are setting up in the wood line. Blackfoot is moving across the LZ and setting up an ambush. Pick up your shit. Let's get going. I want to be set up before dark."

"With a company of NVA soldiers in the area, why aren't we setting up in company size?" I asked.

"The decision has been made, and there's nothing I can do about it," he replied. That was a saying I would hear a lot from him.

"It would have been logical to set up in a company size," I said to Mateo.

"Nothing is logical in this war. You'll be all right. See you in the morning."

"Yeah, wish us luck. We're going to need it," I said.

I slung my rucksack over my shoulder and followed Lieutenant CJ and Cartwright across the LZ. It started to rain when we entered the wood line.

Cartwright hesitated when he discovered a well-traveled trotter leading into the jungle. There was an aroma of cooked rice. The decision to set up on the other side of the LZ had "disaster" written all over it. Lieutenant CJ decided not to travel too far into wood line and ordered everyone to quickly put out their night work.

"I can't believe Lieutenant CJ didn't make the effort to convince the CO to set up in company size. It would have been a hell of a lot safer," I said to Sundance.

"Get your night work out, One Shot, and tell the others to keep the damn noise down," he replied.

I took a position between Brother Charles and Sundance. The rest of second squad filled in. Lieutenant CJ requested both machine guns be placed facing the jungle.

I shook my head in disbelief as I rolled out the claymore wire. Brother Al, the newly assigned platoon RTO, was calling in coordinates as I left the perimeter. With my M-16 and a bandolier of ammo wrapped around my chest, I ran the claymore wire from the guard station and headed for a nearby tree.

"I'll cover you while you put out your night work," said Sundance, scanning the jungle.

"This place scares the hell out of me," I said.

"I know. There are fucking hot trotters everywhere."

"No shit. I can even smell the dinks cooking rice. This is crazy. Why are we staying here tonight?"

"The CO specifically requested Blackfoot to set up on this side of the LZ. Hurry up and get back to the perimeter," said Sundance.

I dropped to one knee, leaning my weapon against the tree. Placing my claymore on top of the trip flare, I inserted the blasting cap into the detonator well.

Claymore in place, I slowly stepped back and started toward the perimeter. Within two steps, an enemy rocket whistled past my head and exploded nearby. It sent a shockwave through the jungle. I was thrown to the ground. Scrambling for cover, I was pinned down by enemy machine gun fire.

I managed to crawl to the base of a nearby tree, hidden from view. All I could do was pray I wouldn't be hit.

Sundance tried to return fire but was attacked with a barrage of AK-47 fire. Duggy also wanted to return fire, but he didn't know Sundance's position. His M-60 machine gun remained silent.

The blast from the B-40 rocket left me temporarily deaf. When the enemy's Chicom machine gun jammed, Sundance saw an opportunity to empty a thirty-round clip in the direction of the fire. The remainder of the platoon took the opportunity to move forward.

"One Shot, are you all right?" shouted Sundance. He emptied another thirty-round clip into the jungle. I could hear the enemy reloading their machine gun. This gave me the opportunity to return fire.

"Where's the dinks?" shouted JC.

Sundance gave JC a direction as the rifle team began firing a barrage of M-16 rounds over our heads. Joe Gun and his assistant machine gunner managed to position their gun near Sundance. Lieutenant CJ ordered Duggy and his assistant machine gunner to protect the right flank as he called in fire support.

"Get that gun smoking!" shouted Sundance. Joe Gun began laying down a suppressive volume of fire.

"Hold your fire! Hold your fire! They're friendly's," shouted Lieutenant CJ.

"What the hell are you talking about? Get down!" cried Sundance.

For a brief moment I thought the madness would end. But how could the platoon leader mistake the distinct sound of enemy machine gun fire for our own?

The nightmare started all over again with machine gun rounds ricocheting everywhere. When the enemy's machine gun jammed again, I took the opportunity to spray thirty more rounds of automatic fire in the direction of the contact. I reached for another clip. When I discovered an empty bandolier, I shouted for someone to throw another. Sang, the platoon's Kit Carson scout, located an M-72 LAW and tossed it over.

It landed a few feet away. I managed to pull it in. I extended the rocket launcher and rested it on my shoulder, I took aim. Peering through the crosshairs, I pressed the firing mechanism. There was a loud back blast, followed by an explosion.

"Someone, get me a bandolier!" I shouted.

Determined to keep us from gaining fire superiority, the enemy began attacking our right flank. They were met by a barrage of machine gun fire from Duggy and his assistant machine gunner. The enemy retaliated by launching a B-40 rocket. It exploded near Duggy's position. Shrapnel took out the assistant machine gunner. Duggy returned fire, turning back the enemy.

"Is anyone hit over there?" shouted Lieutenant CJ.

"The situation is under control, Lieutenant! I just lit up the bastards, but you better call for a medevac for Peter Gun. He's down!" shouted Duggy.

The assistant machine gunner had taken shrapnel in the arm and was lying on the ground, bleeding and in shock. JC began launching grenades. They made a *thump, thump* as they left the barrel of JC's over and under (combination M-16 and grenade launcher). The first grenade penetrated the enemy's position, but the second caromed off the trees, exploding near Sundance.

"Incoming!" shouted JC as shrapnel ricocheted over Sundance's head.

"What the hell are you doing, JC?" Sundance shouted.

"Sorry!"

JC fired two more grenades, penetrating the enemy's perimeter. Holt had taken cover in the middle of the perimeter and was severely shaken. Brother Charles tried to assure him that he was going to be all right and to move forward.

"Why are they shooting at us?" cried Holt, hugging his rucksack.

"Shut the fuck up and watch where you're pointing your weapon!" cried Brother Charles.

Wet from the day's monsoon rain, I was still huddled behind the tree.

"One Shot, here comes a bandolier!" shouted BJ. Unfortunately, it landed considerably short. BJ attempted to throw another, and it landed just short of my reach. I tried to retrieve it anyway, but a single shot from a sniper whistled over my head.

"Go for it, we'll cover you!" shouted Joe Gun.

"When we start firing, grab the bandolier!" shouted BJ.

Joe fired a burst of M-60 machine gun rounds. But when I reached for the bandolier, his machine gun jammed.

"Sorry, my fucking bolt broke!" cried Joe.

"Don't worry, boss, I have another," said BJ, pulling a spare out of his pocket.

I reloaded my M-16 and waited for an opportunity to fire. When Joe Gun got his M-60 machine gun back in action, the enemy started to flee the area. Just when I thought the firefight was over, I heard the sound of a striker pin being released from a grenade. I prayed it was one of our own. It turned out to be the enemy's.

The grenade landed in front of my position. I placed my body in a fetal position and braced for the blast. I knew I was about to die. I expected my life to flash in front of me, but honestly, my only thoughts were focused on my death breaking the hearts of loved ones. In anticipation of being mortally wounded, I cried out, "God, help me!"

It seemed like eternity as I waited for the blast, but in reality it was only a few seconds. I slowly opened my eyes, realizing my life had been spared once again.

"One Shot, are you all right?" shouted Sundance from across the way.

"I think so!" I replied.

Uncertain if it was safe to return to the perimeter, I remained on the jungle floor. Although Blackfoot regained fire superiority, the enemy escaped without casualty. Had the enemy stayed any longer, they couldn't have escaped the wrath of the gunship the enemy referred to as "Whispering Death."

"Excellent job. I'm proud of all of you. Get me a casualty report. Sundance, there's a medevac on the way," said Lieutenant CJ.

"We have two severely wounded soldiers," said Sundance.

"How about One Shot?" asked Lieutenant CJ.

"He's under that tree."

"Hey, One Shot, where you at?" called the lieutenant.

"Down here."

"Are you all right?"

"Wow! That was close. It's going to take a little time for me to get over this firefight," I replied.

Lieutenant CJ ordered everyone to empty ammo into the contact area for a minute. After the mad minute, everyone was ordered to cease firing. He threw a canister of yellow smoke on the ground as a low-observation Huey hovered over the jungle, searching for the fleeing enemy. Brother Al brought over two canisters of smoke to help guide the gunship.

Lieutenant CJ set his radio frequency to match the gunship pilot's push.

"7-6 Planters Family, 7-6 Planters Family, this is 7-7 Scorpion, do you read me? Over," said the gunship pilot.

"This is 7-6 Planters Family, go ahead 7-7 Scorpion," answered Lieutenant CJ.

"I identify First Cav yellow, over."

"That's a solid copy, go ahead, over."

"I'm going to let the low-observation Huey work out for a while, then I'll make my runs from east to west. Over," said the gunship pilot.

The Huey pilot identified two dead enemy soldiers. When the pilot drew fire, the Huey pulled back and let the gunship take over.

"7-6 Planters Family, pop a can of smoke and keep your head down, over," said the gunship pilot.

"7-7 Scorpion, you're clear to make your runs from east to west. Over," answered Lieutenant CJ.

The pilot identified the yellow smoke marking our position and came in for his first run. Everyone hugged the ground as he ejected rockets from the pods.

After the first run, Lieutenant CJ instructed the pilot to drop another fifty meters.

"Damn, that's close!" shouted Sundance, finding cover behind a nearby tree.

"Take cover, I know what I'm doing," replied Lieutenant CJ.

The pilot turned the gunship around and came in for a second run, releasing his rockets.

"Perfect," said Lieutenant CJ to the gunship pilot.

The pilot made two more runs, completing the fire mission. "7-6 Planters Family, come in. Over," he said.

"Go ahead, 7-7 Scorpion," replied Lieutenant CJ.

"7-6 Planters Family, I'm out of rockets so I'm heading back. Good luck. Over."

"That's a solid copy. Over." Lieutenant CJ handed the horn back to Brother Al. "All right, guys, let's get the hell out of this place."

The retreat to the LZ wasn't a sign of defeat, but a celebration of life. When I reached the LZ, I looked to the heavens, grateful to have survived the ordeal. The encounter ended as the sun was setting. Blackfoot was fortunate to escape with only two casualties. Peter Gun took shrapnel in the arm, and first squad's RTO caught an AK-47 round in the shoulder. Holt, taking refuge in the middle of the perimeter, had thought he was wounded, but he was only shaken.

"Pop smoke, birds inbound!" shouted Lieutenant CJ.

The medevac arrived as a heavy downpour dampened the LZ. Blackfoot loaded up the wounded and said farewell.

"You're going to be all right, shammer," I shouted as we lifted Peter Gun into the waiting medevac. I waved as the helicopter cleared the treetops and headed for the field hospital.

I envied the two wounded soldiers because they were out of the field, probably for good. For the remaining members of Blackfoot, it would be another wet, hungry, sleepless night.

"Get it on, guys," said Lieutenant CJ. "We're linking up with Cheyenne and Aztec for the night."

Spending the night in company formation was a relief, knowing the enemy remained in the jungle nearby. Aztec and the main CP were on their feet, awaiting our arrival. The CO shook everyone's hands as we entered the perimeter. Curious to know about the encounter, Aztec must have been frustrated at not being able to provide fire support.

With a hug, Mateo handed me a warm canteen cup of hot cocoa.

"I thought my luck had finally run out," I told him, taking a welcome sip.

"When I heard that B-40 rocket go off and then enemy machine-gun fire, I knew you guys were in trouble. I just prayed no one was killed," said Mateo.

I laid my rucksack next to Mateo's air mattress and settled in for the night. Wet and exhausted, I took off my rain-soaked fatigue shirt and slipped into a wool nightshirt.

"You're bleeding," Mateo said.

"Where?"

"Your back."

"I don't feel any pain," I replied.

"It looks like you were hit with a piece of shrapnel," said Mateo.

"It must have been from the B-40 rocket that exploded at the beginning of the ambush."

"I'll tell the CO to put you in for a Purple Heart," said Mateo proudly.

"The two guys who were severely wounded today deserve Purple Hearts, not me," I replied.

Mateo pulled out a bandage from his rucksack and placed it over the wound. I changed into my dry wool nightshirt and settled in. Not allowed to put up a hooch, I huddled under my poncho liner, trying to keep warm. It was going to be a long, damp night.

"Keep your head down. The CO is calling in artillery," whispered Mateo.

"Good. I hope they kill all the bastards."

The first marking round exploded above our heads, signaling the beginning of the fire mission. I pulled my poncho liner over my head as a barrage of 105 artillery rounds whistled over our heads. All I could think about was going back to the safety of my sanctuary—Vung Tau Village.

***

July 14. At dawn's first light, everyone was packed, waiting for orders from the CO. Soaked with the night's rain and smelling like wet dogs, we were grateful when the sun came out and dried us off. Knowing the low-observation helicopter had spotted two bodies, the battalion commander requested Blackfoot to return to the contact area for a body count.

"If the battalion commander wants a body count, he can get his ass down here and get it himself," I said angrily.

"You know that isn't going to happen. Just get it over with so we can go to Vung Tau," said Mateo.

"What if the enemy is waiting for us?"

"After the barrage of artillery shells last night, I don't think so," said Mateo with confidence.

"Yeah, that's what they said when Blackfoot Platoon was ambushed on February 7."

Uncertain of what the point team would encounter, Cartwright headed for the wood line. He took a different path from the day before. I could see the palm tree that had shielded me from the enemy. It was riddled with holes. I wondered how I survived.

Cartwright made his way toward the enemy's position and came to a halt.

"What's the matter?" asked Sundance.

"Bunkers, lots of bunkers," replied Cartwright.

We had walked into a U-shaped bunker complex. The enemy machine gunner had been set up on top of a bunker with a perfect line of sight. Lieutenant CJ realized his platoon would have been wiped out if the enemy had allowed his point team to walk any farther into the jungle.

Cartwright noticed something lying on the trotter. When he reached what appeared to be a body, he discovered it was only a black canvas rucksack. The enemy must have dropped it as they fled the area.

A thorough search of the bunker complex didn't reveal any bodies, but blood on the jungle floor indicated the enemy had been seriously wounded. The two bodies identified by the low-observation helicopter pilots were nowhere to be found. Lieutenant CJ suspected a body count, but believed the bodies had been carried off. Discouraged that no bodies were accounted for, the battalion commander ordered Blackfoot to return to the LZ for extraction.

Episode Twenty

Birthday Celebration in the Village

July 14. Another life-threatening mission came to an end. Bravo Company was extracted and dropped off near Highway 1. Everyone was looking forward to China Beach, especially after the way the mission had ended for Blackfoot.

Now that we were on our way for a little fun and relaxation, I was going to celebrate my twenty-first birthday. I accepted the fact that I was going to remain in the field, and dealt with it the best I could, but for the moment my thoughts were focused on the village.

It was turning out to be another hot and humid day. Everyone gathered under the shade of a nearby tree. Growing impatient for transportation to arrive, Holt wanted to be part of the excitement. Like everyone else, he looked forward to three days of rest.

Holt decided to join some of the guys having a conversation. He became agitated when Clint ignored him. He tried to get Clint's attention but was pushed aside. Holt wasn't going to stand for Clint's actions and punched him in the arm.

"Now you'll listen to me," said Holt with a look of vengeance.

"Why did you hit me, you big dumb bastard?" shouted Clint.

"Because you didn't talk to me!"

"Why should I? You're stupid."

"Knock it off, Clint!" I shouted.

"Leave it alone. It's not your business," Brother Al warned me.

Clint wasn't going to stand for Holt punching him in the arm. He took a step back and punched Holt on the side of the head. Holt was knocked to the ground. Clint stood over his body

243

shaking his hand in pain. Tucker tried to revive Holt as he lay unconscious.

Outraged, I felt an obligation to defend Holt. I was no match for the well-built soldier, so I picked up my weapon and started after Clint.

Brother Al positioned his body in front of mine. "What the hell are you doing? It's not your fight. It's theirs. Besides, it's not worth going to Long Bien Jail over."

"I wasn't going to shoot Clint. I just wanted to scare him," I said.

"Let it go. It's not your problem."

Realizing Brother Al was right, I placed my weapon down. Concerned about Holt, I walked over to see if he was all right.

"What the hell happened?" muttered Holt, slowly regaining consciousness.

"Clint punched you on the side of your head," I replied.

"Why?"

I helped Holt to his feet and dusted off his boonie hat. He remained dazed but would survive the blow to his head. I turned and looked at Clint with disgust.

"What you looking at, Garcia?" asked Clint angrily.

"Say you're sorry, you big dumb bastard!" I said.

"Why? He started it."

"You didn't have to hit him. Apologize."

Clint started toward me with his fist clenched. I stepped back, ready to defend myself, but Clint reached for Holt's hand and apologized.

"What's going on?" asked Lieutenant CJ.

"Ask Clint," I said.

"Nothing, Lieutenant," said Clint.

"What's wrong with Holt?" asked Lieutenant CJ.

"Tell him what happened," I said to Holt.

"I passed out from the heat," said Holt.

Desperate to be accepted by the members of his platoon, Holt refused to tell Lieutenant CJ the truth. Brother Al shook his head and walked away.

"I told you not to get involved," said Brother Al.

"Someone had to say something to the big ox," I said.

"I thought Clint was going to kill you," said Brother Al, pulling a cigarette out of a newly opened pack.

"Pop smoke, birds inbound!" shouted Lieutenant CJ.

A Chinook transport landed on Highway 1, lowering the ramp for Blackfoot to board. Arriving at Vung Tau Airport, everyone promptly boarded the bus to take the familiar road to the R & R compound. Everyone was eager to enjoy three days of rest.

The entire company assembled at the R & R center for another orientation. This would be the final trip to China Beach for Brother Theo and Brother Kelly, so I agreed to join them at their favorite hangout, the Soul Bar. Located on the outskirts of the entertainment area, the nightclub was a popular hangout for the blacks in the battalion.

Brother Theo wanted to visit a friend before returning to the States. All of us agreed to accompany him for a brief visit. Brother Theo flagged down a Lambretta, and the five of us squeezed in. He gave the driver directions, and we drove off in search of his friend's apartment.

Main street traffic made for an interesting ride through the village. Locating the two-story apartment building, the five of us exited the Lambretta and made our way upstairs. Brother

Theo's friend answered the door and embraced him. He was introduced to us as Brother Murphy.

Pleased to see a familiar face, Brother Murphy offered everyone a decanter of his fine Hennessy brandy and a carton of cigarettes.

"Why would anyone stationed in China Beach want to live in the village?" asked Brother Theo.

"Let me show you why. Honey, come here!" shouted Brother Murphy.

An attractive Vietnamese girl walked into the room and was introduced as Ginger. "This is why I live in the village. I can't live on the base with Ginger, so I decided to rent an apartment," said Brother Murphy.

"What kind of Vietnamese name is Ginger?" I asked jokingly.

"I named her Ginger because she's tall and thin, like Ginger on *Gilligan's Island*," said Brother Murphy.

After a brief visit, Brother Theo invited his friend to join us at the Soul Bar, but Brother Murphy declined. Brother Theo flagged down another Lambretta, and we headed for the Soul Bar for his farewell celebration.

The four brothers entered the Soul Bar and were greeted by Mama-san.

"He no soul brother," said Mama-san, looking at me as I entered behind them.

"This is my brother from another mother. He's number one soul brother," said Brother Al, placing his arm around my shoulder.

"He no number one soul brother, he number ten," said Mama-san.

The girls were excited to see the brothers return for another visit. It was obvious why the brothers enjoyed coming to the cheerful bar. They were appreciated by Mama-san and her girls.

I followed Brother Al to the bar and took a seat.

"How about a drink for my brother?" asked Brother Al.

"Why you call him brother? He no soul brother," said Mama-san.

"Show Mama-san the dap," said Brother Al.

After seeing us perform the soul brother handshake, Mama-san shook her head and served us. "Okay, you can stay, but if you no dance like soul brother, you have to go," she said, laughing.

Mama-san pressed the play button on the cassette player and the celebration began. The sound of sweet soul music filled the bar as everyone enjoyed Motown and many more.

When the popular 1960s hit, *"Ain't Too Proud to Beg"* by the Temptations, played, I started singing to Mama-san. *"If I have to beg, plead, for your sympathy ..."* The brothers sang along.

"Okay, you no more number ten, you number one," said Mama-san with a smile.

Knowing they were leaving soon, I watched as Brother Theo and Brother Kelly enjoyed for the last time the friends they had lived and fought alongside.

Then I fixed my eyes on an attractive Vietnamese girl entering the bar. She was wearing a nicely fitting silk dress and had glistening hair and big, beautiful green eyes. She took a seat at the end of the bar. Infatuated with her beauty, I had to meet her.

"You no soul brother, why you sing?" said the hooker in a sensual voice.

"What's your name?" I asked.

"Manoi. What your name?"

"They call me One Shot."

"You want to talk to Manoi, you buy tea," said Mama-san, placing a small glass of mint-flavored tea on the bar.

"Why you come to Soul Bar?" Manoi asked.

"These are my friends," I said.

"Look around, you see brother rab?"

"I'm not a brother rab."

"Then why you come to Soul Bar?"

Trying to convince Manoi I was loyal to the brothers, I continued to buy tea. I enjoyed her company until it was near curfew. I wanted more, but I felt she would turn me down because I wasn't black.

"Where are you staying tonight?" Brother Al asked.

"I'm going back to the Mi Lien," I replied.

"Come with us. We're catching a Lambretta," he offered.

Manoi walked up from behind me, placing her arms around my waist. "You come home with me tonight."

"Did you just get lucky?" asked Brother Charles.

"Hurry, we go now," said Manoi, rushing me out the door.

"I think your friend be sorry," I heard Mama-san say as the brothers left the bar.

I followed Manoi to her scooter. "Get on," she said, jump starting the motor.

I climbed on wrapping my arms around her tiny waist. As she maneuvered in and out of traffic, I hung on tight.

Manoi sped through the village ending up at the front door of a small apartment. Placing her bike on the kickstand, she opened the door. Entering her living room I was surprised to see a red velvet sofa and red shag carpet.

"You like?" asked Manoi.

Manoi's apartment was nicely furnished, but it was the framed photographs of seven soldiers from different military branches that caught my attention.

"Yeah, but who are the guys in the photographs?" I asked.

"Boyfriends, and now you boyfriend too," replied Manoi, heading for the bedroom.

Manoi talked with someone as I waited in the living room. Curious, I decided to take a look. When I entered the bedroom, Manoi was cradling a baby and having a conversation with a young Vietnamese girl.

"This is my sister and my son. They live with me," said Manoi.

"What's his name?" I asked.

"Todd," she answered proudly.

Manoi kissed the baby on the cheek and handed him back to her sister. Speaking Vietnamese they headed for the front door. Her sister waved and started laughing.

"What was that about?" I asked.

"I tell you tomorrow," said Manoi, escorting me back to her bedroom.

The following morning, I was awakened by the aroma of sizzling bacon and the sound of a crying baby. I jumped into the shower, preparing for another day in the village. I joined Manoi in the kitchen as she cooked breakfast. Her sister was breast-feeding the baby.

"Why is your sister breast-feeding your baby?" I asked.

"You ask too many questions," said Manoi in an angry tone.

"But shouldn't you be breast-feeding your baby?"

"I'm not baby's mother."

"Why did you claim to be the baby's mother?"

"Sister only sixteen, too young to be mother, so I say I'm baby's mother," said Manoi.

"Then who is the baby's father?"

"Baby's father already gone home. He promise to come back and take sister and baby to America. Never happen, GI," cried Manoi.

Because the father had abandoned her sister and child, she didn't want the child to be considered a leftover of the war. She knew the child would never know his father and didn't want him to be abandoned at the gates of an orphanage. Unfortunately, the infant was just another illegitimate child fathered by an American soldier, discarded like a speck of dust.

Manoi served eggs and bacon, along with a cup of Vietnamese coffee.

The plan was to spend the day celebrating my birthday with Brother Al and Brother Charles and join Manoi at the Soul Bar later.

"You stay with me tonight?" asked Manoi.

"Sure I'll stay with you tonight," I answered.

"You promise," said Manoi, putting her arms around my waist.

"Yes, I promise. I'll see you later at the Soul Bar."

Together we walked to the street and flagged down a passing Lambretta.

"I enjoyed being with you last night," I said, holding her.

"Stay with me today and we see Buddha in the morning," said Manoi.

"Why Buddha?"

"We get married!"

"Why would I want to get married?"

"Because you love me," said Manoi.

"I like you, but I don't love you. Sorry, Manoi, but I think I better go."

In a desperate attempt to keep me from climbing into the Lambretta, Manoi grabbed my fatigue shirt and pulled me back. "If you marry me, you can stay when you come back to village," she pleaded.

"I have to be married to spend the night with you?"

"All boyfriends pay to stay with me," said Manoi.

"Is it money?" I asked, reaching into my fatigue pocket for a handful of piastres. Counting out five thousand, I placed the money in Manoi's hand.

"Is this all you pay?" she replied, throwing the piastres on the ground.

"What did you expect?" I asked.

"Two hundred MPC, like all husbands pay," cried Manoi.

"Husbands? You said they were your boyfriends," I said, climbing into the Lambretta.

"Yes, all husbands pay two hundred when they come to see me, and now you pay two hundred too," she said, extending her hand.

Now I understood how Manoi could afford to furnish her apartment and drive a scooter. Needless to say, I wasn't going to be added to her list of husbands. I ordered the driver to leave.

Manoi pleaded with me as the driver sped away. She picked up a rock and hurled it at the Lambretta.

"She crazy," said the driver.

"You're telling me, brother," I replied.

The Lambretta driver shook his head and headed for the Mi Lien Hotel.

Once again I had fallen for a hooker. I was definitely going to see her again. For now, it was in my best interest to let her cool down. I wondered if one of her husbands fathered her sister's baby.

Brother Al and Brother Charles were waiting in the lobby of the hotel when I arrived.

"How was your date, Jarcia?" asked Brother Charles with a big grin.

"Great, until she wanted to get married," I said.

Brother Al placed his arm around my shoulder, taking a drag off his cigarette.

"After you left the bar last night, Mama-san said Manoi was looking for a husband to take her back to the States. I tried to warn you, but you were already on the back of her scooter."

Episode Twenty-One

Back to the World

July 19. Bravo Company returned to Fire Base Mace and then boarded a convoy to the newly constructed Fire Base Jefferies. It appeared the same two soldiers were back for another shot of penicillin.

The company clerk confirmed my request for a two-week leave. I was scheduled to leave Tan Son Nhut Air Force Base on August 19. I was excited, but at the same time concerned about returning to civilian life. I had endured a number of life-threatening experiences and didn't know if I was ready to return.

Lieutenant CJ authorized a pass to Bien Hoa Airport so I could purchase an airline ticket for my return to the States. Company headquarters had recently moved from Fire Base Mace to Bien Hoa Air Force Base. I hoped this meant the transition of responsibility to South Vietnam had begun.

The price of a round-trip airline ticket was three hundred and fifty dollars. It was a large amount of money, but well worth the expense for two weeks of peace of mind. When I arrived at Bien Hoa, I stopped in at finance to withdraw that amount of combat pay and a little extra to spend.

I located the nearest EM club for a well-deserved drink. After a few cocktails, I was ready for the airport. The terminal hadn't changed since the beginning of my tour. I located the Pan American ticket agent and made my purchase. I had no problem handing over that amount of money for a trip back to the world.

New arrivals were waiting for transportation to Tan Son Nhut Processing Center, just as I had done six months ago.

Although my battalion hadn't received any replacements since February, new troops were still arriving daily.

I knew how it felt to be a new arrival. The only friends you had were the friends you arrived with, and you wouldn't be accepted until you proved yourself.

I returned to the EM club and enjoyed a few more cocktails before returning to the company rear. I held my airline ticket in my hand tightly as I sipped my drinks. It was comforting knowing I would be home soon. It would be good for my parents to have me home safe, even if it was just for a short time.

***

August 16. Back on the fire base on the eve of my departure, I stopped for a visit with Mateo. Mateo congratulated me on my Silver Star recommendation, and we celebrated with a beer.

"I can't believe the CO put me in for another Silver Star. The June 8 ambush was my most frightening experience so far."

Romeo heard the laughter and joined in the conversation. Mateo passed out more ice-cold beers as I discussed my trip home.

"Why would you want to go home?" asked Mateo.

"I need to get the hell out of this place."

"I wouldn't come back," said Romeo.

"That's for sure," said Mateo, taking a drink of beer.

"I'm not coming back," I said casually.

Mateo and Romeo laughed, not taking me seriously.

"Not you, One Shot. You love Vietnam, especially Vung Tau Village," said Mateo.

"You're right about that," I replied.

"Hey, I heard a cargo plane carrying US mail crashed on the way to Bien Hoa," said Mateo in an excited voice.

"Maybe that's why I haven't received any mail lately," I replied jokingly.

The evening movie featured the popular documentary *Woodstock*. We grabbed a couple beers and took a seat on a row of sandbags.

Woodstock is considered one of the most pivotal moments in popular music history. The three-day festival featured thirty-two acts, performing for over half a million concertgoers. Watching the documentary brought back memories of time spent with my favorite cousin in North Hollywood. Her irresistible smile and big brown eyes could light up any room.

***

August 17. After a night of celebration, I opened my eyes to a painful hangover. Managing to keep breakfast down, I packed my things. I said good-bye to the guys in Mateo's hooch.

"It's been nice knowing you, Mateo," I said jokingly.

"Why, you're not coming back?"

"Why would I want to come back?"

"You have to come back. What's Blackfoot Platoon going to do without you?" said Mateo in an encouraging way.

"Just kidding. I'm too scared not to come back," I replied, laughing.

I gave Mateo a hug and headed for the LZ. The supply bird would be my transportation to Bien Hoa Air Force Base. Brother Al and Brother Charles walked down to the LZ to keep me company. I could only hope they would stay out of harm's way while I was gone.

The bird touched down, and the door gunner unloaded his supplies. I gave the brothers the familiar handshake before climbing aboard.

"Have a good time in Canada!" shouted Brother Al.

"What do mean, Canada?"

"Because that's where you're going to live if you don't come back."

I waved to my friends as the bird lifted off the LZ. I would miss the guys in Blackfoot, but I wouldn't miss the war at all. Now that I was officially on my way home, I was going to forget about the war and enjoy my time at home. I didn't know if I'd made the right decision to return to the States, but at least I would be safe for two weeks.

Arriving at battalion headquarters, I stored my rucksack and weapon. Pate issued my orders and instructed me to report to the First Cav R & R center promptly at 10:00 a.m. I persuaded Pate to join me for a drink at the EM club. Pate didn't spend much time with Blackfoot, but remained respected as a grunt.

A five-member Vietnamese band was playing a popular Creedence Clearwater song as we entered the club. Pate and I joined a couple members of Aztec Platoon, who were enjoying a drink before leaving for Thailand in the morning.

Pate stayed for a couple drinks and called it a night. I enjoyed the band as they played the popular songs of the day.

At closing I returned to the company barracks for a needed rest. Knowing I was on my way home in the morning, I slept through the entire night.

***

August 18. I was up early and showered. I put on a pair of tailored jungle fatigues and enjoyed a mess hall breakfast. I had a quick visit with Pate and then headed over to the First Cav R & R Center. Promptly at 9:45 a.m., I arrived and checked in. Transportation to Tan Son Nhut arrived at ten, and I was on my way to Camp Alpha.

The driver took the route through the First Team Academy Training Center, bringing back memories of when Jet and I had gone through seven days of jungle warfare training, only to be separated at the end.

The route to Tan Son Nhut was the usual drive down Highway 1. The drive through the compound reminded me of the time I spent with Little Joey—the last time I saw him alive.

The driver arrived at Camp Alpha, rolling up to the special services office. Everyone was eager to enter the building and sign in. After my orders were processed, I was given a barracks assignment and instructions to attend a mandatory 7:00 p.m. orientation.

Since there were no restrictions on clothing, I decided to shop for civilian clothes for the trip home. Located on the other side of the compound was the base PX, the largest in Vietnam. I had to ask directions just to locate the clothing department.

There wasn't much of a selection, but I did manage to find a pair of bright yellow bell-bottoms with green pinstripes, along with a lime-green collared shirt. I made the purchase and returned to the compound.

After dinner, I attended the orientation for soldiers returning to the United States. The officer presented the group with information about military courtesy, troop appearance, and conduct while out of the country. He also discussed the consequences of AWOL. Absence without leave was considered a major offense in the military and was dealt with severely during the war.

The orientation officer brought the meeting to an end by informing us we would board the bus at 7:00 a.m. the next day to be transported to the Tan Son Nhut Air Base. I returned to the barracks, avoiding the EM club, for a decent night's rest.

***

August 19. Awakened by everyone preparing for departure, I climbed out of bed and headed for the shower. I was dressed by six thirty. I took my time and enjoyed a hearty breakfast. From the mess hall, I walked over to the bus terminal and waited with the other soldiers for the transportation to arrive.

Driving through the streets of Tan Son Nhut, I wondered if I was doing the right thing. One thing was for sure: I wasn't going to miss the filth and undesirable odors. Now that I was on my way home, I should have been thrilled, but knowing I would eventually have to return was a little depressing.

The Pan American jetliner was waiting on the tarmac as we drove through the security gates. Customs agents thoroughly inspected my luggage, searching for drugs, weapons, or any other illegal items. When everyone cleared customs, the group was cleared to board the plane.

At the top of the stairs, I was greeted by an attractive blonde stewardess wearing a tight-fitting Pam Am uniform and cute hat. "Welcome aboard, soldier," she said with a kind smile.

Infatuated by her beauty and the scent of her perfume, I realized the stewardess was the first round-eyed woman I'd seen in six months. She escorted me to my seat, only to find a sailor sitting in it.

"Excuse me, you're in this gentleman's seat," said the stewardess.

The sailor looked up at the number posted above his seat and replied, "I'm sorry," realizing he had taken the wrong seat. The sailor introduced himself as I sat down and buckled my seat belt.

"Where are you stationed?" asked the sailor.

"In the bush," I replied.

"No, seriously."

"I'm a grunt."

"How is it out there?"

"It's not as bad as Tet, but there's still killing going on. What's your job?"

"I don't do anything like you. I'm stationed in Saigon. If you don't mind, I'd like to know more about life out there."

The tower cleared the pilot for takeoff, and the plane began to taxi down the runway. When the plane lifted off, I was relieved to be on my way home, but concerned about returning to civilian life in the middle of a war. I was able to talk about the war, so I didn't mind telling the sailor my story.

He listened enthusiastically as I related my bloody Vietnam experience in detail. I continued to describe it until we reached Yokota Air Force Base. The sailor shook my hand and thanked me for sharing my story.

It had been six months since my previous visit to Yokota Air Force Base. Nothing had changed, not even the weather. The jetliner remained in Yokota long enough to refuel and replenish the meals and supplies.

The plane was cleared for takeoff and the jetliner taxied down the runway. The pilot turned on the "Fasten seat belts and extinguish all cigarettes" sign as the stewardesses prepared for takeoff. Our next destination was the Philippine Islands.

I slept most of the flight, getting up once to use the bathroom. On the descent into Manila International Airport, the captain announced we would be delayed due to an engine malfunction. Turbulent air currents midway through the flight must have rattled the jet engine. The pilot encouraged us not to worry about connecting flights, because we shouldn't be delayed very long.

The jetliner touched down on the runway and taxied over to the Pan American aircraft hangar. The airline mechanics lined up the hydraulic platform and started checking the jet engine. Everyone was invited to depart the plane and wait in the terminal. The sailor, Randy, and I found the nearest bar and enjoyed a drink.

Randy bought all the drinks as we waited for the mechanics to complete their inspection. Concerned about the delay, I located a Pan Am ticket agent. "How much longer before we can board the plane?" I asked.

"Don't worry. I'll call you when it's time. It shouldn't be too much longer," said the agent.

Finally, after an hour and thirty minute delay, the Pan American ticket agent announced we could board the jetliner. Our next destination was Honolulu International Airport, on the island of Oahu.

Ahead of us was a two-hour flight. The pilot lifted off and headed for Honolulu. When we arrived, we were informed that we needed to depart the plane to clear customs.

Clearing customs meant another delay. Showing identification took time for an entire plane of travelers. After clearing customs, I stepped outside the terminal to enjoy a view of the bay.

Having a little time before boarding the next plane, I took a seat on a bench. I lay back to enjoy the warmth of the Hawaiian sun and accidentally dozed off. When I opened my eyes, I panicked. Forty-five minutes had gone by. Fearing I had missed the flight, I ran through the terminal until I reached the Pan American counter.

"Are they still boarding the flight to Los Angeles?" I said, out of breath.

"They're closing the door. You better hurry," said the counter agent.

I waved my arms in desperation at the gate, trying to get the ticket agent's attention.

"We just about left you, young man," she said, opening the door.

"That was close," I replied as the door closed behind me. My carelessness could have cost me a night in Honolulu, delaying my arrival in Bakersfield one day. I quickly took my seat and buckled my seatbelt.

"Where have you been?" asked Randy.

"You won't believe this, but I fell asleep," I said, chuckling.

Once we were back in the air, the pilot apologized for the delay but remained confident everyone would make their connecting flights.

"Where you headed?" Randy asked.

"Bakersfield, about two hours from Los Angeles," I replied.

"You're lucky. I have to catch a connecting flight to Boston. I won't be home until tomorrow."

"I'll be lucky if I make it home by tomorrow," I said jokingly.

The plane taxied to the runway and prepared for takeoff. The pilot was cleared and went full throttle. Everyone remained awake for the flight across the Pacific Ocean to Los Angeles International Airport.

With no further delays, the jetliner arrived in Los Angeles and circled the airport, waiting for authorization to land. A thin layer of fog made it difficult to see the streetlights clearly. With landing gear fully extended, the pilot approached the runway. When the plane touched down, everyone cheered with excitement.

The flight arrived an hour and a half later than scheduled. Soldiers living in the Los Angeles area were fortunate to be home. Soldiers with connecting flights didn't know when they would be home.

The plane taxied over to the Pan American terminal and powered down the engines. I made my way to the exit, but the stewardess was having trouble opening the door. She encouraged me by saying there wouldn't be a problem making my connecting flight.

After a few agonizing minutes, she got the door open, and we were allowed to depart the plane. I rushed down the ramp and looked at the flight monitor, searching for my United Airlines flight to Bakersfield. The monitor indicated the commuter plane had already taken off from gate A, located on the other side of the terminal. I ran the entire way.

The agent at the counter was preparing to leave for the evening when I arrived. "Excuse me, sir. Will there be another flight to Bakersfield tonight?" I asked the ticket agent.

"I'm sorry, you just missed the last flight of the evening," he said, pointing to the plane taxiing down the runway.

"Can you please stop the plane?" I pleaded.

"Sorry. I can put you on the first flight in the morning," said the agent.

"I just arrived from Vietnam on a flight that was delayed an hour and a half. I was told everyone would make their connecting fights," I explained.

"Sorry, young man, there's nothing I can do for you tonight. I can put you up in a hotel and have you on the seven o'clock flight in the morning. Or you might consider the Greyhound bus. Let me check if there's a bus scheduled for Bakersfield tonight."

The agent looked over the bus schedule as I hopefully waited. Then, "Sorry, the last bus was scheduled to leave at eight."

"My parents are expecting me. I don't know what I'm going to do now," I said, shaking my head.

It appeared I was stranded in Los Angeles for the night, and there was nothing I could do about it. In desperation I pleaded with the agent one more time. "Are you absolutely positive there isn't another flight leaving for Bakersfield tonight?"

"I'm sorry, young man, there's nothing I can do. Can I get you a room for the night?"

"No, thank you," I said, turning away disappointed.

I was grateful the agent had tried to find a solution to my dilemma, but none of the solutions put me on a flight to Bakersfield. I was desperate and needed to get home at any cost, I even considered hitchhiking.

My duffel bag was checked through to Bakersfield. There was no need for me to go to baggage claim. I tried to contact relatives with no luck. I would have to call my parents and give them the discouraging news.

With no solution to my problem, I headed down the corridor leading to the exit. Unexpectedly, I heard a voice calling out for someone. "Excuse me, you in the yellow bell-bottom pants!"

I was wearing a pair of yellow bell-bottom pants, so I quickly turned around. To my surprise, an unfamiliar face headed in my direction. I was the only person in the entire terminal wearing a pair of bright yellow pants; he had to be addressing me.

"Who, me?" I asked.

"Did you say you needed a ride to Bakersfield?" asked the stranger.

"Yes!" I replied enthusiastically.

"I just got off work and I'm driving home. I live in Bakersfield. You're more than welcome to ride with me."

"Oh, my God, this is a miracle! Of course I would," I replied in disbelief. I couldn't believe someone was still looking out for me.

"What's your name, young man?"

"Ricky Garcia, what's yours?"

"My name is John, John Lackey," said the stranger.

"I'm so grateful to meet you, John."

"I heard you say you just arrived from Vietnam. Are you home for good?"

"No, I have to return in two weeks," I replied.

"Ouch! That's too bad. But I would like to thank you anyway for your service. It will be a pleasure to give you a ride home."

John located his 1968 Volkswagen in the employee parking lot. I climbed into the passenger seat and John started the engine. "I have to make a quick stop at my girl's house. I hope you don't mind," he said.

"Don't worry about me. I'm just grateful have a ride home."

On the drive to the girlfriend's house, John pulled into a liquor store parking lot. "I bet you could use a cold beer," said John.

"After what I've been through today, I would die for one," I replied.

John returned with a six-pack of Budweiser in bottles. "This is on me. Enjoy," he said.

He drove down the street and parked in front of his girlfriend's house. "I won't be long. I'll leave the radio on," he said as he jumped out of the car.

"Take your time. I'll enjoy a beer or two and listen to the radio. It's been a long time since I've had a cold bottle in my hand," I said.

John didn't stay very long—just long enough for me to listen to my favorite disc jockey, Wolfman Jack, on XERF Radio and enjoy a couple beers.

"I hope I wasn't too long. You know how girls are when you're saying good-bye. Are you ready to go home?" John asked.

"You don't know how ready I am," I said.

John started up his Volkswagen and headed for the freeway on-ramp.

"How did you know I needed a ride to Bakersfield?" I asked.

"I overheard your conversation with the ticket agent."

"Yeah, I was desperate."

"I work for United Airlines, and I had just finished my shift. I was passing by the desk and heard what you said. I knew there weren't any more flights scheduled for Bakersfield tonight, so I decided to offer you a ride."

"Boy! I was lucky," I said.

"Not luck, fate," he said.

"Fate or luck, it brought us together tonight."

John asked if I would mind talking about my experience in Vietnam. I didn't mind, so I gave him a timeline of the events during my tour. Like others, John was amazed at the number of times I had defied death. He said I was as lucky as a cat with nine lives.

Like many American civilians, he was angry about the way the government was handling the war, and believed the troops should be pulled out before any more lives were lost. He also believed the antiwar movement was just an excuse for the protestors to avoid the draft.

"Will you be able to forget about the war while you're home?" asked John.

"I'll just have to take it one day at a time," I said as we headed down the grapevine into the valley.

In the distance, I could see my hometown lights shining brightly. What a wonderful sight for a homesick kid. As we entered the city limits, I wondered how civilians could lead a normal lifestyle while the nation was in turmoil over the war. When the Vietnam War was over, our government would continue to protect our interests in other countries.

John pulled up in front of my home shortly after midnight. I reached into my pocket and pulled out a hundred-dollar bill. I placed it in John's hand. "You don't know how grateful I am for the ride. I will never forget your generosity," I told him.

"No, the pleasure is mine. It was an honor bringing you home tonight. I'm grateful for you risking your life for a nation that doesn't appreciate you. Good luck, my friend, and return home safe," said John.

I offered him the money again, but he refused it. He said good-bye and drove off into the night.

Standing in front of the home where I once lived, I wondered if Mom and Dad were still awake. The porch light was on, but the house was dark. Dad knew my flight was scheduled to arrive in Bakersfield at 8:30 p.m. When they didn't see me step off the commuter plane, they must have been worried sick.

Dad peered through the curtains and saw me standing on the porch. Recognizing me, he quickly opened the door.

Eager to see my dog, DI, I listened for his bark. DI was a loving Lakeland terrier I had rescued on a cold winter night during my thirty-day leave.

"Honey, Ricky's home!" Dad shouted with joy.

Mom ran into the living room and gave me a loving embrace. She didn't say a word. She just held me tightly.

"Where's DI?" I asked.

Mom placed her hand over her mouth and began to sob.

"We didn't want to tell you, son, because it was too close to Little Joey's death," said Dad.

"Where's my dog?" I asked in a firm voice.

Dad glared at Mom.

Grabbing Mom by her shoulders, I asked, "What happened, Mom?"

"DI was killed by a car," said Mom, weeping.

"It was an accident, son," said Dad.

"Who killed my dog?" I said.

"Your sister's boyfriend," said Dad in a guilty voice.

"How could you let this happen?"

"We'll get you another dog," said Mom.

"I don't want another dog. I loved the little guy and he loved me," I said, tears running down my cheeks.

I sat down, my hands pressed to my forehead. With the recent loss of Little Joey and now learning of my dog's untimely death, I was overwhelmed with grief.

I explained why I had arrived late and how I was fortunate to have been given a ride. Although I was exhausted, I had to know one thing. "Tell me about Joey's funeral."

"It's late, son. We'll talk tomorrow," said Dad.

"No, I want to talk now."

"It was a sad day when we were informed of Little Joey's death," said Dad with tears in his eyes.

"I know the feeling. Little Joey wrote me a letter on the day he was killed."

"We were hoping you could escort the body home," said Dad.

"It would have been an honor, but the military wouldn't allow me to—I'm not a family member. Besides, by the time I received the news, Little Joey had already been laid to rest," I said, every word full of the remorse I felt.

"You better get some rest, son," my mom said, concerned about me.

"How was his family notified?" I asked.

"The army dealt with the situation in the usual way. Army personnel were sent to the home to deliver the news. When the military vehicle pulled up in front of their house, Joey's parents knew exactly why they were there," said Dad, wiping the tears from his eyes.

"Did Little Joey receive the military funeral he deserved?"

"Yes. It was a dignified funeral. Joey was laid to rest in the veteran's section of Union Cemetery. His coffin was draped in an American flag. The color guard played 'Taps' and gave him a three-gun salute. At the grave site, the priest spoke proudly of him."

"The priest didn't know Joey. How did he know what kind of person Joey was?"

"After the funeral, the family invited us to attend a modest reception," said Dad, ignoring my question.

"How are Little Joey's parents dealing with his death?" I asked.

"Little Joey's father took me aside and said in Spanish, 'I'm saddened by the loss of my son, but for you to lose your only son would be more tragic.' I respected Little Joey's father for being concerned about you," said Dad.

My parents grieved for Little Joey's family, knowing it could have been their only son who was laid to rest that day.

My head hit the pillow and I fell into a deep sleep. I dreamed of Little Joey jumping on my bed, trying to wake me as DI barked with excitement. I opened my eyes, only to realize it was a dream. For a brief moment, I had thought my entire Vietnam experience was just a bad nightmare. The dream was a reminder of the war I had to return to.

The following morning, I had a cup of coffee as I waited for Mom to serve breakfast. It felt great having Mom prepare breakfast, as she had many times before. Mom joined me at the table with a cup of coffee and a look of despair.

"Your grandfather suffered a massive heart attack a few days ago, and it doesn't look good," she said.

"Why didn't you tell me?"

"I couldn't write, because you were already on your way home," said Mom. "It would make him happy if you saw you."

I had spent a considerable amount of time with Grandpa when I was a child. One of my favorite childhood memories was chasing chickens around his backyard. When it was time to prepare his favorite meal, Grandma's delicious chicken mole, Grandpa would jerk a chicken's neck until the head was severed from its body. The headless chicken ran around the yard until it collapsed. I would help Grandpa pluck the feathers and then watch in amazement as he sliced through the chicken's belly, pulling out its internal organs.

I loved Grandpa dearly and wanted to be by his side when he needed me most. I agreed to visit and drove Mom to the hospital. On the way, Mom gave me the details of her father's condition. "Your grandpa is very sick, so don't be alarmed when you see him."

"Believe me, Mom, I've seen a lot worse. I'm in the middle of a war, remember?"

We took the elevator to the third floor. An elderly nurse, wearing a name tag that read *Beulah*, stood at the entrance to the intensive care unit.

"This is my son. He's here to see his grandfather," said Mom.

"I'm sorry, but we are only allowing one person at a time to see your father. He is not doing very well."

"Is my grandfather going to die?" I asked.

"At this moment, it's up to your grandfather if he wants to live or die. Maybe seeing you will help," replied the nurse.

I encouraged Mom to visit Grandpa first. Knowing he was in intensive care made me think we could lose him. Mom whispered in her father's ear that I had returned from Vietnam just to be with him. A few minutes later, she returned with a smile on her face.

"He smiled when I told him you were here to see him," she said with a glimmer of hope.

I entered the intensive care unit and stood at Grandpa's bedside. He had once been a strong, hardworking man, but now he appeared thin and frail, fighting for his life.

I wasn't prepared to see him this way. I had been a witness to death, but Grandpa's appearance affected me more than anything I had ever seen. I couldn't imagine living without him. I just wished there was something I could do to make him better.

I leaned over the railing and kissed his forehead. "Grandpa, you're going to get better. Everything is going to be all right. I promise."

Grandpa looked over his shoulder and smiled. He took my hand as tears rolled down his cheek.

I stayed at Grandpa's side until he fell asleep. He held my hand the entire time. Leaning over the railing, I said, "Good-bye."

I placed my arm around Mom and left the hospital.

"Thanks for seeing your grandpa. He always loved you the best," she said.

"Don't worry, Mom. He'll be all right."

"What are your plans today?"

"I'm going to the cemetery."

"You're going to visit Little Joey?"

"I have to."

I dropped off Mom and headed for the cemetery. I entered the familiar gates and headed for the military plots. A chill ran through my body as I drove alongside the veteran's section of Union Cemetery.

Following Dad's directions, I searched for Little Joey's grave site. I counted six trees that lined the veteran's section, and parked. Little Joey's headstone was located near a tree that stood between two majestic pines.

Disturbed soil and wilted flowers marked his grave site. Kneeling on one knee, I brushed away the dirt covering his name. I could only imagine all the friends and family grieving over his casket, draped with the American flag he had defended so proudly.

I couldn't hold back the tears as I read his name. I asked Little Joey to protect me when I returned to Vietnam. Nearby was the grave of a childhood friend, which added to the pain.

***

The following morning, Mom informed me that her dad had been removed from intensive care and placed in a private room. He was sitting up in bed, eating, and joking with the nurses. The nurses couldn't believe his miraculous recovery.

Grandpa boasted to the nurses that his grandson had come all the way from Vietnam to heal him. If Grandpa believed I had healed him, so be it. I was just happy he was going to be around for a while.

Two friends decided it would be best to have a party on my behalf. They rented a room at the rear of the Westerner Hotel, a perfect location. My friends meant well, but I believed the party was for their own benefit. Although the room was a little small, it had enough room for a hi-fi console.

The guys placed a chilled keg of Budweiser in the bathroom tub and iced it down. The pump was installed, and we started pouring the beer. I placed a vinyl album on the turntable. I tried not to think about the war, but it was difficult not to think of the guys in Blackfoot Platoon. It was just something you couldn't forget.

As guests arrived, the hotel room quickly became crowded. Some of the guests I recognized; others I had never met. As I greeted guests, an attractive girl with a golden tan approached the door.

"You must be the one who just returned from Vietnam?"

"Who are you?" I replied.

"I'm Paula."

"Where did you get that beautiful tan?"

"I'm Italian," said Paula.

"Excuse me for staring at your chest, but I've been in the jungle for six months. I don't get to see very many attractive girls like you."

"You've been away too long."

"Are you alone?" I asked.

"No, I'm waiting for my boyfriend."

Another attractive girl arrived, wearing a pair of tight shorts, her hair neatly styled. "What's your name?" I asked.

"Yvonne," she replied.

I couldn't help but admire her perfectly shaped body as she entered the room.

Everyone was enjoying the party. With a room filled with friends and guests, I should have been having a good time. Instead I was withdrawn and feeling claustrophobic. With the overcrowded room making it difficult to have a conversation I decided to go for a walk.

"Where you going?" Paula asked.

"I'm leaving this cluster-fuck."

"Cluster what?"

"A cluster-fuck is a crowd," I explained.

"Are you okay?"

"It's just a little too crowded."

A stranger with long, curly hair handed me a marijuana cigarette. "Do you want hit?"

I agreed and inhaled the smoke. It was obvious his homegrown pot wasn't as potent as the marijuana in Vietnam.

"Good shit, huh?" said the young man.

"Are you kidding? You think this is good shit? Boy, you don't know what good shit is until you've been to Vietnam," I answered sarcastically.

"You're the dude from Vietnam? I hear there's some powerful weed killer over there."

"All the drugs are powerful over there," I said and returned to the party.

I managed to squeeze into the bathroom to fill my cup with beer. On the way out, I noticed two Hispanic girls standing against the wall. I didn't hesitate to introduce myself.

"What's your name?" I asked.

"I'm Carol and this is my friend Teresa. Are you the one who just got back from Vietnam?"

"Yes, I am. Are you having a good time?" I said, shouting above the laughter and music.

"How does it feel to be back?" Carol asked.

"Honestly, I feel like I don't belong in this world anymore," I replied.

"I'm sorry. I wish there was something I could do to make it better," said Terri.

"That would be up to you. What would it cost to spend the night with you?" I asked.

"Are you crazy? Do I look like a hooker?" she exclaimed.

"I'm sorry. I forgot where I was for a moment," I said.

I don't know if it was the alcohol or the fact that I had been in a combat zone for six months, but I realized I had said something inappropriate. I apologized to the girls and left the party.

I headed for the nightclub located at the front of the hotel and took a seat at the bar. Cigarette smoke lingered in the air as the band entertained an enthusiastic crowd.

"What would you like to drink?" asked the bartender.

"Budweiser in a bottle," I said.

"Can I see some ID?"

"I just returned from a war. I don't have any ID," I responded.

"Sorry. No ID, no alcohol," the bartender rudely replied.

"That's the problem with this country. Nobody gives a damn about the soldiers fighting in Vietnam. Kiss my ass!" I shouted angrily.

The bartender leaned over the bar, pointing his finger in my face. "I don't give a shit where you've been, asshole. You raise your voice one more time, I'm throwing you out." He walked away.

Although I wasn't allowed to drink, I stayed to listen to the music. Unexpectedly, the bartender tapped me on the shoulder and handed me a Budweiser in a bottle. "This is from the guy across the bar," he said with a smirk on his face.

I raised my bottle of beer and acknowledged the individual for his generosity. Curious to know who he was, I walked over to the other side of the bar.

"Thanks for the beer," I said, extending my hand.

"I heard you shouting at the bartender. When he didn't serve you, I decided to buy you a beer. It's the least I can do for a grunt," said the stranger.

"How do you know I'm a grunt?"

"It takes one to know one."

I sized him up and realized the thin Hispanic man was a Vietnam vet. "When were you in Vietnam?"

"I just got back. How about you?" he replied.

"I'm on a two-week leave. I have to return for another five and a half months."

"Sorry about that, man. Hopefully, it will go by fast."

"What's your name?" I asked.

"Jesse. What's yours?"

"Ricky, but they call me One Shot."

"What unit are you with?"

"First Cav," I replied.

"I was with the 101st Airborne Division, stationed in Thua Thin Province," said Jesse.

"Did you say Thua Thin?" I asked.

"Yes, why?"

"I had a friend who was killed there."

"What's his name?"

"Little Joey. Did you know him?"

"No, but I'm sorry about your friend," replied Jesse.

I enjoyed listening to Jesse talk about his Vietnam experience. It was good to hear from someone whose story was a lot like mine.

Unexpectedly, someone embraced me from the rear. "Where you been, party boy? I went to the hotel room looking for you, but no one knew where you were at. I figured you would be at the bar. How's everything hanging, brother?" asked Roger.

"I needed some fresh air, so I decided to have a drink," I replied.

"I heard you were in town. I wanted to have a drink with a war hero. Let's go to the Golden Lion. You can tell me about the war."

"I better get back to the party. Everyone's probably wondering where I'm at," I replied.

"Man, those punks don't care if you're gone. Let's go. It'll be like old times," said Roger.

"Want to join us, Jesse?" I asked.

"No, you guys have one for me," Jessie replied.

"Who's your friend?" asked Roger.

"Just another grunt," I replied.

At the door of the Golden Lion, I was asked for my ID. I informed Roger that I didn't have any.

"You don't need any; you're with me," replied Roger.

He placed his arm around the bouncer's shoulder and slipped a five-dollar bill into his hand. The bouncer smiled, allowing me to enter the club.

The bar was filled with patrons. The dance floor was packed with dancers. "This is my kind of place," said Roger. "Let's find a table."

He located an empty table next to two attractive girls. Flirting with the cocktail waitress, Roger ordered the first round.

"What would you like to drink?" asked the waitress.

I looked over at the girls enjoying mixed drinks. "That looks good. I'll have what they're drinking."

"Whisky sour it is," said the waitress.

"Same for me. I'm going to ask that good-looking chick to dance. See you later," said Roger.

"What's your name?" I asked the girl remaining at the table.

"Terri, and that's my friend Mary your friend is dancing with," said the attractive girl, who wore stylish black-framed glasses.

"Do you come here often?" I asked.

"Not really, I'm not even twenty-one," said Terri.

"Would you like to dance?"

"Sure."

I took Terri's hand and led her to the dance floor. I was greeted by friends who wished me well. I was enjoying myself. Then I noticed an angry young man glaring at Terri.

"What's his problem?" I asked.

"Don't pay attention to him. He's my ex-boyfriend."

We remained on the dance floor and so did the angry ex-boyfriend. When the music ended, we returned to the table. The angry ex-boyfriend followed. Obviously intoxicated, he continued to glare at Terri.

"What is your problem?" I asked.

"That's my girl you're dancing with," he replied.

"Look, punk, you need to get lost," I said in a firm tone.

"You guys come back from Vietnam thinking you're bad."

"Asshole, I don't think I'm bad. I'm just trying to have a good time. Now get lost," I replied.

The angry ex-boyfriend stepped back, raising his fists. "Come on. Show me some of that kung fu they taught you in the army."

Everyone in the area was focused on what I was going to do next. Roger noticed I was about to get into an altercation and rushed over. Jumping over a chair, he flipped a table and grabbed the intoxicated troublemaker by his shirt,

"Get lost, punk, or I'll kick your fucking ass!" said Roger, glaring into his eyes.

The ex-boyfriend slowly walked away, leaving the nightclub. Terri took my hand and led me back to the dance floor. "I broke up with that clown last week. He thinks we're still together. Sorry for the hassle."

"Don't worry. I've had to deal with a lot worse situations in Vietnam," I replied.

"I think your friend scared the shit out of him. Maybe he'll leave me alone now."

Roger decided it was time to return to the party. I invited Terri and Mary, but they declined the invitation.

"Did you see the look on that punk's face when I flipped the table over?" said Roger, laughing hysterically.

"You scared the crap out of him!" I replied.

"I'm not going to let anything happen to you. You have enough crap to worry about." He pulled into the Westerner Hotel and parked, with the engine idling.

"Are you going to join me for a beer? We'll tell everyone about the fight we almost got ourselves into?" I said.

"No, I better head home. Little Mamma is waiting for me. Besides, you're a better storyteller than me any day," said Roger.

"Thanks for coming by, Roger."

"Kill a few of the bastards for me. You better come home alive, punk." He embraced me and drove off.

When I returned to the party, most of the guests were gone. Only a few friends remained. I walked over to the hi-fi and placed *The Four Tops Greatest Hits* album on the turntable. I laid my head on the bed and fell asleep.

The remainder of my leave passed quickly. Grandpa recovered from his heart attack and was released from the hospital. He religiously believed that God was responsible for bringing me home to miraculously heal his heart. Grandpa made me promise I would attend his church to tell the story when I returned.

***

September 1. On the morning I was scheduled to return to Vietnam, Mother was deeply troubled. Until my safe return, she would have to live in constant fear of losing her only son. After spending two weeks at home, I was inspired to return to Vietnam to complete my tour.

Mom and Dad accompanied me to the airport. I gave Mom a big hug and a kiss on her cheek. She didn't want to let go. "Promise you'll be careful," she said with tears in her eyes.

"Sorry, Mom. My destiny is in God's hands," I said.

I boarded the small commuter plane, ready for takeoff. At the top of the stairs, I hesitated to wave good-bye. Mother laid her head on Dad's shoulder and cried.

I was scheduled for a brief layover at LAX. Mom had made sure I wouldn't wait alone. A brief visit with relatives living in the area was very emotional.

Episode Twenty-Two

The Radar Site

September 1. The return flight made stops in Honolulu, Manila, and Tokyo, and then it was back to Tan Son Nhut Air Force Base. We arrived ahead of schedule, late in the evening. Everyone quietly departed the plane and boarded the waiting transportation.

The drive revealed the familiar sights and sounds of Vietnam, but for some strange reason it felt good to be back.

The group spent the night at Camp Alpha and returned to Bien Hoa Air Force Base in the morning. I could only hope the remaining months of my tour would pass as quickly as the previous two weeks at home.

***

September 2. I was out of civilian life and back into the war. With five and a half months remaining, it appeared I would be in the field until the end of my tour. My only hope was an early release for Christmas.

I returned to the company rear to retrieve my weapon and rucksack. The company clerk was shuffling paperwork when I entered the room. "Look who's back," he said, smiling as if he was glad to see me.

"Is that my transfer to the rear?" I asked jokingly.

"Honestly, do you think the CO is going to take you out of the field?"

"I guess the only way I'm getting out of the field is in a body bag."

"There's a bird leaving for Fire Base Jefferies in thirty minutes. Bravo Company is being resupplied tomorrow."

"I hope there was no trouble while I was gone?" I asked.

"No more than usual."

It didn't take long to get back into the war because I never forgot about it. I placed my rucksack over my shoulder and headed for the LZ. Bravo Company was in the field when I returned to the fire base. I was resupplied with food and ammo and briefed on the current operation.

***

September 3. I returned to the field on the first bird. I joined Blackfoot for the remaining three days of the mission. Everyone welcomed me back and was eager to hear about my experience in civilian life. Like a family reunion, it was good to see everyone.

Sergeant Tomas had rotated to the States while I was gone. Since he was a career soldier, he would probably find his way back to Vietnam for another tour.

It was unfortunate that I didn't have a chance to say good-bye to the leader who had become my friend and mentor. Knowing Sergeant Tomas, he was probably enjoying his thirty-day leave by lounging in his La-Z-Boy recliner with a can of beer, the television tuned in to his favorite show, *The Real McCoys*.

The new platoon sergeant would never fill the shoes of Sergeant Tomas. He was overweight and had no experience leading a light infantry weapons platoon. His belly hung over his fatigue pants and he waddled like a duck. Besides perspiring heavily, he was constantly out of breath.

"What do you think of the new platoon sergeant?" asked Brother Al.

I replied, "How long do you think he'll last?"

"He'll be lucky if he makes it through the rest of this mission," said Brother Charles, laughing.

Brother Al joined in. "Hell, the first day in the field, we had to stop three times for the sergeant to catch his breath. I thought he was going to have a heart attack. Finally the platoon leader gave him a break and set up for the night."

"Once the platoon sergeant sat his fat ass down, he never moved the rest of the night," added Brother Charles. "Not only is he out of shape, he snores like a pig. It was so loud, someone had to constantly wake him up to keep from giving our position away."

Somehow the new platoon sergeant managed to complete his first mission with Bravo Company. The company was extracted from the field and returned to the fire base to pull base security. Personally, I didn't think the sergeant would last much longer.

After a short stay, Bravo Company returned to the field. Sergeant Smith remained as the platoon sergeant. Our missions were getting shorter, but so was our time on the fire base. Although the South Vietnamese Army was taking on more responsibility for the ground war, our missions remained classified as search and destroy.

The second day of the mission, the platoon came across a field where a large-scale battle had taken place. A number of enemy trenches lined the battlefield, and empty ammo boxes cluttered the area. It appeared the battle had taken place during the 1968 Tet Offensive. Scars from US air attacks were visible in the surrounding trees. The enemy clearly had fought valiantly to hold their position, but it wasn't enough to hold off American firepower.

Human remains protruded through the jungle floor. The enemy soldiers who died in the battle had been hastily buried in shallow graves. Was it worth it? For the enemy, it probably wasn't. For the United States, it was another victory over a determined hostile force.

***

September 26. The mission ended abruptly for Bravo Company. The company was ordered to a pickup zone and extracted from the field. The first platoon to leave the field, Blackfoot was transported to Fire Base Jefferies. Touching down on the LZ, I stepped off the skid and entered the fire base.

I dropped off my rucksack and joined in the gathering at the big green cooler, curious to know the reason for the sudden change in mission. Sundance tossed me an ice-cold can of Black Label beer, and I took a seat on the sandbags. I was waiting for the mail and clean clothes to arrive.

Mateo came over for a visit. "Hey! One Shot, we missed you around here. I made a bet you wouldn't come back."

"Believe me, I thought about it," I replied.

"It's was actually boring around here while you were gone."

"I'm back, so let's enjoy a cold beer!"

The new platoon sergeant waddled over with beads of sweat dripping from his forehead. "Here comes trouble," said Sundance.

"How about a cold beer?" I asked the sergeant.

"No, thank you, I don't drink. Second squad, listen up. I got some bad news for you. Pick up your mail and a three-day log. You're being convoyed over to a radar site to pull security," said the sergeant.

"Wait a minute, Sergeant Smith. Why does second squad have to go? It's not our turn to go on patrol," said Sundance in an angry tone.

"I don't know and I don't care. Pick up your shit and head over to the LZ."

"Where is this radar site located?" asked Sundance.

"Somewhere near Highway 1."

"What's on this radar site?" I asked.

"Two soldiers monitoring the radar equipment. If you want hot chow, I suggest you take plenty of LRPs. Now pick up your shit, the convoy is waiting," said the sergeant, extremely irritated.

I loaded my rucksack with plenty of LRPs, beer, and sodas. When the clean clothes and mail were distributed, I gathered up my equipment and headed for the convoy. Once everyone was aboard the trucks, the convoy headed south on Highway 1. Not knowing where we were headed, I sat back and enjoyed the ride.

Signs indicated we were headed for Xuan Loc. The convoy turned off Highway 1 and headed for a small fire base.

There was no room to turn around inside the radar site, so the convoy stopped at the entrance. The small fire base provided shelter for the radar personnel, along with four guard bunkers on the perimeter. There weren't any sleeping bunkers or shitters on the site. It was going to be an interesting experience.

Sundance collected five dollars MPC from everyone and sent the Kit Carson scout to purchase additional food and drink from the nearest village. "Don't forget the hookers," I said jokingly as the scout headed for the highway.

It would take a little ingenuity to build a roof over my head to sleep under. Selecting a position near the perimeter, I set out to find materials for a hooch. Over the dirt berm, I discovered several pieces of discarded metal. I collected them and began the task of building.

Curious onlookers watched as I drove the largest pieces into the ground as main supports. I secured my poncho to the ground. I draped my mosquito net over the top and blew up my air mattress. The self-made hooch would provide shade in the heat of the day, shelter from the monsoon rain, and adequate cover. Others chose to lay out their air mattress with no protection from the sun or rain.

Although the monsoon season meant wet, miserable nights, everyone welcomed the rain during the day. The rain cooled down the landscape, leaving a cloud of fog lingering along the ground.

***

September 27. In the early morning, I was abruptly awakened by an excited Brother Charles.

"It's only four thirty. Why are you waking me?"

"There's VC in the jungle," said Brother Charles.

"Where?"

In the wood line."

"Why didn't you wake up Sundance?"

"I want you to check it out first."

"All right, let me put my boots on." I grabbed my weapon and followed Brother Charles to the guard station. Searching the wood line, I saw no evidence of Viet Cong. "Why did you think there were VC in the wood line?"

"They were using some kind of code," replied Brother Charles.

"Probably Morse code," I said sarcastically.

"Yeah, I saw a light flashing off and on. I saw it, honest."

I persuaded him that there were no VC in the jungle, and he returned to his sleeping area.

During my watch I began to wonder if Brother Charles really had seen something in the jungle. The moon appeared and the monsoon clouds disappeared to the southeast. By the light of the moon, I was able to see the wood line. The tranquil night provided enough silence to hear the faint thunder of B-52 bombers striking communist targets.

As dawn transitioned from dark to light, I noticed a bright light flickering off and on. It appeared the enemy was sending a coded message. Concerned that they could be planning an early morning attack, I quickly alerted Sundance. "Wake up, there's dinks in the wood line."

"I told you," said Brother Charles, rubbing the sleep from his eyes.

Sundance and I returned to the guard bunker as the sun was rising over the mountain range. We searched the wood line but saw no evidence of the enemy. "I'm going to call Lieutenant CJ. He's going to want us to patrol the wood line," said Sundance.

Everyone was locked and loaded as Sundance communicated with Lieutenant CJ back on Fire Base Jefferies. Just as suspected, the platoon leader requested a patrol. The point team was given an azimuth and headed for the wood line. Boot prints, empty LRP packages, C-ration cans, and aluminum soda cans led us to believe American troops had recently occupied the area.

A thorough search of the wood line revealed no evidence of the enemy. Sundance ordered the patrol to return to the radar site and await further orders. The bright light in the wood line remained a mystery for now, but if it returned, we were instructed to fire up the wood line.

The squad returned to the radar site and prepared for another day. Morning was the only decent part of the day. I decided to enjoy a game of spades.

Brother Charles pulled out a new pack of cards and started the game.

"Why hasn't the Kit Carson scout returned from the village?" I asked Brother Al.

"He'll be back, you'll see," he replied.

"Yeah, One Shot, what makes you think he won't come back?" asked Brother Charles.

"I just don't trust ex-NVA soldiers, even if they are working for us," I replied.

After lunch, a bus stopped on Highway 1. When the dust settled, there stood the Kit Carson scout. He entered the radar site with a cardboard box, accompanied by an attractive Vietnamese girl in black pajamas.

"Here's your girl," said the Kit Carson scout.

"How did you convince her to come to the radar site?" I asked.

"No sweat. I pay, she come, no problem," he replied, chuckling.

"What's her name?"

"Her name is Dung."

"Lieutenant CJ is going to shit when he finds out about the hooker," said Sundance.

"No worry, Dung no tell," replied the scout.

"Look, Dung, I'm sorry you had to come out to the radar site. Here's ten dollars MPC so you can take a bus back to your village."

"Sorry, GI, no more bus today. You pay, I stay," said Dung, shaking her head.

"I guess she's stuck here for the night," said Sundance.

"Where I sleep?" asked Dung.

"Yeah, One Shot, where's she going to sleep?" wondered Brother Charles.

Feeling guilty about Dung having to spend the night, I escorted her to my hooch.

"You sleep here tonight," I said to Dung.

"That no place to sleep," said Dung.

"Sorry, it's the best you get."

"Why you want girl? You have no bed," said Dung.

"I'm sorry. I didn't think anyone would come out here to work, even if you are a hooker."

"No problem. I sleep with you tonight," said Dung.

She took shelter under my hooch when it started to rain. I remained in the rain, enjoying a cold Tiger 33 beer. "You crazy, GI. Why you stay in rain?" Dung asked.

"Because it feels good," I said.

I finished my beer and joined Dung sitting on my air mattress. Together, we listened to the rumble of the thunder as the rain rolled off my poncho.

"Dung, that's an unusual name. What does it mean?" I asked.

"It means *beautiful* in Vietnamese."

"Where do you live?"

"I live in village near Xuan Loc."

"Do you live with your family?"

"Yes, I live with Mama-san and two sisters. Papa-san killed by VC," said Dung, turning away for a moment.

"Did your father fight with the South Vietnamese Army?" I asked.

"No, Papa-san rice farmer. He killed because he no help VC. Two brothers join South Vietnamese Army to kill VC for Papa-san."

"Does Mama-san know you're a hooker?"

"No, she thinks I work in laundry factory."

"How about your brothers?" I asked.

"I no see brothers for two years. Don't know if dead or alive," said Dung.

"What about your sisters, will they be hookers?"

"No want sisters to be hooker. I want sisters have better life."

Dung was concerned about the uncertainty of her family's future. She believed the American troops would abandon South Vietnam, allowing North Vietnam to win the war and eventually kill everyone who worked for the Americans.

Dung boasted that she studied geography and knew the name of all fifty states in America. I was impressed since I could only remember half. Dung was saving her money to move her family out of Vietnam. Her dream was to live in the United States.

Dung fell asleep as the rain continued to fall. I covered her with my poncho liner as I watched her sleep. I fell asleep lying next to her and didn't open my eyes until it was time to report for guard duty.

Dung remained asleep while I made my way to the guard station. The rain stopped and the monsoon clouds disappeared into the skyline.

"Did you see anything?" I asked Brother Charles.

"Not tonight," he answered.

I pulled guard until dawn's early light. When guard duty was over, I headed back to my hooch to prepare a hot cup of cocoa. Dung was heading for the highway.

"Dung, wait a minute," I hollered. "I want to give you something for staying with me."

"No sweat, GI. I sleep in worse place," replied Dung.

"Here's forty dollars MPC. It won't get you to America, but I hope it will help you find a way out of this place." I could only wonder what the future held for Dung and her family. I watched as she climbed aboard the crowded bus. When the bus sped away, I returned to my hooch.

I prepared breakfast—a hot cup of cocoa and a can of scrambled eggs with minced ham.

***

September 28. As the morning sun rose over the mountains, I prepared for another day at the radar site. Thumbing through the pages of a *Playboy* magazine, I memorized all the names of the girls. At times I wished I were back in the bush.

Lieutenant CJ requested second squad run a patrol across the highway. Everyone picked up their weapons, along with a bandolier of ammo. Sundance took point and led the squad across the highway.

Sundance headed for a large mound of dirt. On the far side of the mound, he discovered a rectangular excavation filled with clear rainwater. Hillbilly wasted no time taking off his fatigues and boots, diving in headfirst. Everyone started undressing, taking advantage of the cool rainwater on a hot day.

"Wait a minute, someone has to pull guard!" said Sundance.

"Go ahead, I'll set up the gun in the shade and keep a lookout," said Duggy.

"I'll join you," replied Bart.

Sundance undressed and dived in. Hillbilly passed around a bar of soap, and everyone took the opportunity to lather up. After a couple hours of playful relaxation, Sundance decided it was time to return to the radar site.

Sundance reported to Lieutenant CJ that we patrolled the area across the highway but didn't see any signs of the enemy. He felt there was no need to tell our leadership we had gone swimming.

***

September 29. Once again Lieutenant CJ ordered a patrol across the highway, this time to investigate a logging road leading into the jungle. Sundance advised everyone to bring lunch because we would be out there past mealtime.

Sundance led the patrol by the swimming hole and followed the logging road. Dense triple canopy covered both sides of the road as we entered the jungle. Sundance led the patrol two hundred meters in and ordered a short break so he could report to Lieutenant CJ.

There was no sign the logging road had been used by anyone recently. Lieutenant CJ ordered Sundance to continue the patrol. When the point team reached an area brown with disease, the patrol came to a halt. Wilted leaves were falling from trees, and the foliage was stripped as far as I could see. The other side of the logging road was rich with vegetation. Everyone was curious to know what caused the destruction.

"All right everyone, take a break and chow down!" hollered Sundance.

I took a seat next to Sundance on a fallen tree.

"Hey, what happened to the jungle?" I asked.

"I heard that the military was spraying chemicals to flush out the dinks," he said.

"What kind of weed killer would do this kind of damage?" asked Duggy.

"Agent Orange, brother, Agent Orange," offered Hillbilly.

"What the hell is Agent Orange?" Holt asked.

"Powerful," whispered Hillbilly.

The military used Agent Orange from 1961 to 1971 to deprive the enemy of cover and keep the peasant farmers from growing crops. We were fortunate Agent Orange was in our hands and not the enemy's.

I dropped a cracker from my B-2-1 unit on the jungle floor. I picked it up and was just about to put it in my mouth when I decided it might not be safe to eat. The powerful herbicide was just another discomfort of the Vietnam War.

"Pick it up. We're heading back. There's a convoy on the way to take us to Fire Base Jefferies," Sundance announced.

"It's about fucking time!" cried Hoskie.

Episode Twenty-Three

The Replacements

September 29. Second squad was convoyed back to Fire Base Jefferies. After three days of C-rations and LRPs, everyone was eager for a shower and a hot mess-hall meal. Sergeant Smith reported to the rear with an injury, never to return to the field.

Blackfoot spent the night on the Fire Base Jefferies and was scheduled to begin a new mission in the morning. After three boring days on the radar site, the bush was welcome. Blackfoot's next objective was to work out of Fire Base Jefferies. Due to recent mortar attacks on the fire base, battalion ordered Blackfoot to sweep the north side of Highway 1.

***

September 30. With first squad leading the way, Blackfoot crossed the highway and entered the wood line. Twenty-five meters in, the point team discovered an enemy observation post. It appeared the enemy had been spying on the fire base.

The point team followed the trotter leading away from the observation post. Lieutenant CJ received a call from the CO and was ordered to send a squad back to the fire base to pick up seven replacements. Blackfoot was about to be introduced to seven new faces.

"Finally, someone to take over the gun," boasted Duggy, the experienced machine gunner.

"Yeah, maybe I can find someone to take over the grenade launcher too," said JC.

The platoon was definitely in need of additional manpower. Since the tragic losses on February 7, Blackfoot had never regained full strength. The last replacements to join Blackfoot had been my group back in February. With a number of grunts leaving in less than thirty days, it was time to rebuild.

Everyone waited eagerly to meet the new members of Blackfoot. Static from the radio indicated an incoming call.

"Keep an eye out for first squad. They're heading our way," said Lieutenant CJ.

"Are the new guys transfers or FNGs?" I asked.

"Definitely FNGs," he replied.

The replacements strolled into the perimeter wearing new fatigues and shiny black boots. It was obvious they had recently arrived in-country.

Standing in the center were five blacks, one Hispanic, and one white soldier. Seeing the replacements for the first time reminded me of when I first joined Blackfoot. No one then had wanted anything to do with us.

None of the new recruits looked like they could survive the field, but that's what had probably been said about me when I first joined Blackfoot. There would be plenty of disappointment before the replacements would be respected as jungle-wise grunts.

Brother Al introduced himself to the five new blacks in the platoon and gave them the brotherhood handshake. They were introduced as Bush, Short Round, Shake, DC, and Stretch. The one Hispanic was introduced as Billy, and the white soldier was introduced as Donny but wished to be called Sarge.

"Bush, is that your real name?" asked Brother Al.

"That's what everyone calls me," replied the new soldier.

Those of us who had joined the platoon in February were now responsible for leadership. I was fortunate to have survived until now. It was time to consider a rear job.

Lieutenant CJ assigned four of the replacements to second squad, with the remaining three assigned to first squad.

"One Shot, you're in charge of the cherries. Make sure they have their shit together before we move out," said Lieutenant CJ.

"No thanks, lieutenant. I'm too short to be responsible for anyone but myself," I replied.

"It's not a request, it's an order."

"Why do I get to babysit the new guys?" I complained.

"Someone has to do it," said Lieutenant CJ and walked off.

Although I wasn't pleased with the platoon leader's decision, I had no choice in the matter.

"All you new guys, listen up. Before we move out, you have to learn a few things. Has anyone worked in the bush before?" I asked.

"No," replied Billy.

"I didn't think so. Does everyone have plenty of ammo?"

"Yes," said Short Round.

"Does everyone have plenty of food and water?"

"I hope so," said Billy.

"All right, this is how it works. Always assume the enemy is around the corner. That way, you're always mentally prepared to engage the enemy. It works for me. You have to be ready to do battle at all times. If you let your guard down, that's when you get your shit blown away."

"The company clerk said Blackfoot hasn't seen much action lately," said Billy.

"Just because we haven't had any contact lately doesn't mean there isn't killing going on. We're dealing with a determined enemy force that's on the move. Although the enemy is working in smaller pockets, if they run into us, they're going to inflict as much death as they possibly can. Don't ever forget it," I replied.

"When are we going back to the fire base?" asked Billy.

"You're lucky. This is a fairly short mission. We're scheduled to go back to the fire base in six days."

"That's a long time," said Billy.

"Hell, that's nothing. Blackfoot has been known to stay in the field for twenty-one days."

"How do you handle the fear, knowing you could be killed any moment?" asked DC.

"If I thought about being killed every minute of the day, I would have killed myself a long time ago," I replied.

"All right, One Shot, get the FNGs together. We're moving out in five mikes," said Lieutenant CJ

"You heard the lieutenant. We're moving out in five minutes. I'm only going to say this once, so pay attention. First squad is pointing out. Leading the squad is the point man, followed by the slack man, and then the LT and RTO. Filling in the rest of the squad are the riflemen, and bringing up the rear is the drag position. Slack is responsible for looking out for the point man, and drag is responsible for pace count and protecting us from the rear. All we expect from you is to do your job. Now pick it up," I said.

"Where do you want us?" asked Billy.

"Fall in behind the assistant machine gunner. If you have any questions, just ask. Now get your shit on and get ready to move out."

Duggy walked up to Billy and handed him the machine gun. "Here you go, shithead."

"Who are you calling shithead, and why are you giving me the machine gun?" Billy replied.

"Because I can," said Duggy.

"Why me?"

"I'm making you the new machine gunner," said Duggy and reached for Billy's M-16.

Duggy convinced Billy it was a privilege to carry the M-60 and selected Short Round as his assistant machine gunner. Duggy had carried the gun for nine months, never complaining.

Billy wasn't impressed with his new assignment. "This gun is heavy!"

"You'll get used to it," said Duggy and walked away.

"Hey, keep the noise down. There's movement ahead," said Lieutenant CJ.

He gave the order to move out, with first squad leading the way. At the two-hundred-meter pace count, the point team discovered a discharge of fresh human waste. Footprints indicated we were on the trail of three to four enemy soldiers.

"See that?" I said to Billy, pointing to the human waste as we walked by.

"Yeah, it looks like someone took a shit?" replied Billy, panting with exhaustion.

"No, it means a dink just took a shit. We're on his trail, so you better pay attention!"

Billy had a lot to learn, but I was determined to teach him how to survive in the jungle.

"Where you from?" I asked.

"Colorado," Billy replied. "Where you from?"

"California."

"What part?"

"Bakersfield."

"Bakersfield? Where in the hell is Bakersfield?"

"Two hours from Disneyland," I said.

"I'm miserable. How do you handle it?"

"You'll get used to it. Now, stay up with the others."

Basic and advanced infantry training had taken a few pounds off Billy, but it hadn't prepared him for the jungle. His equipment hung everywhere but in the right place. Machine gun ammo was falling off his rucksack, and his claymore hung off the side. His fatigue pants were unbloused, and his fatigue shirt was hanging out of his pants.

Lieutenant CJ ordered a short break. I took the time to remove a couple straps from Billy's rucksack. I quickly demonstrated how to blouse his fatigue pants and adjusted some of his equipment. "Now you look like a grunt, so act like one."

"Why did you do that?" asked Billy, looking a little puzzled.

"Two reasons. To keep your pants from getting caught on wait-a-minute vines, and keep the snakes from crawling up your ass."

"There's snakes out there?"

"That's not the only thing you have to worry about."

"What else do I have to worry about?"

"I'll tell you later. Right now we have to get going and keep the barrel of the machine gun out of the dirt," I said.

Billy continued to fall behind, getting tangled in wait-a-minute vines. When he stopped to rest, he jammed the barrel of the M-60 machine gun into the ground. The enemy could have walked up and he wouldn't have been capable of firing.

At the four-hundred-meter count, Lieutenant CJ called for another break. Billy couldn't get his rucksack off his back fast enough. "It's about fucking time!"

"Hold down the fucking noise! You want every fucking dink in the jungle to know our position?" said Duggy angrily.

After a short break, Lieutenant CJ gave word to move out. With a look of despair, Billy tried to get to his feet. "Oh no, not again!" He leaned over and decided he'd had enough. He threw the machine gun on the ground, took off his rucksack, and refused to move.

"We're just as tired as you are, but we have to keep going, so get your shit on and let's get the hell out of here before I kick your ass," threatened Duggy.

"I'm sorry. I can't go any farther," cried Billy, shaking his head.

Lieutenant CJ came by to see what the commotion was about. I tried to encourage Billy to put on his rucksack, but he refused.

"What the hell is going on?" asked Lieutenant CJ in an angry tone.

"I'm tired, I can't go no farther!" replied Billy.

"It's that or we'll just have to leave your ass," said the lieutenant. "Pick it up, let's get going."

The lieutenant wanted to set up before dusk, and Billy was determined not to move. I had never known anyone to refuse to move because they were too exhausted. Everyone was eager to see how this was going to turn out.

The M-60 machine gun was heavy and awkward to carry, but it appeared Billy could handle it. I guess he was the wrong selection for the duty. Lieutenant CJ waited five minutes, then gave the word to move out. "Tell that cherry to get his ass up, because we're moving out with or without him!"

Somehow Billy managed to get to his feet. The machine gun was returned to Duggy, and Billy was handed his M-16.

"You're not man enough to handle the gun," said Duggy.

"Man, give me a break," replied Billy.

"Not in the bush," Duggy said.

Without any further delays, the platoon leader located a position for the night. Lieutenant CJ instructed us to get our night work out and secure the perimeter. I walked over to Billy with claymore and trip flare in hand.

"This is what we do every time we set up our perimeter. Grab your claymore and trip flare and follow me."

"I have a claymore, but not a trip flare," replied Billy.

"You've got to be kidding. Supply didn't issue you a trip flare?"

"No. Was I supposed to get one?"

Cole overheard the conversation and threw over his trip flare. "Don't lose it," he said.

I instructed Billy to follow close behind and pay attention. I walked out of the perimeter and headed for a nearby tree. "Go over there and set up your claymore and— Where's your weapon?"

"Back at the perimeter," replied Billy.

"That's the number one rule in the bush! Never go anywhere without your weapon. Now let me show you how to set up your night work."

Afterward, Billy and I returned to the perimeter and settled down for the night. I watched as he unloaded an assortment of C-rations, LRPs, and personal belongings, along with a pair of fatigues. Not to mention ten quarts of water.

Although I had my work cut out for me, I was determined to have Billy trained before the next mission.

Episode Twenty-Four

The Encounter

October 2. Blackfoot completed their objective, returning to Fire Base Jefferies. Monsoon season was coming to an end. I managed to survive the wet season without being infected with jungle rot or any other infectious disease.

I was looking forward to an upcoming R & R in Sydney, Australia. Having experienced Australia, Brother Theo encouraged me to stay at the Bay View Apartments, a modern high-rise apartment. If I wanted soulful hospitality, the Cheetah Room with attractive Aborigine cocktail waitresses would be the choice.

After a short stay on Fire Base Jefferies, the CO informed Lieutenant CJ his platoon would be flown to a mini fire support base to provide security.

After a few challenging experiences, Billy and the other FNGs were beginning to adapt to life in the field. In time, they would be accepted as jungle-wise grunts.

***

October 13. In the early morning, Blackfoot was ordered to the LZ to wait for transportation to our new objective.

"The platoon is scheduled to pull base security for the next five days," announced Lieutenant CJ.

"Where at?" asked Sundance.

"A small fire base containing a single artillery and mortar unit," said Lieutenant CJ.

"Is there a mess hall?" I asked.

"Pack a three-day log, that's all I can tell you," he said.

The Chinook transport landed alongside Highway 1. The ramp was lowered and the platoon filed in. With the thrust of the powerful twin rotary engines, the Chinook transport was airborne. The pilot turned the nose of his aircraft and headed west.

An unusually long flight time got the best of everyone's curiosity. A natural watercourse on the horizon made everyone believe the Chinook transport was headed for the Mekong Delta, near the Cambodian border.

The United States had launched a major ground attack against NVA forces in Cambodia the previous year. Known as the "Cambodian Incursion," the purpose was to deny sanctuary to NVA and VC navigating the Ho Chi Minh Trail to hide in neutral Cambodia and Laos.

The Ho Chi Minh Trail was a well-traveled network, over 9,600 miles long, extending from North Vietnam down into South Vietnam. It was composed of truck routes, bicycle paths, and jungle trails used by the enemy to move supplies and reinforcements. Originally known as the Duong Truong Son Road, the Ho Chi Minh Trail was nicknamed "the Blood Trail."

The success of the Cambodian Incursion had supposedly eliminated any cross-border threat, so why was Blackfoot Platoon working so close to the border?

The twin-engine Chinook transport circled the mini fire base and headed for the LZ. The pilot landed the aircraft and lowered the loading ramp. Everyone departed the transport and entered the fire base. Lieutenant CJ met with the platoon leader from Delta Company as his platoon boarded the Chinook transport.

"Good luck, guys. It's been crazy the last few nights," said the Delta Company platoon leader.

The Chinook transport lifted off the LZ. The isolated fire base was equipped with a single 105 howitzer and a single 80 mm mortar tube.

"Boy! Are we relieved to see you," said the artillery sergeant. "There's been incoming the last two nights, and we caught a dink in the wire, trying to penetrate the perimeter."

"Hear that, guys? Let's get out there and secure the perimeter. Sundance, make sure the barbed wire is in place and all trip flares are in working order. First squad, make sure there's plenty of ammo and illumination flares in every guard bunker," shouted Lieutenant CJ.

"Are we going to be overrun?" asked Holt.

"I'm too short to be in the middle of nowhere," complained Brother Al.

That evening, everyone remained awake anticipating an attack on the fire base. The FNGs were concerned because it could be their first confrontation with the enemy. Lieutenant CJ posted two guards at every guard bunker.

That evening the moon was out and the night was quiet. We would be able to see and hear the enemy if they tried to attack.

Around eleven o'clock, bunker number six called in an illumination round, claiming there was movement in the wood line. Six mortars were fired near the suspected movement. We hoped this would distract the enemy from attacking the fire base.

Brother Al and I were assigned to bunker number one at the main entrance. Devoting our full attention to listening for signs of the enemy, there wasn't much conversation. After midnight, Brother Al and I took turns dozing until the early morning light.

***

October 14. After very little sleep, everyone congregated around the grunt hooch. Built by the previous platoon, the thatched roof provided shade during the heat of the day. To discourage the enemy from attacking the base, Lieutenant CJ ordered a patrol of the wood line. First squad would patrol the first half of the perimeter, with second squad patrolling the second. First squad leader assembled his men and entered the wood line on the east side of the fire base.

The patrol came to a halt when the point team discovered an enemy observation post from which 60 mm mortars had been launched into the fire base. First squad continued the patrol, discovering signs that the enemy had been in the area, and returned to the fire base.

"Sundance, prepare your squad to patrol the remaining half of the perimeter. One Shot, you're leading the point team," said Lieutenant CJ, placing his arm around my shoulder.

"You have to be insane, asking me to take point."

"Don't worry, it's a piece of cake," said the platoon leader, handing over the compass.

"Thanks for nothing," I replied.

Since I had no choice in the matter, I placed the sling of my weapon over my shoulder and drew a deep breath. I put my hand on the pistol grip. With the safety mechanism on full automatic, I headed for the wood line.

This was not the place I had intended to be with less than three months remaining in-country. My position was at drag.

Now I was in the most vulnerable position in the platoon—at point.

I cautiously entered the wood line approximately where the morning patrol had ended. Fortunately, it allowed a clear path through the jungle.

"Remind me to never agree to this position again," I said to Sundance, who was following close behind.

"Just keep pushing. I'm right behind you," he said.

I maintained a steady pace until I reached a heavily vegetated area. Sundance and I chopped through. When we broke out on the other side, we discovered a small enemy base camp. The campfire was still warm.

"7-6 Bravo, come in. Over," said Sundance over the radio.

"7-6 Planter's Family, go ahead. Over," replied Lieutenant CJ.

"We have come across a small enemy camp that has recently been occupied. I strongly suggest we head back to the fire base and call in mortars," said Sundance.

"Negative, continue to patrol the remaining perimeter of the wood line. Over," said Lieutenant CJ.

I had a gut feeling something was about happen. With two-thirds of the wood line patrolled, the remaining one-third would take the longest. The jungle had become difficult to navigate. Sundance decided to find an alternate route.

Heading in a new direction, I came across a shallow stream. Pieces of shrapnel scattered throughout the area and a spent rocket embedded in the stream bed indicated a recent air attack by a gunship.

I quickly waded across the stream and climbed the bank. The discovery of a recently traveled trotter and the smell of cooked rice confirmed my worst fear—the enemy was nearby.

The discovery concerned Sundance, who halted the patrol. Fearing a confrontation with the enemy, Sundance called Lieutenant CJ again.

"7-6 Bravo, we just crossed a stream, and there is definitely enemy in the area," said Sundance in a concerned voice.

"7-6 Planter's Family, the enemy will continue to attack the fire base unless we eliminate the threat. Continue your patrol, but keep me posted. I repeat, continue the patrol, over," said Lieutenant CJ.

Disappointed that the platoon leader hadn't authorized his squad to return, Sundance turned to Sang for advice.

"What do you think?" Sundance asked the ex-NVA soldier.

"Go back to fire base," Sang replied.

"Thanks, you're no help," said Sundance. "Okay, this is what I suggest. One Shot, check out the trotter. Sang and I are right behind you."

Fearing a command-detonated mine, I moved forward exploring the trotter. Low-hanging vines prevented me from keeping my boonie hat on my head, so I pulled out an olive-drab handkerchief, wrapping it around my forehead. Sang started to laugh.

"What's so funny?" I asked.

"You look like VC."

"You say I look like you. That's just great," I said jokingly.

"Not me, VC," said Sang.

At the end of the trotter was an opening leading to an abandoned logging road. I decided to take a quick look. "Wait here. I'm moving ahead," I said to Sang, who took a position on one knee.

Placing my finger on the trigger, I moved forward. Thinking I could be killed at any moment, I slowly peered through the opening.

I quickly pulled back into the wood line when I noticed three VC insurgents seated on a fallen tree. They were sharing a bowl of rice and not aware of my presence. Six AK-47s leaning against the tree indicated there were others in the area. I could have taken out the three I saw, but without the support of my squad, I decided to play it safe.

Suddenly, one the VC insurgents made eye contact. I anticipated he would reach for his weapon, but he only smiled. "*Ban coy toy*," he said.

Outnumbered, I quickly stepped back into the jungle, fearing the enemy would retaliate. I retreated to warn the others.

"What happen?" said Sang.

"Don't ask, I'll explain later," I replied, looking over my shoulder.

"What you see?"

"VC," I said nervously.

"Why you no kill VC?" he said as we approached Sundance and the rest of the squad.

"Too many!" I cried.

I warned Sundance about the situation, and he agreed we needed to leave the area immediately. I located an opening and headed for the fire base. Sundance alerted Lieutenant CJ we were on our way in.

Sundance entered the fire base and met Lieutenant CJ.

"What happened out there?" asked Lieutenant CJ

"I encountered six VC insurgents, and one of them talked to me," I said.

"What he say?" asked Sang.

"I don't know, but it sounded like *ban coy toy.*"

Sang repeated the words a few times and then smiled. "That no Vietnamese, that Cambodian. *Ban cua toi* mean friend in Cambodian. He think you Cambodian," said Sang, laughing.

"Why didn't you fire them up?" asked Lieutenant CJ.

"I could have taken out three VC insurgents, but without knowing where the other three were, I didn't want to get pinned down without the fire support of the rest of the squad."

Sundance gave the mortar platoon a line on the enemy's position, and they went to work aligning their mortar tubes. "Hold your ears," said the mortar team leader, covering his own. *Thump* went the mortar round as it was launched.

Everyone followed the mortar round into the air and watched as it returned to earth and exploded.

"Close enough!" shouted Sundance.

Mortar platoon launched a barrage of rounds into the wood line. Whether the mortars inflicted any damage remained to be seen. We hoped it was enough to convince the enemy flee the area.

The mortar explosions did manage to frighten a herd of Asian elephants.

"Hey, look at the elephants!" I shouted. For some reason, I was the only one excited about the herd.

The afternoon turned out to be a peaceful resolution to a dangerous situation. I was just grateful I didn't have to take another life.

***

October 15. After breakfast, Lieutenant CJ ordered second squad to return to the area where the confrontation had taken place. A thorough search of the area revealed no sign of the six VC insurgents.

Lieutenant CJ suggested everyone clean their weapons in preparation for another night of defense. The majority of the platoon congregated in the shade of the thatched roof, breaking down their weapons. After a thorough cleaning, I assembled my weapon and locked and loaded a fresh magazine of M-16 ammo.

Lieutenant CJ requested Brother Al and I head for the LZ and wait for the resupply bird. "They're bringing in the mail, clean clothes, and hot chow."

"All right, hot chow! Let's go!" I shouted with enthusiasm.

"Pop a can of smoke; the bird is coming in," said Lieutenant CJ.

I picked up a canister and rushed out to the LZ. I pulled the ring and threw the canister off to the side. Above the tree line, a Huey approached. The pilot was about to set the skid on the LZ when three 60 mm enemy mortars exploded simultaneously.

Amid the pilot's effort to get his helicopter back into the air, the door gunner kicked out the mail bag, along with three canisters of food. Though he'd been hit by shrapnel, the pilot managed to get his helicopter safely back to Fire Base Mace.

Lieutenant CJ ordered everyone to fire blindly into the wood line. After a minute of firing, the order was given to cease fire. When the smoke cleared, all that remained was the red mail bag and three canisters of hot chow. Although two of the canisters were lying on their sides, they appeared undamaged. If we wanted a hot meal, all we had to do was retrieve canisters. Everyone was hesitant, fearing another mortar attack.

Sundance tapped my shoulder with a grin on his face. "You know, One Shot, with that amount of fire power we just emptied into the wood line, those dinks must have fled the area."

I knew exactly what Sundance had on his mind. Without any regard for his life, he jumped up and ran for the food. Though I had absolutely no reason to endanger my own life, I followed, with Brother Al joining in.

"Come back!" shouted Lieutenant CJ. "You're going to get yourself killed!"

Brother Al retrieved a canister of food. Sundance picked up a second canister, and I retrieved the mail bag. Everyone cheered as we returned to the safety of the fire base.

"What the hell were you thinking?" Lieutenant CJ asked us.

"I wanted hot chow!" said Sundance.

Everyone enjoyed a serving of mashed potatoes and turkey, smothered in gravy. As reckless as we had been, the hot chow was well worth the chance we took to retrieve it.

Our remaining time on the fire base was spent running daily patrols, trying to eliminate the threat of mortar attacks. Cartwright returned to point, and I returned to my position at drag. No one was certain if the enemy would attack again, but we remained alert, ready to defend the fire base.

After our daily routine, Sundance started a game of two-card guts. If you enjoyed gambling, you played two-card guts. The object of the game was to end up with the two best cards. The best hand won the money, and the players who lost had to match the amount of money in the pot.

Sundance managed to round up six players. None of the FNGs were interested in playing, but they looked on. After a few hours of card playing, I had made money and lost money. The game totally consumed our time, and before long it was dusk.

The game was temporarily interrupted to make candles so we could continue to play. From the wax liners of 105 artillery canisters, we molded candles to provide light throughout the night.

At midnight, the players took a break to prepare a meal and a canteen of hot cocoa. The longer we played, the more money was at stake.

***

October 16. The game that had started at 1:00 p.m. the previous day lasted until six in the morning. Everyone was exhausted but determined to continue the game.

"All right, guys, I don't know about you, but I'm dead tired. I don't care who wins this pot; I just want this game to be over," said Sundance.

Sundance dealt the hand, hoping it was the final game of the night. There were five of us remaining in the game. Brother Al had dropped out and was sitting by my side as a spectator. Two players decided to play the cards they were dealt, and three players drew a single card each.

Sundance dealt the final three cards to each of us. I picked up my card and looked my hand over. I was holding an ace of spades and drew a ten of clubs. Brother Al, looking over my shoulder, gave me a nudge, revealing a king of spades under the table. Hoping the hand would end the game, I took the card.

"Read 'em and weep," said Sundance, laying down his hand. With an ace of spades and a queen of hearts, Sundance smiled, thinking he had won. But when everyone showed their cards, my ace of clubs and king of spades had won the hand. Totally exhausted from lack of sleep, no one question the hand and walked away from the table.

I smiled as Brother Al gathered the money. "I feel bad winning that way," I said.

"No one cares who won the money. They just wanted the game to be over."

"Yeah, it' a lot of money."

"Sure it is, and half is mine," said Brother Al with a smirk.

"How much you win, Jarcia?" asked Brother Charles, returning from guard duty.

"Enough to afford the best-looking girls and all the alcohol you can drink," I said. We walked off to prepare breakfast.

***

October 17. It was our final day on the tiny fire base. Everyone was relieved that our replacements were arriving in the morning, especially the FNGs. If we could make it through the night, we would be on our way to China Beach.

The night turned out to be peaceful. The following morning, Lieutenant CJ sent first squad to patrol the wood line, preventing a mortar attack when the transport Huey arrived.

"Pop smoke, the shit hook will be here any moment!" hollered Lieutenant CJ The Chinook transport flew over the trees and landed safely on the LZ. Our replacements filed out from the rear loading ramp and entered the fire base. Blackfoot boarded the empty transport and prepared for liftoff.

Episode Twenty-Five

Adela

October 18. Blackfoot was flown to Fire Base Jefferies to link up with sister platoons Aztec and Cheyenne. I looked forward to telling Mateo and Romeo about my confrontation with the six VC insurgents. The company would spend the night and be transported to Vung Tau in the morning.

After dinner, the squad leaders assigned guard times. Assigned to the 11:00 p.m. watch, I decided to play a game of spades. After an hour of card play, I went to get a little rest before guard duty.

Shortly before eleven, I was awakened by Brother Charles to pull the next watch. Grabbing my weapon, along with a bandolier of ammo, I headed for the guard bunker facing Highway 1. I was equipped with an M-60 machine gun, starlight scope, and an M-72 LAW. I settled in and made myself comfortable.

I focused on another visit with Manoi. Brother Al stuck his head in the bunker and advised me, "There are hookers in bunker number three."

"Thanks, but I can wait until tomorrow," I replied.

There was an 11:00 p.m. curfew, so no vehicles were on the highway. Shortly before midnight, I stepped outside the bunker and glanced at my watch. As I was about to locate my replacement, I heard an engine approaching. I hoped it was military. I picked up the horn and notified the main CP.

"7-6 Bravo, 7-6 Bravo, this is 7-6 Hotel, over."

"7-6 Hotel, go ahead, over," responded the main CP.

"7-6 Bravo, there's a vehicle coming down Highway 1. Over."

"7-6 Hotel, curfew is at 11:00 p.m., stand by, over."

315

The view through the starlight scope revealed a Volkswagen bus approaching the fire base.

"7-6 Hotel, come in, over," said the main CP.

"Go ahead, 7-6 Bravo," I responded.

"7-6 Hotel, fire a couple warning shots. If the vehicle doesn't stop, fire it up. Over."

"That's a solid copy. Over," I replied, hanging up the headset.

As the VW bus neared the fire base, I fired a two warning shots. The driver fired a burst of green tracers that cracked over our heads. I extended the M-72 light antitank rocket launcher and took aim. When the VW bus sped past the fire base, I squeezed the firing mechanism. The LAW skidded along the pavement, exploding at the rear tires.

With orders to return fire, everyone opened fire on the Volkswagen.

"Hold your fire, hold your fire!" shouted the CO.

The night returned to silence as illumination rounds lighted the fire base. We hoped to get a glimpse of the charred remains of a Volkswagen bus, but a brush fire made it impossible to see anything. The CO considered sending a patrol, but decided to wait until morning.

***

October 19. At dawn's early light, the last guard completed his watch. The smell of freshly cooked bacon brought the fire base to life. Eager to see the outcome of the previous night's encounter, Lieutenant CJ ordered Sundance to assemble second squad to check out the damage.

The sun slowly rose above the mountains as the point team made their way toward the burned wreckage. When the point man reached the pavement, there wasn't any sign of the Volkswagen bus.

"I don't know how that bus survived that gauntlet of firepower," said Sundance, placing his arm over my shoulder.

"Yeah, but I bet we scared the hell out of them," I replied.

The enemy had escaped the wrath of an M-72 LAW and a barrage of M-16 and M-60 machine gunfire, surviving another day. Morning traffic began flowing steadily as second squad returned to the fire base to prepare for another visit to China Beach.

Bravo Company was convoyed to a runway near Fire Base Mace and flown to Vung Tau Airport. The C-130 transport plane landed safely, and everyone was escorted to the R & R center. After several visits to China Beach, you would think we could avoid the familiar orientation from the officer. The only soldiers listening were the FNGs. The rest of us ignored the redundant speech.

After the officer's orientation, I headed for the barracks for my usual visit to Mama-san to clean and starch a pair of jungle fatigues and spit shine my worn-down jungle boots.

Prepared to enjoy my first day in the village, I headed for the exchange shack. Brother Charles and Brother Al accompanied me. The current exchange rate was seven hundred piastres to the dollar, and I had seven hundred dollars. I vowed to spend it all in the village. The soldier at the exchange shack counted out 490,000 piastres in stacks of five hundred.

The brothers and I boarded a waiting Lambretta and instructed the driver to drop us off in front of the Mi Lien Hotel. When the Lambretta pulled up in front of the hotel, I handed the driver a generous tip.

"You already pay, GI," said the driver.

"That's for you," I said.

"Thank you, thank you," replied the driver, climbing back into his vehicle with a big smile.

I entered the lobby, requesting three of the best rooms in the hotel. I paid the receptionist in piasters and received three keys. I gave Brother Al and Brother Charles their room keys and climbed to the third floor, revealing an upscale level of the hotel I hadn't been aware of. Our rooms were located on the same floor. Everyone dropped off their personal belongings, and we set out to enjoy the day.

The three of us entered the Hong Kong Club for a visit with Qui and a round of drinks.

"You come see me," said Qui, sitting at the bar.

"I always come to see you," I replied.

"Pay Mama-san and I be with you tonight," said Qui convincingly.

"You promise?" I asked sincerely. "Hey, Mama-san, here's twenty dollars MPC. Buy tea for all the girls."

"You number ten, GI," said Qui sarcastically.

The three of us went from bar to bar, flirting with the girls and buying tea and drinks for everyone in Bravo Company. I rolled up smaller amounts of piastres and tossed them to the village children as we walked.

That evening, the three of us returned to the top of the Mi Lien Hotel. The nightclub there was a popular hangout for Bravo Company, providing attractive girls and the best entertainment.

"A round of drinks for everyone," I said to Mama-san.

"What you celebrating?" asked Billy.

"Besides being twenty-one, I'm officially a two-digit midget," I replied.

"What's a two-digit midget?" asked Billy.

"Let's just say, I'm so short, I have to wear crutches to keep the ants from pissing on me," I said to Billy, laughing hysterically.

Curfew rolled around, and the band played their last song of the evening. Not knowing where Brother Charles had run off to, Brother Al and I headed down to the room. I opened the window and noticed a street vendor pushing a sandwich cart down the street.

"Hey, Papa-san, can I buy a sandwich?"

"Yes, what kind you want?" shouted the vendor.

"What kind do you have?" I shouted back.

"I have ham sandwich."

"I'll take two sandwiches, please."

The only problem was the street vendor was three floors below.

"Bring the sandwiches to the third floor?" I asked.

"No can do, GI. Hotel no let me in after curfew," replied the vendor.

"How can you get them to me?" I asked.

"No problem. You pay, I throw," he said, confident he could accurately toss a sandwich up three floors.

I tossed the piastres down to the street vendor, and he tossed up the first sandwich. The tightly wrapped sandwich landed perfectly in the palm of my hand. I handed the sandwich to Brother Al and waited for the other to come up.

The vendor tossed the second sandwich, but it came up a little short. In an effort to retrieve it, I extended my body out the window and snagged it. Brother Al grabbed the seat of my pants and pulled me back in. "That was dumb! Why did you do that?" he asked.

"I wasn't going to fall out! Besides, I'm hungry," I replied.

"No, you're drunk."

Brother Al and I enjoyed our ham sandwiches, sipping on a cold beer. Brother Charles strolled into the room with an attractive date hanging on his arm. Brother Charles, wanting to show off his girl, introduced us and joined us for a beer.

Brother Charles's date was incredibly attractive. She was well dressed and didn't appear to be a typical hooker. "Where did you find your girlfriend?" I asked.

"She was sitting in the lobby," said Brother Charles.

"How much did you pay Mama-san?" I asked.

"Twenty MPC, and your friend say you pay," said the attractive hooker.

"Yeah, One Shot, you said you would pay for the girls," said Brother Charles.

"Yeah, One Shot, where's my date?" said Brother Al.

"No problem, Mama-san have girl for you too," said the attractive hooker, leaving the room. She returned with Mama-san and two more girls. I gave Mama-san her normal fee along with additional piastres for beer. I pressed Play on the cassette player and enjoyed the company of our dates.

My date was attractive, but not what I was looking for. I decided to search for a girl who would exceed all expectations, regardless of the cost.

Brother Al danced with his attractive date as we listened to *The Four Tops Greatest Hits* cassette. Taking my date's hand, I attempted a slow dance.

"Why are you laughing?" I asked Brother Charles.

"I didn't know you could dance!" he said.

At one in the morning, Brother Charles decided it was time to escort his attractive date to his room. Brother Al took the opportunity to leave as well. Too intoxicated to keep my date entertained any longer, I rested my head on the pillow and didn't open my eyes until the following day.

I managed to stumble out of bed around one o'clock. My cute little Vietnamese friend had already left the room. With a bathroom and running water, I was able to enjoy a decent shower. I was ready to search for the girl who would be the envy of all my friends, and set out to enjoy the day.

I was dropped off at the Soul Bar to enjoy a brief visit with my friend Manoi. I was greeted at the door by Mama-san and joined two of my friends enjoying the company of Mama-san's girls. I handed Mama-san a large sum to provide drinks for the guys and tea for the girls.

Manoi appeared, walking out of the back room with a flower in her hair. She embraced me, and we made our way over to a table.

Although I paid for the conversation, I welcomed every moment with Manoi. Our relationship hadn't started very well, but it developed into a meaningful friendship. Nevertheless, she wasn't what I was after that day. I began to search for the girl who would be the envy of all the others.

After visiting several bars, I stepped into the Blue Angel Club. The bar was made out of ash wood, glistening with a thick coat of varnish. The cocktail lounge was ideal for enjoying one of Mama-san's attractive girls.

Seated at the end of the bar and playing a game of cards was Mama-san. Older than most, Mama-san was well dressed and wore her jewelry proudly. "What you like to drink?" she asked, a cigarette hanging from her mouth.

"What do you have?"

"I have all kinds. What you like?" she asked.

"Budweiser," I said.

Mama-san opened her cooler and brought out a bottle of Tiger 33.

"I said Budweiser."

"You drink, all beer taste same," said Mama-san, returning to her card game.

I was impressed with Mama-san's rough attitude and decided this would be the place to begin my search. Mama-san nodded at one of the girls to join me. The bar hooker took my hand and led me to a table. She would have been the envy of many soldiers, but for me she was just another Vietnamese hooker.

Mama-san brought tea for the conversation and another Tiger 33. A barefooted Vietnamese shoe-shine boy approached the table. He was wearing tattered clothing and was blind in his left eye.

The boy sat down on his shoe-shine box. "Hey, GI, shine boots for you?"

"How much, little boy?" I asked.

"For you, GI, one MPC."

"How about five MPC?"

"You pay five MPC for shoe shine, okay with me, GI," the boy replied, grinning widely.

With enthusiasm, he went to work on my worn-down jungle boots. I enjoyed another beer as I watched him bring my boots back to life. "Good job, little man."

"I sing for you too, GI," he said.

"Yeah, what do you sing?"

"Number one song."

I expected *"Yankee Doodle Dandy,"* but the boy belted out the entire lyrics to *"Love Potion Number Nine"* by the Searchers.

I hugged the child, tears filling my eyes. I knew there was nothing I could do to restore his sight, but at least I could make his poverty-stricken life a little more bearable. I counted out seven thousand piastres and placed them in the palm of his little hand.

"Wow, thanks, GI. You number one," said the boy, running out of the bar and forgetting his shoe-shine box.

I would have given all of my piastres to the shoe-shine boy if it meant getting his eyesight back. It was only money, and I had plenty of it.

"Why you give shoe-shine boy so many piastres? Pay Mama-san and I take you upstairs for short time," said the bar hooker.

"Because I enjoyed giving it to a boy who needs it more than Mama-san," I said.

"You no want to be with me?" she said sadly.

"It's not you. Today I'm looking for someone special," I replied.

"You number ten," said the bar hooker and walked away.

She went to Mama-san and whispered something in her ear. Mama-san came to the table with a sarcastic look on her face and another Tiger 33.

"So you want special girl," said Mama-san.

"Yes, and I don't see her in your bar," I replied.

"Why you no want my girl? All girls very pretty."

"Yes, all your girls are very pretty. It's just that I'm looking for someone different."

"You pay more money and I find number one girl for you. You wait here, I be back before you finish beer," said Mama-san, making her exit through the back room.

Mama-san caught my attention when she returned with a girl that would draw the attention of any American soldier. The olive-skinned brunette fit perfectly into her long, white silk dress.

"Ah, you like French girl," said Mama-san, wearing a big grin.

The beautiful young lady, about five foot three, stood in front of me, lighting a cigarette. Her perfume disguised the smell of the cigarette. I couldn't resist smelling her long, well-groomed hair.

"Mama-san say you look for special girl tonight," said the hooker.

"What's your name, sweetheart?" I replied.

"Adela."

"You speak good English, Adela."

"That's because my father is French and my mother is French-Vietnamese. They taught me English."

"Why is a beautiful girl like you working as a bar hooker?" I asked.

"No work in bar," boasted Adela.

"Okay, I'm impressed. Can I buy you tea?"

"What's your name?" asked Adela.

"They call me One Shot, but my real name is Ricky," I replied.

She leaned over and gave me a kiss on the cheek, extending an invitation. "Do you want to take me upstairs?"

"What's this going to cost?" I asked curiously.

"Pay Mama-san and we go," said Adela.

"How much?" I asked Mama-san.

"She number one girl. You pay for all night. Adela no do short time," said Mama-san.

Counting out 28,000 piastres, I laid them out neatly on the counter. "Is this enough?"

Adela took my hand and quickly escorted me upstairs. She led us into a room furnished with a full-size bed. Taking a seat next to the bed, I watched as she undressed. Adela's flawless complexion and nicely tanned body were a pleasure to look at. But just as she completely undressed, someone knocked on the door.

"Who's that?" Adela asked, pulling the blankets up to her chest.

"I don't know," I replied.

I opened the door, and there stood Brother Al. Staring into the room, he noticed Adela lying in bed. "She's beautiful," he said around the cigarette in his mouth.

"How did you find me?" I asked.

"A shoe-shine boy was telling a story about a GI giving him seven thousand piastres for singing a song at the Blue Angel. I had a hunch it was you."

"Your friend busy, go away now," said Adela.

"I can't believe how beautiful she is, One Shot. You must have paid a lot of money for a girl who isn't Vietnamese," said Brother Al.

"More than usual, but worth every penny," I replied.

"I'll be at the bar," he said, heading downstairs.

The joy of being with Adela that afternoon was everything I had been searching for. Once again I had become infatuated with a hooker, but this time I knew better than to fall in love. I could have spent the entire day with Adela, but I had promised Brother Al we would celebrate our last night in the village together. I made arrangements with Adela to meet her later in the evening. I joined Brother Al and Brother Charles, who were sitting at the bar and entertaining Mama-san and her girls.

"You like Adela?" asked Mama-san.

"Yes, she's exactly what I needed," I replied.

"You didn't fall in love again, Jarcia?" said Brother Charles, chuckling.

The three of us returned to the Mi Lien for an evening at the rooftop bar. I bought drinks for the guys and paid Mama-san for two of her best-looking girls to keep Brother Al and Brother Charles entertained. Meanwhile, I returned to the Blue Angel to spend the night with the attractive French girl named Adela.

The following morning, I returned to the Mi Lien Hotel. Brother Al and Brother Charles were sitting in the lobby, waiting for me.

"Where you go last night?" asked Brother Al.

"I was tired, so I went to sleep early," I said.

I refused to admit that I had fallen in love with another hooker.

Episode Twenty-Six

Night Encounter

October 21. Another memorable trip to Vung Tau Village had come to an end. This late in my tour, I wasn't sure if there would be another. Bravo Company returned to the fire base and pulled base security for four days. When Bravo Company returned to the field, I would be on my way to Sydney.

I received a letter from a hometown friend. It was promising, stating his unit had stood down. Because he didn't have enough time in-country, though, he would be transferred to another unit.

The good news was he had managed to get transferred to Blackfoot Platoon. This meant we would spend our remaining time in Vietnam together. His arrival date indicated that he was already on his way. Hopefully, I would be able to see him before I left for Sydney.

"I understand my friend will be joining us soon?" I said to the company clerk.

"What's his name?"

"Jet," I replied.

"He's in the rear, but isn't scheduled to come out for another three days."

This meant Jet would be arriving on the day I was scheduled to leave. Maybe Lieutenant CJ would allow me to leave a day early to spend time with a friend.

Life on the fire base had become a ritual for everyone. Everyone knew the drill and did their job without complaint. For me, the only difference was eagerly awaiting Jet's arrival.

Everyone in Blackfoot pulled work detail during the morning and enjoyed their time off in the afternoon. In the evening, everyone watched a movie and ate a meal prepared by the mess hall, served promptly at ten o'clock. Every soldier pulled guard duty, including squad leaders. The only soldiers exempt from guard were the platoon leader and platoon sergeant.

***

October 23. Everyone completed their morning work detail and headed for the mess hall for a lunch break. With the next torrential downpour not scheduled to arrive until late afternoon, the squad leaders organized a game of football between Blackfoot and Cheyenne.

We gathered around as the squad leaders selected their teams. Holt was excited because he had been selected to play on the line. The last selection for Sundance was between Billy and me. Sundance studied his options and decided it would be me. Billy was probably the better choice, but Sundance wouldn't select an FNG over me.

The field was flooded by the early morning monsoon rain, making the game interesting. Each team sloshed up and down the field without scoring. Everyone was covered in mud but enjoyed playing the game.

Both teams were on the scrimmage line, ready to snap the ball, when Lieutenant CJ ran out to the field with bad news. "Hate to break up the game, but Delta Company just hit the shit again. Get your shit together and meet me on the LZ, ASAP. The birds are on their way!"

I had only three days before R & R. Why did Blackfoot have to be the choice for the quick reaction force? Everyone was frantically packing their rucksacks and replenishing their ammo.

I could only hope Lieutenant CJ would realize I was going on R & R and allow me to stay behind.

"One Shot, why are you standing around with your head up your ass? Get your shit on and get out to the LZ!" Lieutenant CJ shouted.

"Lieutenant, I'm going on R & R in three days. Have a heart," I pleaded.

"I need you out there! Now get your shit on!"

I arrived on the LZ as Lieutenant CJ began briefing his point team. "Delta Company's first platoon has encountered a battalion of NVA. Our objective is to provide additional manpower to help stabilize their situation. Get it on gentlemen, we're going into a hot AO."

Although a battalion of NVA soldiers was considerably weaker than one of our own, I remained fearful of an encounter with a force that size.

"Pop smoke, birds inbound! Sundance, Cartwright, One Shot, and the RTO, on the first bird with me!" shouted Lieutenant CJ.

There was no way to avoid a confrontation with the enemy in this situation. The LZ was not prepped prior to our arrival, and there was a good chance the first bird might be ambushed. But it didn't happen. When everyone was safely on the ground, Lieutenant CJ assembled the platoon and ordered the point team to move into the wood line.

The point team headed for the killing zone, with the sound of enemy fire leading the way. At the hundred-meter pace count, a call came in ordering us to change direction and approach the enemy's flank.

Anticipating an encounter at any moment, everyone was prepared to blast anything that moved. The point team continued to push forward, hoping the enemy would break contact before we arrived.

As the point team drew closer, minimal AK-47 fire indicated Delta Company had possibly broken contact. Lieutenant CJ was on the horn as Blackfoot moved into position.

Everyone dropped to their knees when the sound of fleeing NVA soldiers crashed through the surrounding jungle. We didn't want to fire without a clear shot. The sound of breaking brush eventually faded. Knowing the NVA soldiers had come that close to our position, I feared the platoon would get caught up in the cross fire between Delta Company and the enemy.

The point team neared the contact area, and Lieutenant CJ encouraged them to proceed with caution. He kept in contact with Delta Company's main CP in order to avoid friendly fire. The point team eventually linked up with Delta Company's first platoon. Blackfoot quickly secured the perimeter and waited for the Max gunship to arrive.

With the situation on the ground stabilized, Max brought additional fire support from the air. After several runs, Max forced the NVA to seek refuge in another area. Blackfoot Platoon's task was to help Delta Company carry their wounded back to the LZ.

The sight of the dead was a frightening reminder of death lurking in the doorway to hell, clipping his nails. Blackfoot and Aztec secured the LZ as the wounded were lifted onto the medevac and extracted from the field. I could only hope Blackfoot would return to the fire base when this was over.

Unfortunately, Delta Company's first platoon was ordered back into the wood line to continue their search for the enemy, meaning Blackfoot and Aztec would remain in the field as reinforcement. With monsoon clouds gathering above, Lieutenant CJ and his point team returned to the wood line in search of a location for the night.

Thick vegetation made for an ideal night defensive position. Everyone quickly placed their night work and settled down.

As the first watch about to begin, a series of claymores exploded in the distance, followed by a heavy barrage of machine-gun fire. My heart rate accelerated as sporadic enemy AK-47 fire indicated Delta Company had engaged another enemy force.

A call came over the horn that a small number of NVA soldiers had walked into a Delta Company ambush. One dink was killed but three NVA soldiers managed to escape. Fearing the enemy was headed in our direction, everyone prepared for a firefight.

Although the three enemy soldiers never crossed our path, Blackfoot remained alert throughout the evening. Delta Company's CO ordered an artillery strike as a torrential downpour fell on the jungle. Marking rounds confirmed Delta Company's position, and then it rained 105 artillery shells.

Hot pieces of shrapnel ricocheted off nearby trees as 105 rounds exploded within a hundred meters of our position. I pulled my poncho over my head and hugged my air mattress, preparing for a wet, sleepless night.

***

October 24. Early Sunday morning, everyone was packed, waiting for the word to pull in their night work. Rumor had it that Blackfoot would remain in the field and assist Delta Company for another two days. My only concern was making it through the ordeal for two more nights.

On high alert, there was no time for breakfast. Lieutenant CJ ordered everyone to pull in their night work and prepare to move out. With a determined enemy force in the area, it was imperative that the platoon be prepared for battle.

Blackfoot and Aztec were ordered to continue sweeping to the north, forcing the enemy into Delta Company's ambushes. Well-traveled trotters indicated we were on the trail of a large number of NVA, but no contact was made. At the end of the day, Blackfoot was ordered to set up a platoon-size ambush. Aztec, working two hundred meters to the west, would do the same. Everyone put out their claymores and trip flares and prepared for another wet, sleepless night.

***

October 25. Exhausted from a sleepless night, everyone awakened to the pitter-patter of the monsoon rain falling on the jungle. Although I was soaked by the previous night's rain, my only concern was making it through one more night.

A quick meal and everyone pulled in their night work. Blackfoot was ordered to move two hundred meters to the east to check out an abandoned logging road. Low-observation helicopters suspected the enemy had been using the road as a route of travel during the night.

Chopping through thick triple canopy for two hours was hard on morale but good for defense. The point team reached the logging road midafternoon. Footprints verified it had recently been traveled. Lieutenant CJ decided to set up a night defensive position nearby. With half the claymores facing the road, the enemy would have to face a gauntlet of firepower if they crossed our path.

The majority of second squad was ordered to set up facing the logging road. Brother Charles and Brother Al set up on the left and Bart set up on the right. I was scheduled for guard at midnight, following Bart. The jungle remained damp because of the recent rain, but with the sun coming out from behind the monsoon clouds, everyone would dry out. Since we were not allowed to set up hooches, I covered my body with my poncho and poncho liner and settled in for the evening.

The pitter-patter turned into a thundering downpour, making it impossible to get any sleep. During second watch, everyone was startled by a trip flare going off near the logging road. Assuming the enemy was about to penetrate the perimeter, I jumped to my knees, reaching for my weapon. I was ready to squeeze the trigger.

Then I was blinded by the bright flame of another trip flare glowing in the dark. I low-crawled to the nearest tree, a thick cloud of smoke making it difficult to see. Brother Charles low-crawled to be by my side.

Together Brother Charles and I waited cautiously as the flare burned in the night. Curious to know what had tripped it, everyone was focused on the road. A shadow was cast on the logging road. Everyone feared it was the enemy. The smoldering remains of the trip flare were reduced to an ember. The sound of footprints continued to approach the perimeter.

A wild boar strolled into the perimeter.

"Damn, that was scary, Jarcia," whispered Brother Charles.

"Yeah, I thought it was a dink," I said nervously.

The wild boar continued on its way as the night returned to dark. Relieved that it was not a battalion of NVA soldiers, I returned to my sleeping position. I pulled my poncho liner over my head and tried to get a little sleep before guard duty.

"One Shot, it's your turn," said a familiar voice.

"All right, I'm up," I answered.

I was handed the illuminated watch and pointed in the direction of the guard station. The perimeter was dark due to a thick layer of clouds hovering above. Standing, I took a deep breath of moist jungle air and felt my way to the guard station.

I stopped along the way to take a piss. I assumed I was going on the jungle floor. Unfortunately …

"What the hell are you doing?" said an angry voice.

"Sorry, I didn't realize anyone was down there," I said regretfully, zipping up my fatigue pants.

The fact I had accidentally urinated on Billy meant I was nowhere near the guard station. Stumbling around in the dark, I frantically felt my way along the jungle floor. It wasn't until I heard static from the radio that I was able to locate the guard station.

Relieved that I hadn't ended up outside the perimeter, I began my watch. I glanced at the illuminated watch every five minutes. Time passed slowly. To help it along, I kept occupied with thoughts of Adela, the attractive French hooker.

With only five minutes of guard time remaining, I managed to do the unthinkable: I fell asleep. I dreamed of a comforting, warm bed. Nothing else mattered.

A sudden roar of thunder brought me back to reality, and I registered the chilling presence of two NVA soldiers only twenty meters away. My heart rate accelerated with fear. Lightning only confirmed their identities. They had their weapons drawn. I was certain they knew of the platoon's presence.

I needed to make a decision. If the enemy penetrated the perimeter, the platoon would no longer be protected by claymores. I didn't want to risk the safety of the platoon not knowing how many NVA soldiers were present.

Placing both hands on the clackers, I waited for the lightning. It came, and revealed the enemy had moved down the road. Bart rolled over and began snoring. I prayed that the heavy monsoon rain muffled the sound of his grumbling snore.

Relieved that the two NVA soldiers had left the area, my heart rate returned to normal. I could have taken out both enemy soldiers, but not engaging the enemy in the dark was the right decision.

It appeared the two enemy soldiers were strays and not part of the battalion Delta Company had encountered. Once again, I was in the right place at the wrong time.

Bart began snoring again, and I quickly covered his mouth. "Bart, wake up!"

"Who's that?" he said.

"Your snoring just about got us killed!"

"Killed? What the hell you talking about?"

"Go back to sleep and don't snore. You just might not wake up tomorrow."

"What did you say?"

"Never mind. Go back to sleep."

Bart rolled over on his stomach and fell asleep. It was fifteen minutes past the end of my guard—time to wake Brother Charles. No one was aware of my encounter with the two NVA soldiers. I probably should have notified Lieutenant CJ, but decided to wait until morning to advise him.

The roar of the thunder and lightning had stopped, making it difficult to find my replacement's sleeping area. I had a general idea, but I became disoriented. Without the help of fluorescent moss on the jungle floor, I had to feel my way.

"Brother Charles," I whispered, hoping someone would hear me. I was getting desperate and starting to panic.

Fortunately, I came across one of the electrical wires leading to a claymore. The wire led back to the guard station. It was my only chance. When I felt a claymore, I knew I was in trouble. I'd followed the wire in the wrong direction and ended up on the logging road. Careful not to disturb the trip flare, I felt my way back to the guard station, hoping no one had heard me.

Relieved to be back at the guard station, I decided to remain on watch. Wet, exhausted, and frightened, I considered myself lucky.

***

October 26. At the break of dawn, Sundance noticed I was on last watch. Curious to know why, he made his way to the guard station to inquire.

"You had the midnight watch; why are you pulling last guard?" asked Sundance, looking puzzled.

"You won't believe what happened last night," I replied.

"It must have been really bad for you to pull everyone's guard duty."

"First of all, I accidentally pissed on Billy. Then there were two NVA soldiers strolling down the logging road. They eventually moved on, but it was a miracle they didn't hear Bart snoring. To make matters worse, when my guard was over, I got lost and ended up on the logging road. By the time I found my way back to the guard station, I decided it was safer to stay and pull everyone's guard."

"With that story, you should be grateful you made it through the night."

"Grateful! There's nothing to be grateful for. I just want to get out of this mess and go on R & R."

"I know something you can be grateful for."

"Yeah, what's that?"

"It stopped raining!"

I could only chuckle. I began waking everyone. When I reached Lieutenant CJ's sleeping position, he looked surprised. "Why are you waking everyone up?"

"Don't ask," I said.

I decided not to tell him about last night's frightening encounter. Besides, he probably wouldn't have believed my story anyway.

Eager to leave the field, I prepared a canteen cup of hot cocoa. When I pulled in my night work, I couldn't believe how disoriented I had become last night. I was lucky no one had heard me and blown a claymore.

The objective for the day was to cut out an LZ. Blackfoot was to remain in the field for another three days. Unfortunately, this was the day Jet was scheduled to join the platoon. I hoped there would be enough time for a visit.

Lieutenant CJ found a suitable location for resupply, and the platoon began clearing the LZ. Several trees were much too large to be cleared by machete, so the CO called in a demolition team.

The demolition team arrived by helicopter, rappelling to the jungle floor. The team quickly determined the trees that needed to come down and wired explosives to them. Everyone pulled back into the jungle.

"Fire in the hole! Fire in the hole!" cried the demolition team leader.

A few seconds later, there were several loud blasts. The trees fell to the ground, and everyone returned to the LZ.

Thirty minutes later, Lieutenant CJ cried out, "Pop smoke, birds inbound!"

I waited eagerly for the first bird to arrive, hoping to see Jet's familiar face. When it touched down, the door gunner kicked out a water blivet, but there was no sign of Jet. The demolition team climbed aboard, and the bird lifted off the LZ.

The second bird delivered C-rations and LRPs, along with the top sergeant, but no one else. "Is there anyone else coming out?" I asked him.

"I'm not sure, but there might be one or two."

The third bird arrived with the mail bag and two duffel bags of clean clothes, but no sign of my friend.

"One Shot, you better be on the backlog bird, or you'll miss your R & R."

Uncertain if I would be reunited with my friend, I waited.

"One Shot, get ready. The last bird is on the way. I'm sorry about your friend, but you better get your ass on that bird!" shouted Sundance.

Reuniting with Jet would have to wait until I returned. The final bird skimmed over the treetops and set down on the LZ. I said good-bye to all my friends and picked up my gear.

As I slung my rucksack over my shoulder, there was Jet stepping off the skid of the helicopter.

It was just like Jet to make an entrance on the last bird of the day. He gave me a big hug, and we were able to talk briefly.

"Where have you been?" I shouted.

"I wasn't in any hurry to come out," said Jet.

"I'll see you when I get back. The guys in the platoon will tell you everything you need to know about Blackfoot."

"Where are you going?" asked Jet, with a concerned look.

"I'm going to Sydney, Australia. Don't worry. The guys will take care of you. We'll talk when I get back."

I climbed into the cabin. Jet's look of uncertainty concerned me as the helicopter lifted off the LZ and cleared the trees.

Episode Twenty-Seven

Kings Cross

October 26. With a clear view of the South China Sea, the pilot set course for Fire Base Mace. I expected that I would spend the night and be convoyed to Bien Hoa in the morning. The pilot circled the fire base several times, waiting for clearance to land. The fire base was under mortar attack, and the landing strip needed to be cleared prior to landing.

Arriving safely, I picked up a pair of clean fatigues and headed for the barracks. Seated on a cot was an unshaven soldier with "Kill a Gook for God" written on the camouflaged cover of his steel pot. Meticulously cleaning his weapon, he hadn't realized I'd entered the barracks.

"You're new around here?" I asked.

"Yep, I just arrived," said the grunt.

"What's your name?"

"They call me Rebel, Reb for short."

"What unit are you with?" I asked.

"Echo Recon."

"You'll fit right in, believe me."

"Where you headed, soldier?" asked Rebel.

"I'm going on R & R."

"I don't take any R & Rs. They're a waste of time. I'd rather be in the field, killing gooks," boasted Rebel.

"How long have you been in country?" I asked.

"Just a month, but it's my third tour."

"Your third tour."

"Yeah, two tours with the Marines and another with the army. When the dinks got me in the leg, it was the end of my

340

second tour. When the Marines refused to send me back, I joined the army, and here I am."

"Why would anyone want to come back to Vietnam?"

"I love Vietnam. Don't you?"

"Hell no, I can hardly wait to get the hell out of this place," I replied.

"Shit! This tour I'll do standing on my head. When I was over here in 1968, I was involved in over 240 firefights. How many firefights have you had?"

"I've had my share."

"Sure you have. You're still a cherry," said Reb, chuckling as he continued cleaning his weapon.

Rebel's name suited him perfectly. Wearing a pair of wire-rim glasses and a boonie hat with the brim folded up on one side, the soldier resembled a young Theodore Roosevelt. He cleaned his weapon like he was making love to a woman. Although Reb was a little strange, his jungle-wise experience would be welcome in Echo Recon.

***

October 27. After breakfast, I was on a convoy headed for Bien Hoa Air Force Base. Two hours later, we rolled into battalion's recently relocated headquarters. I checked in my weapon and rucksack and picked up my mail. I received a letter from Dad and another from a hometown friend.

In the letter, my friend wrote that he was in trouble and needed help financially. I felt he must be in serious trouble. Since I had earned a large amount of combat pay, I didn't mind helping a friend in need.

Stopping by finance, I exchanged MPC for good old American greenbacks. I withdrew an additional amount of cash along with a cashier's check to bail out my friend. Then I was on my way to the First Team Academy storage unit. I retrieved all my civilian clothing along with a pair of dress shoes, and I was ready for R & R.

***

October 29. After breakfast, I went to headquarters to pick up my R & R documents. They authorized me to leave battalion headquarters. I gathered my belongings and headed for the First Cav R & R Center.

The clerk at the center reviewed my orders, authorizing bus transportation to the special services center in Tan Son Nhut. The driver took the usual route through the village and entered the Camp Alpha compound.

The center's personnel directed everyone to the office to turn in orders for processing. We were given a pillow and barracks assignment. Then everyone was free to do as they pleased until dinner.

At dinnertime, I enjoyed a cool green salad with well-seasoned vinaigrette dressing, home-style mashed potatoes, gravy, green beans, and a nicely prepared, medium-rare New York steak, washing it all down with a tall glass of ice-cold lemonade. Although I was pleasantly satisfied, I couldn't resist the rich chocolate cake for dessert.

Required to attend a mandatory orientation, I was directed to the conference room. I took a seat next to a soldier who introduced himself as Stan. We listened to the orientation. The officer discussed all the rules about behavior, language, and standard of dress, along with recommendations for restaurants and hotels in the area.

Stan recommended the Texas Tavern, located in Potts Point.

"Have you heard about the Bay View? I was told the rates are cheap and the location is near the nightlife," I replied.

"I going to stay at the Texas Tavern," said the soldier.

After the boring orientation, Stan invited me to join him for a drink. At the EM club, we found two seats at the bar.

"What's your MOS?" asked Stan.

"11B20, light weapons infantry. In other words, I'm a grunt," I said proudly.

"How many kills do you have?"

"Not enough to get me out of the field."

"How does it feel knowing you killed someone?" Stan asked.

"I deal with it. What's your job?"

"My job isn't anything like yours. I'm a clerk, assigned to a compound in Saigon."

"So you're a REMF."

"Yes, I'm a REMF, and proud of it," replied Stan.

We enjoyed the entertainment until the band played their last song for the evening. I returned to my assigned barracks, and as soon as my head hit the pillow, I was asleep.

***

October 30. I was awakened by an announcement over the loudspeaker. Excited to begin my R & R, I jumped to my feet and headed for the shower.

Showered and dressed in civilian clothing, I headed for the mess hall for breakfast. I enjoyed two over-medium eggs, hash browns, bacon, slightly burned toast, and a strong cup of coffee. I was ready for my visit to Australia. I returned to the barracks to retrieve my personal belongings, then headed for the bus stop.

A representative from Camp Alpha accompanied us to the airport. A Pan American jetliner awaited our arrival.

Prior to boarding, our duffel bags were inspected by customs. Everyone promptly cleared customs and boarded the aircraft. At the top of the stairs were two attractive stewardesses who eagerly welcomed me aboard. I located my assigned aisle seat and prepared for takeoff.

"Fasten your seatbelt, please. We're about to take off," said one stewardess politely.

"Where you from, gorgeous?" I asked.

"I'm from Kansas."

"I know someone from Kansas," I replied.

"Yeah, who's that?"

"Dorothy, the character in *The Wizard of Oz*," I said, chuckling.

"Yeah, that's delightful," she said sarcastically, and attended to another soldier.

The flight tower cleared the pilot for takeoff. The jetliner lifted off the runway, and we were on our way to Sydney.

"Good morning, I'm Captain Kent Ringborn. On the behalf of Pan American Airlines, I would like to welcome everyone aboard flight 927 to Sydney, Australia," said the pilot over the loudspeaker, as the plane ascended to 30,000 feet.

After a longer than expected flight time, we started our descent into the Sydney's international airport. As we approached the runway, I looked out the window, noticing a

344

resemblance to San Francisco, California. The jetliner touched down and taxied to the Pan American terminal. Everyone picked up their personal belongings and eagerly departed the plane.

We were met by an R & R representative and escorted to waiting transportation. The bus took a route along a steep, sloping street. I learned that Australians drive on the opposite side of the road from Americans.

The driver delivered the group to the R & R reception center, where we were escorted to the second-floor briefing room. A navy lieutenant dressed in khakis gave us another lengthy briefing on codes of conduct and standard of dress. For some reason, American troops needed to be constantly reminded how to behave among civilians.

The lieutenant ended his briefing with an invitation. "Tonight, the reception center is sponsoring a 'Get to Know You' dance at 7:00 p.m. If you would like to meet an attractive Australian USO girl, I highly recommend you attend. Coffee and doughnuts will be served, along with a rock and roll band for entertainment. This is one of several events sponsored by the reception center during your stay."

"Can we ask the USO girls for a date?" asked one of the soldiers.

"You'll just have to attend and find out. If you enjoy the dance, you can return for another scheduled on Wednesday. Also, if you are caught swearing or found drunk in public, you might be fined up to eighty dollars, and that's not the way to spend your money while on R & R. All right boys, I'll see you in seven days. If you are not here by the time the bus leaves for the airport, you are considered AWOL. Enjoy your R & R, gentlemen." The lieutenant concluded the briefing by directing everyone to exchange their MPC for Australian currency.

I exchanged the entire amount of American currency in my wallet and received several denominations of Australian bills. Australian currency was larger than American currency, and a lot more colorful. The smaller bills were printed with kangaroos, koala bears, and a strange-looking creature called an emu. The larger bills depicted with some lady of royalty.

"Transportation is leaving for Kings Cross in thirty minutes!" shouted the navy lieutenant.

This gave me time to go downstairs to the men's department store, located in the basement of the reception center, to shop for a few more shirts and ties. On display was a stylish, cream-colored, three-piece suit. Attracted by the vest and bell-bottom pants, I asked the salesman to allow me to try it on. He removed the jacket, vest, and pants from the rack and escorted me to the dressing room.

Slipping into the trousers, I buttoned the vest and tried on the matching coat. I returned to the floor and checked the outfit in the mirror.

"It fits perfectly, sir," said the salesman, brushing the sleeves of the coat.

"Yeah, it fits so nicely, I'm tempted to wear it out of the store," I said jokingly.

"How about a few ties and shirts to go along with your new suit, sir?"

The salesman picked out a few ties and shirts to match and folded everything neatly into a paper bag. "That will be $97.57, sir," he said, punching the keys on the cash register.

I handed him two crisp fifty-dollar Australian bills. The bus was about to depart. I grabbed the bag of merchandise and hurried up the stairs.

"Your change, sir!" cried the salesman.

"Keep it!"

"It's two dollars and change, sir."

"It's yours!" I shouted.

"Thank you, sir, and enjoy your stay in Sydney," said the salesman enthusiastically as I headed out the door.

"Welcome to Sydney, mate," said the bus driver as I stepped onto the bus.

"Thank you," I replied, quickly taking a seat.

"I'll be driving through Kings Cross, stopping at the major hotels. When you see your hotel, let me know and I'll stop," said the driver.

The driver made several stops before arriving at the Texas Tavern. Curious to investigate the popular hotel, I decided to step off the bus. I expected more of a western flare than my quicktour of the place showed me. But after seeing the secluded bar and a stage filled with band instruments, I decided to give the Texas Tavern a chance.

"Can I help you?" asked the clerk at the registration desk.

"I want to check in," I replied.

"Where you from, soldier?"

"Vietnam."

"No, I mean back in the States," replied the clerk, chuckling.

"I'm from California."

"What part?"

"Bakersfield," I answered proudly, expecting he'd never heard of it.

"I know where Bakersfield is. I drove through several times on my way to San Francisco. The room will be twenty dollars for the night or a hundred and twenty for the week," said the clerk.

"I'll stay the night. If I like it, I'll come back and pay for the rest of the week," I replied.

"What's not to like? There's a coffee shop and nightclub, and the hospitality is the best in Kings Cross," said the clerk confidently.

Eager to get to my room, I filled out the registration card and returned it to the clerk, along with twenty dollars. He escorted me to my room.

"What's your name?" I asked.

"Johnny."

"You don't have an Australian accent."

"Because I'm American, like you," he said.

"What are you doing in Sydney?"

"I served in Vietnam in sixty-nine. When I came to Australia for R & R, I fell in love with the country. I met an Australian girl and married her. I've been living in Kings Cross ever since."

Slipping the key into the keyhole, Johnny opened the door. The room was larger than I expected and came with a view of the brick and mortar of the adjacent building. It wasn't the view that interested me as much as the queen-size bed.

"Enjoy your stay at the Texas Tavern. If you need anything, just call the front desk and ask for Johnny."

I handed Johnny five dollars, but he refused the tip and left the room. I tried to plug my cassette player into the wall outlet, but discovered the plug configuration was different from the standard American outlet. Eager to enjoy my R & R, I headed to the coffee shop for a late lunch.

I was greeted by a tall, blonde waitress wearing a pink uniform, who kindly escorted me to a booth. Handing me a menu, she took my drink order.

I hadn't eaten since breakfast, so all the items on the menu appeared appetizing. When the waitress returned to take my order, I decided on a hot turkey sandwich and another large glass of Coke.

In no time, the waitress returned with the meal, placing a napkin and eating utensils on the table. I expected a sandwich with lettuce and tomato. Instead, I was served mashed potatoes on white bread with slices of turkey smothered in white gravy. Never having had the pleasure of eating a hot turkey sandwich, I enjoyed every morsel. After the comforting meal, I was ready for Kings Cross. I tipped the waitress two dollars and paid the bill.

Strolling through the lobby, I was distracted by the sound of music coming from the Texas Tavern lounge. Soldiers from different branches of the military were enjoying a midafternoon cocktail, so I decided to join them. My intention was to have a drink and leave, but a soldier dressed in air force attire involved me in a conversation.

"Are you here on R & R?" asked the soldier.

"Yes, how about you?" I replied.

"I just flew in today. I'm Kenny from Kansas."

"So did I, I'm Ricky from California," I said, shaking Kenny's hand firmly.

"I hear those California girls are really something."

"They sure are. Where you stationed, Kenny?"

"The Royal Thai Air Force Base in Thailand. My squadron is responsible for the majority of air strikes against North Vietnam. Where are you?"

"I'm a grunt. My unit is currently working in Long Kanh Province," I said.

"Do you mind telling me about the war?" asked Kenny.

"No, I don't mind," I replied and began telling my story,

Like others willing to listen, Kenny was enthusiastic, curious to know what it was like to kill or be killed. After hearing my story, Kenny believed I had nine lives—just like a cat.

"That was amazing. That calls for a shot of tequila," he said.

The bartender brought over two shot glasses of cheap tequila. Kenny raised his and made a toast: "Here's to the grunts in the field."

"Thanks," I replied, pouring the cheap tequila down my throat.

"This one's on me, mate. You guys deserve it," said the Australian bartender, placing two more shots on the bar.

After the third shot, I lost count. Unexpectedly, a rugged Australian with a flattop haircut placed his arm delicately around Kenny's shoulder.

"How's it going, mates?" said the friendly Australian.

"Okay, how about you?" Kenny replied.

"Would you like to join me for a drink at the pub down the street? The drinks are cheap and the mates are a hell of a lot friendlier," said the rugged Australian.

Oblivious to the Australian's intentions, Kenny agreed.

"Are you sure you want to go with the Aussie?" said the bartender, as if he was trying to warn Kenny about something.

Kenny and I had no problem taking advantage of the Australian's hospitality and staggered out the front door. The three of us walked hand in hand down the street and entered a pub filled with patrons. The rugged Australian escorted us to the bar, shoving others aside, making room for Kenny and me.

"A round of drinks for my new mates," said the rugged Australian, laughing hysterically as he rubbed Kenny's rear end. Not having a comfortable feeling, I noticed there were no women in the pub. Then I witnessed two Australians fondling each other, and realized this wasn't an average pub. I pushed the brawny Australian aside and reached for Kenny's arm.

"Run, Kenny!" I shouted, pulling him out of the pub.

"What the hell is going on?" cried Kenny, stumbling out the door.

"It's a fag bar!" I shouted, scurrying up the street.

Kenny stumbled with five stout Australians close behind. I helped Kenny to his feet, and we continued to run. When we reached the entrance to the Texas Tavern, the five stout Australians were not allowed to enter.

Exhausted and intoxicated, Kenny and I took seats at the bar.

"I tried to warn you," said the bartender, unable to hide his laughter.

"This is your fault," muttered Kenny to me.

"Wait a minute, air force man. The big Australian was rubbing your ass, not mine!" I shouted.

"Oh yeah? Well, fuck the army!" Kenny shouted.

"What does the army have to do with it?"

"Because I said so," said Kenny, belligerently drunk.

"No, fuck the air force. And if you don't like it, step outside."

"All right, let's go," slurred Kenny, sliding off the barstool.

Kenny and I staggered out the front door. Blinded by the setting sun, I reached back to land the first punch.

The following morning, I opened my eyes to a painful tequila hangover. Unable to remember how I got to the room, I reached for my wallet. Realizing it was missing, I could only blame myself for being so careless. Without any money, I wondered how I was going spend the rest of my R & R.

I managed to get out of bed, and I noticed my wallet lying on the carpet. I didn't bother to pick it up because I knew the money would be gone. Forcing myself to take a shower, I held my head under cold running water, trying to relieve the pain.

As I dressed, I found a few dollars in my pocket. I reached for my wallet. When I looked inside, I was thrilled to find my Australian currency. Relieved that no one had taken the money, I decided to check out of the hotel. Severely dehydrated and with pain radiating from my head to my toes, I packed my duffel bag and headed for the lobby.

"Good morning, Mr. Garcia. How did you sleep last night?" Johnny asked with a big grin.

"I don't know because I was really drunk last night," I replied.

"Boy, you and your friend really got wasted. You guys put on a show for everyone, especially when you passed out in the middle of the street," said Johnny, laughing.

"How did I get to my room?"

"I slung you over my shoulder and carried you."

"Thanks for looking out for me."

"Where you going?" asked Johnny.

"Nothing personal, but the Texas Tavern isn't for me," I replied.

"Where else can you get a good home-cooked meal, listen to music, dance, and pick up Australian girls?"

"I can't, I'm too embarrassed," I replied.

I offered Johnny twenty dollars for hauling me to my room, but again he refused the money. Sorry to see me leave, he recommended a list of nightclubs in the Kings Cross and Potts Point areas. His suggestions included the Groovy Room, Whisky a Go-Go, and, if I was looking for soul, the Cheetah Room. He also mentioned a few bars featuring totally nude dancers. At this point, all I wanted was to check into the Bay View and sleep off my painful hangover.

Nauseated and dehydrated, I headed to the bar for a cold drink. Fortunately for me, there was another bartender on duty. I ordered a Coke with plenty of ice. It tasted disgusting, but I drank it anyway. The smell of cigarette smoke upset my stomach, and I had to rush to the toilet.

I heaved my guts out, trying to relieve the pain. Resting my head on the toilet, I fell asleep. When I opened my eyes, an hour had slipped by. The bus was due to arrive, so I jumped to my feet and rushed for the exit.

"Good luck, Mr. Garcia," said Johnny as I ran through the lobby.

The bus driver was pulling away when he saw me in his rearview mirror. Luckily for me, he stopped and opened the door. "Where you headed, mate?"

"Bay View, please," I replied.

"Bay View it is, but if you want to ride, you better pay the toll mate," said the driver, closing the door behind me.

I paid the toll and headed for the back of the bus. Stretched out on the rear seat, I waited for the driver to announce the next stop.

"Bay View!" shouted the driver.

I grabbed my duffel bag and stepped off the bus. Entering the building, I headed for the lobby.

"Can I help you?" asked the nicely dressed, elderly gentleman working behind the desk.

"Do you have a room available?"

"Certainly."

"What's the rate?"

"Five dollars a night, sir."

"Five dollars a night? That's cheap. I just paid twenty to stay at the Texas Tavern," I replied.

"How long are you planning on staying with us?"

"Six days."

"That will be thirty dollars, sir. Here is your key. Your room is located on the fifth floor. Enjoy your stay with us, sir," said the kind elderly gentleman.

Still nursing a hangover, I stepped into the elevator. To my surprise, I entered a nicely furnished suite that included a living room, kitchen, and bedroom. It had a panoramic view of downtown Kings Cross. I was pleased with my decision to move to the Bay View.

After a couple of hours of desperately needed rest, I was able to stomach a meal. From the window overlooking the street, I noticed a small mom-and-pop store. Making my way downstairs, I headed for the exit. I thought it was safe to cross the street but was nearly hit by oncoming traffic.

"Don't you Yanks ever look where you're going?" shouted an irritated driver.

Not accustomed to seeing vehicles on the left side of the road, I had neglected to look in the opposite direction. I crossed the street and entered the store. The cashier greeted me with a smile, amid the wonderful aroma of rotisserie chicken, I reached into the cold box for a carbonated drink. Grabbing a loaf of French bread, I returned to the cash register.

"Will that be all, mate?" asked the elderly clerk.

"How about a roasted chicken?" I replied.

"You're lucky. I have one left. It's my most popular item."

He placed the roasted chicken into a thermal pouch and bagged the bread and soda. Hungry for a delicious feast, I hurried back to my apartment, this time crossing the road with caution.

I devoured a whole chicken, loaf of bread and bottle of soda. I was ready for the nightlife. In preparation for going out, I hung my three-piece suit on the curtain rod. I hoped the steam from a hot shower would eliminate any wrinkles.

After my shower, I slipped into my cream-colored suit and stood in front of the mirror, admiring a well-dressed young man. Calling down to the elderly gentleman at the front desk, I requested a cab.

"Mr. Rick, you look very nice tonight. Where are you headed?" he asked when I came down.

"I'm going to the Groovy Room," I replied.

"Your cab is waiting."

"What's your name?"

"Call me Jonathan, Mr. Rick."

"Jonathan, thank you," I responded, handing him a generous tip.

The cab driver was waiting with the door open. "Where are you headed tonight?"

"The Groovy Room, please," I replied.

"The Groovy Room it is, young man."

The cab rolled up to the Groovy Room. "Welcome," said the doorman in his long coat and hat.

I entered the club and was greeted by a waitress with attractive long legs and a pair of purple hot pants. She took my hand and escorted me to a table. "What would you like to drink?" she asked.

"How about a rum and soda," I replied.

The band began their set with a familiar number by a popular underground group. The group featured four musicians: a drummer, two guitarists, and vocalist.

The music was great, but there weren't many single girls to dance with. I listened to a few more songs and decided to head for the Whisky.

"Are you leaving?" asked the waitress.

"There's no girls to dance with," I replied.

"The night's young. There will be plenty of girls later. Come back, you'll see," said the waitress.

The doorman directed me to the Whisky. The club was only a few blocks away, so I decided to walk. Besides, it would give me an opportunity to see the window displays. The shops carried clothing with a European flair: stylish bell-bottoms, paisley shirts, and an assortment of colorful men's scarves.

A marquee displayed "Whisky" in lights. Eager to join the party, I wasted no time getting there. A friendly doorman greeted me, and I paid a two-dollar cover charge to enter the popular nightclub. It showcased two bars. I began my adventure in the discotheque on the street level.

"Nice suit," said a cocktail waitress, carrying a tray of drinks.

"Thank you," I replied, scanning the nightclub.

"Would you like to sit upstairs or downstairs?"

"What's going on downstairs?"

"There's a great band," she answered.

I decided to explore the pub downstairs, where an enthusiastic crowd was enjoying the music of a three-piece band. Taking a seat at the bar, I clapped my hands to the music.

"What will it be, mate?" asked the Australian bartender.

"Budweiser, please."

"Sorry, mate, no American beers down here."

"What do you recommend?"

"I recommend one of our finer pale ales."

"Then pale ale it is," I replied.

"What size, mate?"

The bartender pointed to several sizes. I settled for a pint. He served it up with a nice head of foam. It had an oatmeal aftertaste, but it was stout. I felt the effect of the alcohol after the first pint. I ordered another as I listened to the band perform a popular number.

I notice a girl sitting in a booth. She appeared to be alone, so I casually walked over and ask her to dance.

"No thanks, but you can buy me a drink," she replied.

"Are you alone?"

"No, I'm with a friend," she replied.

"What's your name?" I asked.

"Diana."

Diana's friend returned to the table and was introduced as Beth. I ordered a round of drinks and waited for the waitress to return. Diana and Beth were entertaining, but not my type. Knowing I was an American, the girls insisted I stay.

"Where you from, soldier?" asked Beth.

"California."

"We love guys from California," said Diana and starting singing the lyrics to a popular Beach Boys song. The waitress returned with the drinks, and I paid the bill. Eager to return to the party on the first floor, I headed up the stairs.

The popular discotheque was crowded with American soldiers. I noticed a seat next to two single girls, so I wandered over.

"Hi, I'm Ricky," I said.

The girls politely introduced themselves as Sonya and Audra. Like the two girls downstairs, they were also interested in California. I wasn't sure about the attraction, but I surely enjoyed their curiosity.

"Have you been to Disneyland?" asked Sonya.

"Sure, when I was twelve. My parents took me to Disneyland for my birthday. All I wanted to do was ride Mr. Toad's Wild Ride," I said.

"Tell us about Disneyland," said Audra.

The girls were amazed as I described Disneyland's main attractions, and so was the attractive blonde across the way. Seated with an older couple, the girl listened enthusiastically as I described Walt Disney's popular theme park.

"That cute little blonde has her eyes on you," said Audra.

"I guess she's curious to hear about Disneyland too," I said jokingly.

"Why don't you introduce yourself? We're going downstairs," said Sonya.

"Where are you staying?" asked Audra.

"The Bay View," I replied.

"You're more than welcome to join us," said Sonya.

"Thanks for the invitation. I'll see you downstairs later," I said.

The cute blonde's father noticed I was coming his way. He stood up and introduced himself.

"Hello, my name is William, and this is my wife Lily and lovely daughter Sasha," said William.

"Nice to meet you," I replied.

"What's your name?" asked Sasha.

"Ricky," I replied.

"Would you like to join us?" asked William.

Accepting William's invitation, I took a seat next to Sasha.

"I'm happy you decided to join us," said Sasha, reaching for my hand.

"Where are you from?" asked Lily.

"California," I replied.

"That's nice," said Lily.

"Are you Australian?" I asked William.

"Our parents are English, but Lily and I were both born in Melbourne," William explained.

"Are your parents always this nice to strangers?" I asked Sasha.

"I hope you don't think my parents are strange. They just like to extend their hospitality to American soldiers fighting in Vietnam. They understand you're a long way from home and want to have a good time," said Sasha.

"Would you like to dance?" I asked.

"I'd love to," she replied.

I spent the evening with William and his family, never having the opportunity to go downstairs and join Audra and Sonja.

"What are your plans for tomorrow?" asked William.

"I really haven't decided." I replied.

"We would love to show you around Sydney, if you would allow us."

"Sure, why not?"

"Are you staying in Kings Cross?" asked Lily.

"Yes, at the Bay View."

I told William and his family the story about the incident at Texas Tavern, and they laughed. When the disc jockey announced the last song of the evening, it was the perfect opportunity to end the night. I led Sasha to the dance floor, holding her tightly, her head leaning on my shoulder.

"Your hair smells great," I said to her.

"Did you have a good time tonight?" she asked.

"I had a great time. I enjoyed talking with your parents."

The dance ended and we returned to the table.

"It was a pleasure meeting you, Lily," I said as I prepared to leave.

"Why don't you come home with us, and I'll cook you a wonderful meal."

"Yeah, Ricky, Mother is a great cook," said Sasha.

I went against my better judgment and agreed to go. I sat in the backseat of the family car as William pointed out a few landmarks. Sasha held my hand the entire way.

Arriving at their modest two-story flat, William and Lily proudly welcomed me to their home. Built on a hillside, the flat had a breathtaking view of Elizabeth Bay.

Lily headed for the kitchen and William opened a couple Fosters lagers. After a night of cocktails, the size of the can was a little intimidating, but I couldn't refuse William's generosity.

William took a seat as he discussed the itinerary for tomorrow. Lily worked diligently in the kitchen, and Sasha set the table.

"Come and get it," Lily announced proudly.

The servings were generous and the taste was delightful. I feasted on a grilled piece of meat with a slice of buttered French bread, along with deep-fried potatoes and pasta. I had just met William's family, and now I was sharing a home-cooked meal in the family dining room.

After a wonderful meal, Lily and William cleared the table while Sasha and I sat in the living room.

"I better get going. We have a long day ahead of us," I said to Sasha.

"Nonsense, you're spending the night and I don't want to hear anything more about it," said Lily.

"Yes, it's late. Spend the night and we'll pick up your things in the morning," said William as he headed upstairs for bed.

Sasha took my hand and led me upstairs. "You can sleep in the guest room," she said.

Sasha opened the door to a room at the end of the hall and led me in. The room appeared to be occupied by a teenager. It was lined with dusty rock and roll posters and seemed not to have been slept in for a while.

I sat on the edge of the bed, and Sasha sat on my lap, giving me a long kiss. "What's that for?" I asked.

"That's for joining us tonight," replied Sasha.

Listening to Sasha talk, I laid my head on the pillow and fell into a deep sleep.

The following morning, I was awakened by the sun shining through the bedroom window. Sasha was lying beside me. My three-piece suit was neatly folded on the chair beside the bed. I tried to dress without waking Sasha, but she opened her eyes.

"How did you sleep last night?" she asked.

"Wonderfully, thanks to you and your family," I replied.

Sasha led me to the shower. The aroma of fried bacon made its way to the second floor.

Showered and dressed, I met the family downstairs. William was sitting at the kitchen table, reading the local newspaper and drinking a cup of coffee. Lily prepared breakfast.

"How did you sleep, Ricky?" asked William.

"Great, sir," I answered respectfully. I could only wonder if William knew his daughter had spent the night with me.

"How do you like your eggs?" Lily asked.

"You don't have to make me breakfast," I replied.

"Nonsense, you're a growing young man. You need to start the day with a good breakfast. You never know when it could be your last."

"That wasn't appropriate to say to Rick," said William.

"It was just a figure of speech, William. I didn't mean anything by it. How do you like your eggs, Ricky?"

"All right, you talked me into it. Sunny-side up, please."

Lily brought breakfast to the table as William planned out the day. After breakfast, Lily prepared a picnic basket for lunch.

First stop was the Sydney Opera House, still under construction. William was employed by one of the construction companies. William proudly showed us around, pointing out the work he was responsible for.

For lunch, William found a nice, shady location in a nearby national park, where we enjoyed a picnic. Sitting under a tall, native hoop pine, we enjoyed a bottle of Australian wine and food prepared by Lily.

Then William took us down to Elizabeth Bay. Lily shopped while Sasha and I enjoyed a charming stroll along the waters of the harbor. That evening, we dined at an outdoor café overlooking Lavender Bay, ending the evening at the Groovy Room, dancing the night away.

We returned to the flat, exhausted from the day's activities. William and Lily said good night and turned in. Sasha and I stepped onto the balcony and enjoyed the cool Elizabeth Bay breeze.

"I want to thank you and your parents for your overwhelming hospitality. I never expected my visit to Australia to be like this," I said, kissing her cheek.

"My parents enjoy your company," replied Sasha.

"I know, but I feel I'm taking advantage of your family."

"Nonsense, my parents are just trying to show you how much they appreciate you."

"Seriously, I feel like I'm infringing on your family's privacy. I think it's time to head back to the Bay View."

"My mother and father invited you to stay with us because they want you to enjoy your visit. Why can't you understand that?" said Sasha in a firm tone.

"I'm sorry, but I've never been treated so nicely by strangers," I replied.

Sasha leaned her head on my shoulder and began to cry.

"Why are you crying?" I said with sympathy.

"Because my brother was killed in Vietnam, and I miss him," said Sasha, wiping the tears from her cheeks.

"What happened?" I asked.

"My brother was assigned to an APC squadron in the Royal Australian Regiment. He was killed when his APC ran over a land mine. He was my parents' only son. Since then, my parents have only wanted to reach out to the American soldiers fighting in Vietnam."

"I'm so sorry," I replied. As an only son, I understood their pain.

Sasha pleaded with me to spend another day, but knowing about her brother's death only made feel guilty. Sasha convinced me to spend the night and leave in the morning. That night in bed, she wrapped her arms around me and never let me go.

The following morning I was up early. I wanted to offer Sasha two hundred dollars for her family's hospitality, but I knew she wouldn't accept it. So while she was asleep, I placed the money, along with a note, under Sasha's jewelry box. I quietly left the room and flagged down a cab.

On the drive to the Bay View, I seriously considered spending the rest of my R & R with Sasha. I was fortunate to have been taken in by her family, and would probably regret leaving their generous hospitality, but it was a chance I had to take.

Back at the Bay View, Jonathan's familiar face was at the front desk to greet me.

"Good morning Mr. Rick. Where have you been? I haven't seen you in a while. Are you enjoying your stay with us?"

"I've been enjoying your Australian hospitality."

"Oh, by the way, Mr. Rick, two good-looking admirers are waiting for you in your apartment," said Jonathan.

"Admirers ... who can they be?"

"Late in the evening, two good-looking girls approached the front desk, asking for you. They said they were your friends and you were expecting them. The girls seem to know you, so I let them into your apartment. I hope you don't mind," said Jonathan.

Curious to learn who my admirers were, I hurried up to the fifth floor. When I unlocked the door, to my surprise it was Sonya and Audra, the two girls I had met at the Whisky.

Audra was sleeping on the couch in her underwear. Sonya was asleep in the bedroom, totally nude. Reeking of booze and cigarettes, Sonya slowly opened her eyes. "Where have you been? We searched every club in Kings Cross trying to find you," said Audra.

"I'm sorry, I didn't know we'd made plans," I said sarcastically.

Sonya walked into the living room, stretching and yawning.

"We've been looking for you," said Audra again.

"Why?" I replied.

"We wanted to hang out with you," said Sonya.

"How did you know I was staying at the Bay View?" I asked.

"You told us, remember? The nice man downstairs let us in. While we were waiting for you to come home, we drank your bottle of Bacardi rum. I guess we got a little drunk. Sorry."

Audra picked up the bottle and drank the remaining liquor. It was nine o'clock in the morning, and Audra was drinking straight alcohol. I grabbed the empty bottle and tossed it into the trash. "I'm sorry, girls, but you have to go."

"Why? We want to hang out with you," Sonya replied.

"You can't. I have things to do."

I offered the girls twenty dollars for cab fare and another bottle of rum, just to leave the apartment, but they refused to leave. I called Jonathan at the front desk for advice, and he called security. Within five minutes, security arrived and escorted the two girls out of the Bay View.

Later in the day, I walked to an adjoining suburb known as Potts Point. Over the bridge was a small park where peddlers were selling their wares. An elderly peddler was polishing his silver. Looking through his selection of rings, I came across a ring with a symbol engraved in the silver. "What's this symbol represent?" I asked.

"It's an ancient Aborigine symbol for good luck," said the vendor.

Being superstitious, I purchased the ring, along with a friendship ring.

Eager to visit the Cheetah Room, I returned to the Bay View to prepare for another night on the town. I showered and put on a nicely fitting outfit, then called Jonathan to request a cab.

"Have a good evening, Mr. Rick. Your cab is waiting," said Jonathan as I walked by the front desk.

"Thank you, Jonathan."

The driver was waiting with the door open.

"Where are we going tonight?" he asked.

"The Cheetah Room, please."

"The Cheetah Room it is," said the driver and sped off.

The driver turned on Victoria Boulevard, taking the shortest route to the night club. The club's marquee lighted the entire block. Eager to enter, I paid the driver the fare, along with a generous tip. The doorman opened the door to the cab, and I stepped outside.

"Welcome to the Cheetah Room, mate," said the doorman.

"No cover charge?" I asked.

"Not at the Cheetah."

Inside the popular nightclub was a wild decor. The floor was covered in cheetah-skin rugs, and sparkling glass chandeliers were suspended from the ceiling. A five-piece band entertained a crowd while go-go girls dancing inside a gilded cage for the soldiers.

That's when a tall, attractive, Aborigine waitress dressed in a suggestive cheetah-skin outfit took my arm and escorted me to a table. "Hi, I'm Akala. I'll be serving you this evening," she said.

I immediately determined that she was the most beautiful woman I had ever seen. "Are all the girls at the Cheetah Room as good-looking as you?" I said, flirting.

"No, better looking," Akala replied, chuckling. "Can I get you something to drink, honey?"

"That's hard to believe, but you can get me a rum and cola," I said, admiring her tall, shapely body.

That evening, the club was filled to capacity. All the servers were Aboriginal. I was surprised to see an interracial crowd.

I noticed a group of young Australian girls enjoying the music. Wanting to dance, I strolled over to their table. "Would anyone like to dance?"

"Sure," said a brunette, quickly taking my hand. She led us to the dance floor. The band was performing *"Dance to the Music"* by Sly Stone.

"What's your name?" I shouted over the music.

"Alkira, what's yours?"

"Ricky, but my friends call me One Shot," I replied.

"Are you on R & R?"

"Yes, I've been in Kings Cross for three days."

"What do you think of our country?"

"It's great! Everyone has been so kind to me," I replied.

"That's because we love Americans."

"Yes, I noticed."

"Would you like to join us?" asked Alkira.

Alkira's offer was another demonstration of Australian hospitality. But, attracted by my Aborigine cocktail waitress, I returned to my table, hoping to persuade her to join me for a drink.

"It didn't take you very long to find someone to dance," said Akala. "What's your name?"

"Ricky, but everyone calls me One Shot."

"What kind of name is One Shot?" asked Akala, smiling as she served me another drink.

"It's just a nickname. That's the way it is in Vietnam. Everyone seems to have one," I said.

"You Yanks are something else," Akala replied.

Alkira, accompanied by her friends, surrounded my table. "We're headed for the Groovy Room. Like to join us?" she asked.

"Thanks for the invitation, but I think I'll hang out here," I replied.

"We'll be at The Groovy Room if you change your mind." Alkira pinched my cheek as she walked away.

Akala returned to the table with a tray of drinks. "Why aren't you dancing?" she asked.

"I'm waiting for a dance with you," I said, placing a generous tip on her serving tray.

"Sorry, I have to work, darling. Besides, there are plenty of girls to dance with," said Akala.

A quick glance at my watch revealed it was eleven o'clock. I was considering joining Alkira and her friends at the Groovy Room when Akala returned with another drink.

"This is on me," she said, smiling.

"Why don't you join me?"

"I can't. I have to work, sweetheart," she repeated and walked off.

I enjoyed listening to Akala's Australian accent, along with admiring her shapely backside. I continued to tip her generously, hoping to pursue her later.

Unexpectedly, the attractive waitress returned to the table, taking a seat on my lap. "I get off at midnight, darling. Maybe we can have a drink."

"I'll be waiting," I replied, a surprised expression on my face.

Excited about the invitation, I waited impatiently, receiving an occasional wink from Akala. Promptly at midnight, she approached the table. Dressed in purple hot pants and matching top, she was absolutely stunning.

"Wow! You look gorgeous," I said.

"I thought I would slip into something comfortable. Come on, One Shot, I'm off work. Let's have that drink," said Akala. An enticing fragrance of her perfume lingered in the air.

"Where are we going?" I asked.

"Your place, darling."

Stumbling to get out of my chair, I escorted my date out of the Cheetah Room.

"Where you staying, darling?" asked Akala, flagging down a cab.

"Bay View," I replied.

"Bay View, please, and stop at the nearest liquor store," Akala ordered the driver. "What would you like to drink, darling?"

"Whatever you like," I replied.

The driver stopped at the nearest liquor store, opening the door for Akala. I couldn't help admiring Akala's backside and shapely long legs as she climbed out of the cab.

She returned with a bottle of Scotch and a pack of cigarettes. The driver rolled up to the Bay View apartments and opened the door. Akala paid the cab fee, and we entered the lobby.

"Good evening, Mr. Rick," said Jonathan.

"Hi, Jonathan," I replied with a smile.

In the elevator, I was embraced with a hug and a long kiss. Akala took a tour of the apartment. Reaching for a couple glasses from the cabinet, we sat down on the couch to enjoy a late-night drink.

"How do you like your Scotch, straight or on the rocks?"

"With ice for me, please," I said.

"That's the trouble with you Yanks. You don't know how to drink."

Akala proceeded to drink her entire glass of Scotch.

"Sorry, darling, I have to catch up. Would you mind pouring me another while I take off my shoes? My fucking feet are killing me," she said in her seductive voice.

"Get comfortable," I replied.

"What's the matter, darling? You haven't touched your drink. Drink it, you'll sleep better."

After drinking my glass of Scotch, I laid my head on Akala's chest. I awoke thinking I had taken a short nap. I opened my eyes to the aroma of freshly brewed coffee. Nursing a painful hangover, I realized I was in bed alone.

I entered the living room, searching for Akala. Two outfits draped over the couch, along with a small suitcase and a pot of coffee, indicated Akala was planning on staying a while.

"I thought you might have left," I said, embracing her with a kiss.

"Don't worry, darling. I wouldn't leave without saying good-bye. I just needed to pick up a few things. By the way, I enjoyed your queen-size bed. Too bad you fell asleep," said Akala, smiling.

"I must have been really hammered. I don't remember getting undressed."

"That's because you passed out. I had to carry you to bed. Undressing you was easy part," said Akala, pouring herself a cup of coffee.

"Sorry about that."

"Don't worry, darling. We have plenty of time to be together. Now get dressed. I made arrangements with my boss to take a few days off to show you around."

Our day started at a secluded beach for breakfast. Located in Bondi Bay, the white sand beach was a favorite place for Akala to hang out. Akala took in the sun as I waded in the surf, nursing an Australian beer.

That evening we returned to the apartment to change, and then went to a waterfront restaurant named Dundee's.

The next day, Akala drove me to a koala sanctuary, where we fed koalas and kangaroos. I got a little too close and a wallaby took a punch at me.

After that amusing visit, Akala and I enjoyed a late lunch at a nearby pub. That evening we enjoyed dining at one of her favorite restaurants. Located near the Sydney Opera House, she insisted on a table with a view overlooking the bay.

Within thirty minutes, we were seated at a table well worth the wait. Akala, familiar with wines, ordered an Australian cabernet, along with a tasty appetizer. She recommended the restaurant's signature lobster dish, complemented by a baked potato and fresh green beans. We ended the meal with a rich chocolate cake and a steamy hot cappuccino. Akala even paid the check.

"How was your dinner, darling?" she asked.

"It was great. That was the first time I ever tasted lobster, and I loved it," I replied.

After dinner we returned to my apartment and entertained ourselves with conversation and a good bottle of Scotch. The following morning, Akala left the apartment early to take care of some personal business. She said she would return in the afternoon.

I decided to take one last opportunity to revisit the sights I had become familiar with. Turning onto Main Street, I began to reminisce about the events that had made my stay a memorable one.

I entered the lobby of the Texas Tavern to visit Johnny, the desk clerk. Down the street was the pub where Kenny and I joined the muscular Australian for a pint of beer. The only problem was he preferred men to women.

Then I headed up Victoria Street, stopping in at the Groovy Room and Whisky nightclubs. Continuing onto Elizabeth Street and turning right on Goulburn Drive, I was tempted to visit the Cheetah Room. I continued to explore Potts Point until it was time to return to my apartment for a final evening with Akala.

On the way, I met Sonya and Audra walking on the opposite side of the street. Trying to avoid a conversation with the girls, I flagged down a cab. Unfortunately, the girls recognized me, shouting my name. I didn't hesitate to jump into the cab.

"Where to, mate?" asked the driver.

"The Bay View, the long way, please."

Returning to the Bay View, I entered my apartment and waited for Akala. A knock on the door indicated she had returned, with two bags of groceries in her arms. Akala greeted me a kiss.

"What's this?" I asked.

"It's our last night together. I'm going to prepare you a meal you'll never forget," said Akala, smiling.

Pulling out a bottle of French wine, we began the evening with a glass of wine. She claimed it was from the Bordeaux region and was an excellent wine to accompany dinner.

Akala stirred her sauce as it simmered on the stove. Pouring another glass of wine, she proposed a toast. "Here's to your safe return, darling."

"Here's to the best-looking girl in Sydney," I replied.

"How much more time do you have to spend in Vietnam, darling?"

"Three long months," I replied.

"Hopefully, it will go fast."

"I have something for you, Akala." I placed the dainty friendship ring on her left ring finger.

"What's this, darling?" she asked.

"It's a token of my appreciation," I replied.

"I can't believe I've fallen for a Yank who's going back to Vietnam and I'll probably never see again. I usually don't date

Yanks, but I can honestly say I've enjoyed being with you. I'm going to miss you."

"I came to Australia to live like a civilized person again. I met an attractive young lady, saw a beautiful country, and partied like crazy. You went out of your way to make me feel incredibly welcome, and I will never forget you for that," I said, gazing into her beautiful brown eyes.

"Do you think you'll ever come back to Australia?"

"At the moment, I'm only concerned about making it home alive. I don't look forward to returning to Vietnam, but I am looking forward to being reunited with a friend I haven't seen in a long time."

I explained about the death of Little Joey, and how a hometown friend had managed to be transferred into my unit after a nine-month separation.

"I'm sorry about your friend, but I'm happy for your reunion with your hometown buddy."

Akala served a wonderful pasta dish along with a cherry-covered dessert. Besides being attractive, she had proved to be an excellent cook.

"Where did you learn to cook?"

"Mother. Her idea of keeping a man was with her cooking," said Akala.

"How old is your mother?"

"My mother passed away two years ago, but if she were alive today, she would be forty-five. That's why I left early this morning, to visit her grave. It's her birthday. My mother was a beautiful woman and proud to be Aborigine. Unlike my father, who didn't deserve my mother's love," said Akala sadly.

Akala had learned well from her mother, because her cooking was amazing. When I had chewed the last morsel, I raised my glass and made a toast.

"Akala, I want to thank you for the time I've shared with you. You have made my visit everything I wanted it to be, helping me forget the horrible war I will have to return to."

"Now it's my turn. Here's to a Yank who unexpectedly came into my life. From the moment you walked into the Cheetah Room, there was something that drew me to you. You're funny and kind, and have made my life a little more enjoyable. I hope your remaining time in Vietnam passes quickly and you return to your family safely," said Akala, tears rolling down her cheeks.

I wiped away the tears and embraced her. I reached in my pocket and placed two hundred dollars in her hand. "This is for you," I said.

"What's this for?"

"Please take it. It's a little something to show my appreciation," I said.

"You don't have to give money. I wanted to be with you. That's the trouble with you Yanks. You think everything is for sale," said Akala.

She placed the money back into my hand and removed the plates from the table. When she walked into the kitchen, I slipped the money into her purse.

That evening, I experienced romantic love and affection. Although my visit to Australia had been incredible, I looked forward to the reunion with Jet.

The following morning I was awakened by the aroma of fresh coffee. It was time to report to the R & R reception center.

Akala insisted on accompanying me back to the center. When everything was packed, I called for a cab.

I closed the door behind me and entered the elevator. In the lobby, Jonathan was awaiting my arrival.

"Are you sure you want to leave, Mr. Rick?" Jonathan asked.

"I have no choice," I replied sadly, extending my hand. "It was a pleasure meeting you. Thanks for putting up with me and my friends. I will definitely remember you and the Bay View." I placed forty Australian dollars in his hand and said good-bye.

"Thank you very much, Mr. Rick. You're a generous young man. I will miss your cheerful smile around here. Your cab is waiting."

Akala joined me in the backseat of the cab.

"Where to, mate?" asked the cab driver.

"R & R reception center, please," I said.

Akala put her arms around me, holding me tightly as the driver drove through the streets of Kings Cross. The bus was waiting to take me to the airport when the driver arrived at the center. Soldiers seemed eager to get back to their duty stations. I could only wonder if they had had as much fun as me.

"I'll miss you, Akala," I said, gazing into her eyes.

"I'll miss you too, Mr. One Shot," said Akala with a big smile.

"All right guys, it's time to get back to reality," said the navy lieutenant.

I gave Akala a hug but didn't want to let go.

"I'll remember you forever. Here's my military address. You can write if you like," said Akala.

I climbed aboard the bus and waved good-bye. Like Sasha and her family, Akala made my visit to Australia a wonderful memory I would never forget.

Episode Twenty-Eight

The Reunion

November 8. The return flight arrived at the Tan Son Nhut Airport late in the afternoon. Everyone cleared customs, and the group was promptly escorted to Camp Alpha. Soldiers returning to Bien Hoa were transported to the air force base, where I spent the night.

***

November 9. I boarded the first log bird and was flown to the field to join Blackfoot. Eager to see Jet, I stepped off the skid, searching for him. I located him sitting on a log. Jet and I embraced each other, happy to be reunited after nine months.

Well tanned, with his wavy blond hair over his eyes, he was a sight for sore eyes. It was a good to see a familiar face from home.

With Thanksgiving around the corner, it appeared Jet and I would be celebrating Christmas in Vietnam.

Jet was well received by the members of Blackfoot. I had known they would like him. He just had that kind of personality.

"How did it go while I was gone?" I asked.

"We walked into a bunker complex, but we were lucky it was abandoned. We spotted two dinks, but no shots were fired," said Jet.

"Why not?"

"No one had a clear shot."

"What do you think of the guys in the platoon?" I asked.

"They're a bunch of great guys, but that Bush character never smiles." Changing subjects, Jet said, "The guys were telling me about Vung Tau Village. Do you think we'll go again?"

"If we remain in the field, there's a good possibility," I replied.

Jet had never had an opportunity to visit Vung Tau Village. I described the adventures I had experienced on previous visits.

Resupplied and ready to move out, Lieutenant CJ discussed the day's objective with his team leaders. After the briefing, Lieutenant CJ gave the point man an azimuth and ordered the platoon to move out. Placing our rucksacks on our backs, we followed the others into the wood line.

***

November 16. Bravo Company completed the mission without confrontation. Lieutenant CJ ordered the platoon to link up with Aztec and Cheyenne at the pickup zone and prepare for the extraction.

The company was extracted from the field and flown to Fire Base Jefferies. Unexpectedly, the platoon was informed of Lieutenant CJ's replacement.

Lieutenant CJ had exceeded his time in the field and was rotating to the States. Although somewhat reserved, Lieutenant CJ was an outstanding leader. He allowed no nonsense in the field, but had a sense of fun and playfulness off-duty. Lieutenant CJ would be missed, not only by me, but the entire platoon.

Jet and I claimed a hooch and headed for the big green cooler for a cold drink and to meet the new platoon leader.

"Listen up everyone. I would like to introduce my replacement, Lieutenant Tamale," said Lieutenant CJ.

"This is not good. With two months remaining in-country, I can't believe we're breaking in a new platoon leader," I said angrily.

"Yeah, we'll just have to show him the meaning of time in-country," said Jet with a smirk.

"We'll have to teach him a few things before he gets us killed."

In my opinion, the newly assigned platoon leader was just another FNG. He had never been in charge of a light weapons platoon and had no field experience—a grave concern for the short-timers.

Jet and I spent most of our time together. There wasn't much of the brotherhood left in the platoon. Brother Kelly and Brother Theo had left for the States. Brother Al and Brother Charles had been pulled out of the field and assigned rear jobs. With the majority of the platoon's members returning to the States, there weren't many experienced grunts left in the field.

***

November 17. The following morning, Jet and I woke to the aroma of cooked bacon. We laced our boots and headed for the mess hall. After breakfast, Jet and I were determined to avoid work detail, especially with a new lieutenant in charge of the platoon.

The new leader decided everyone was going string wire around the fire base. The grunts with time in-country sensed he was trying to impress the higher-ups by volunteering his platoon for work detail.

Jet and I avoided stringing wire, but were assigned the job of loading the mule and delivering the wire to the platoon members stringing it outside the fire base. A mule was a small, flatbed, four-wheeled military vehicle with a modified Volkswagen engine. Equipped with a single driver's seat, the vehicle was considered a workhorse on the fire base.

Being the driver, I would wait in the shade until a spool of wire was requested. When needed, I would fire up the engine and drive to the storage area. Jet and I would load a spool of wire onto the mule and deliver it to the guys working outside the fire base.

On our final run of the day, I veered off to the side of the road and lost control. Jet was thrown from the mule, landing on his knee. He lay on his back, clutching his knee, severely injured.

"Are you all right?" I asked.

"I think I blew out my knee!" Jet grimaced.

Although Jet was in severe pain, he managed a smile and hopped back onto the mule. I rushed Jet to the medic's hooch to determine how seriously his knee was injured. When we didn't return with the wire, the new platoon leader was furious.

"What the hell is going on? We're waiting for the wire!" snapped Lieutenant Tamale.

"Jet's knee is injured," I replied.

"Jet wouldn't have injured his knee if you weren't screwing around. Now get back to work! The guys are waiting for wire."

That's when I realized the new lieutenant was a take-no-nonsense leader.

Jet was diagnosed with torn cartilage. The medic instructed him to stay off his feet until the swelling went down. I returned to work detail.

Jet's injury wasn't serious enough to have him sent home, but it did allow him to remain on the fire base for Thanksgiving. He could thank me for that.

***

November 20. Bravo Company completed their stay on the fire base and returned to the field for a twelve-day mission. I tried to encourage the new platoon leader to let me stay on the fire base with Jet, but he insisted I would be more useful in the field.

Although Bravo Company's missions were getting shorter, they were no less stressful. We had less than two months remaining in-country; it was difficult to understand why Jet and I remained in the field.

Another R & R to China Beach was scheduled for December 6. That meant Jet would have an opportunity to visit the village that had become my sanctuary.

I was assigned to the last helicopter of a five-bird gaggle. Everyone waited anxiously for the birds to arrive.

"Lieutenant CJ said you and Cartwright are my most experienced grunts, and I can rely on you for advice," said Lieutenant Tamale.

"Although I've had two Silver Star recommendations, I'm just a soldier who happened to be in the right place at the wrong time," I replied jokingly.

"That's not what I've been told."

The five-bird gaggle set down on the LZ, and everyone in Blackfoot climbed aboard their assigned bird. I waved to Jet as the birds lifted off and headed for field.

Bravo Company would spend Thanksgiving in the field. Without Jet, the holiday would be just another day. There wasn't a day I didn't think of Akala and the time we had together. I had looked forward to reading her letters, but when my letters went unanswered, Akala became just another memory of the war.

***

November 25. Thanksgiving Day arrived. The CO ordered Bravo Company to assemble in company size for a hot turkey dinner to be brought out to the field. The main CP found a secure landing zone, and battalion delivered the food.

Shortly after 12:30 p.m., the resupply bird arrived with canisters of turkey, gravy, stuffing, and cranberry sauce, along with cases of soft drinks. Although we were in the field for the holiday, the meal gave us something to be grateful for.

The holiday passed and Bravo Company continued its mission. Battalion was currently working out of Fire Base Jefferies. Since joining Bravo Company, battalion had worked out of nine fire bases: Mace, Fontaine, Fanning, King, Donna, Hall, Silver, Billy, and Jefferies.

Our current area of operation was working the flatlands, a sanctuary for VC insurgents launching attacks on military installations near Xaun Loc. Downsizing the number of US troops in Vietnam, our government had only 133,000 US servicemen in-country to assist the South Vietnamese soldiers.

Although the enemy was avoiding large-scale battles with US forces, small confrontations remained a threat in the south. NVA and VC insurgents were fierce fighting soldiers, determined to defeat the Americans at any cost.

***

November 30. On log day, Jet returned to the field. He was walking with a slight limp, but looked well rested.

"How's your knee?" I asked.

"The knee still hurts, but I thought I better get back to the field," he said.

"Why?"

"I didn't want to miss my only trip to Vung Tau Village."

"You didn't have to come to the field. We're going back to the fire base before going to China Beach."

"It doesn't matter. I was bored and wanted to get back to the field," said Jet.

"I rather be bored than killed," I said jokingly.

Most of the morning was taken up by resupply. Six days remained in the mission. Jet was looking forward to China Beach. Resupplied with three days' rations, the platoon moved off the LZ. The new lieutenant ordered us to hump two hundred meters to the south and set up for the night. Concerned about our safety, Jet and I set up our sleeping positions nearby.

At the end of the day, Jet appeared exhausted. Beads of sweat were dripping from his forehead as he set up his night work.

"Are you all right?" I asked.

"I'm tired, but I'm okay. I just need a little rest."

Jet and I returned to perimeter and settle down for the night. I had started sleeping in a hammock. I seemed to sleep better, although I had trouble getting in and out.

After an early morning watch, I felt my way back to my sleeping position for a little more sleep before sunrise. I took off my boots and slipped back into my hammock. I was about to doze off when something landed on my chest. Fearing it could be a spider, I quickly brushed it aside.

The following morning I slipped out of my hammock to put on my boots. Lying on the ground was the largest spider I had ever seen, with long legs and big orange spots on its back. It must have been what fell on my chest last night.

Episode Twenty-Nine

Farewell to My Sanctuary

December 6. Another mission came to an end without confrontation. Bravo Company was safely extracted from the field and flown to Fire Base Jefferies. The company would spend the night, and in the morning fly to Vung Tau Airport. My final visit to China Beach would be sentimental because I would have to say good-bye to the village that had become my sanctuary from the war.

The following morning, everyone was up early, anticipating the flight. After breakfast, we retrieved our rucksacks and weapons, gathering outside the fire base to wait for transportation.

A comfortable Vietnam morning quickly turned into brain-scorching heat. Soldiers in Blackfoot headed for the shade of a nearby tree to enjoy a can of cold beer. There hadn't been much drug use in the platoon since Son-in-Law left for the States.

After two hours of anticipation, our transportation finally arrived. "Pop smoke, birds inbound!" shouted the platoon leader.

The rumble of the twin-engine Chinook troop transport approached the pickup point and descended. The transport landed on the highway and lowered its ramp.

"Are you ready for some fun, troop?" I said to Jet, accompanying me up the ramp.

"I'm ready as I'll ever be, troop," Jet replied.

After thirty minutes of flight time, the Chinook touched down at Vung Tau Airport and lowered the rear loading ramp. Everyone eagerly departed for the buses.

Along the route to the China Beach R & R Center, I pointed out bars, clubs, hotels, and eating establishments that had become familiar to me. In front of the R & R center, everyone assembled and listened to the orientation officer's lecture.

Then Jet and I headed for the barracks to locate Mama-san. As usual, Mama-san was standing outside the barracks, smoking a cigarette, chewing on betel nut. I gave her a kiss on her forehead as she giggled with embarrassment. I handed her my boots and fatigues, and as always, she ran off to starch my fatigues and shine my boots.

When she brought them back, I said, "Mama-san, I'm going to miss you."

"Why, where you go?"

"I'm going home soon."

Mama-san smiled with her black-stained teeth, saying in a low tone, "You number one GI to me. I miss you too."

Knowing I would never see Mama-san again, I felt sad. I placed twenty dollars MPC in the palm of her hand, and her eyes filled with tears. She smiled with gratitude and gave me a hug. "You only GI good to me."

Eager to show Jet around the village, I took him to the Beach Comer Club for a drink. A four-piece Vietnamese band was performing, so we stayed for a few drinks.

Jet wanted to walk in the ocean, so we strolled across the compound for a view of the South China Sea. He admired the Vietnamese girls sunbathing as we walked along the beach. We took a seat on a nearby picnic table and enjoyed the scenery.

"My unit never took three-day R & Rs," said Jet.

"You haven't seen anything yet. Wait until we go to the village."

A strong breeze made it impossible to stay for long, so Jet suggested attending the barbecue offered at the R & R center. Having never attended it before, I agreed. We returned as the spoons were grilling up the steaks and laying out the food. Jet fell in line behind the company clerk.

"Hey, it's REMF. How's it going?"

"Why do they call you REMF?" asked Jet.

"Actually, One Shot is the only person who calls me REMF. At one time, I was a grunt like you. I just got lucky."

"Yeah, right, REMF," I said jokingly.

"Hey, One Shot, this is the first time I've ever seen you at the barbecue. What's the matter, the food in the village not good enough for you anymore?"

"I thought I would check it out just once, since it's our last trip to China Beach," I replied.

Jet and I filled our plates with an assortment of food. There were salads, broiled lobster tails, steamed crab, and plenty of juicy grilled steaks. Jet didn't have much of an appetite and served himself small portions.

After the feast, we headed for the exchange shack, converting MPC for piastres. Jet converted forty-five dollars, and I exchanged two hundred. The rate had gone down considerably and was currently at five hundred piastres to the dollar. Jet chuckled when I was handed eight stacks of piastres. "Why are you exchanging so much money?"

"This is my last trip to the village, and we're going to make it a memorable one," I replied.

We climbed aboard a waiting Lambretta. The driver rolled back the throttle and sped down the road. Jet held his boonie hat with one hand, the Lambretta with the other, and laughed hysterically all the way.

The Lambretta ride was always part of the Vung Tau Village experience and well worth the 200 piastre fee. Like Disneyland's E-ticket ride, it was very entertaining. I directed the driver to the Palace Hotel. I wanted Jet to enjoy a room overlooking the South China Sea.

Jet wasn't aware I had checked in to a suite. I wanted to surprise him and spared no expense. The look on Jet's face was priceless when I opened the door to our seventh-floor suite.

I showed him around and then stepped onto the balcony. There was a spectacular view of the South China Sea, along with a bird's-eye view of the village. I wanted Jet to enjoy everything I had experienced on previous visits. That included a tour of the village, so we headed downstairs.

I flagged down a Lambretta and spent the day showing Jet my favorite clubs and bars, stopping occasionally to enjoy a drink and flirt with my favorite bar hookers. After we had covered the entire village, Jet appeared exhausted, so we returned to the hotel.

Not ready to turn in, I caught a Lambretta to the Soul Bar. Although Manoi had insisted on marriage on our first date, I convinced her I was a better friend than husband. After all the brothers in Blackfoot had rotated to the States, I made it a point to visit Manoi. There was just something about those beautiful green eyes I couldn't resist.

Mama-san embraced me when I entered her bar. "Where are your brothers?"

"They all went home, Mama-san," I replied.

"I miss them," she said.

"So do I."

It was important to me to visit with Manoi on this trip, knowing I would never see her again. She sipped her tea as she listened to my stories about the brothers in the platoon. Mama-san continued to serve my favorite drink, playing the songs that reminded her of the brothers in Bravo Company.

After spending the afternoon with Manoi, I stopped by the Blue Angel Nightclub for a visit with another of my favorite girls, Adela. I took a seat at the bar. Mama-san remembered me from my last visit and promptly served up a Tiger 33.

"Is Adela available tonight?" I asked Mama-san.

"Sorry, no can do. Adela with date right now, but maybe later she be with you."

"Tell her One Shot came by to say good-bye."

"Oh, Adela remembers you, One Shot, because you pay boo-koo money to be with her. I tell her you come back later, okay?" said Mama-san.

"Yeah, tell her I'll be back later," I said and walked out the door.

The following morning, Jet and I were up early, enjoying breakfast at the Grand Hotel. I noticed Jet wasn't his usual self. "Are you feeling all right?"

"I'm tired, but I'm okay," Jet replied.

I paid the waiter, and we headed out to enjoy the day. The entire day I was concerned about Jet because he had no enthusiasm.

A street vendor was selling hats, so I thought I would amuse Jet by purchasing a couple bush hats. I placed one on Jet's head and the other on mine, and we strolled around the village.

I persuaded him to join me for a drink at the top of the Mi Lien Hotel, where Mama-san always kept her girls clean and well dressed. This meant they were checked for venereal diseases and always bathed. Since it featured the best entertainment in the village and served the strongest drinks, the Mi Lien was a popular hangout.

Jet and I started upstairs, stopping at every floor so he could catch his breath. By the time we reached the rooftop bar, Jet was exhausted. He tried his best to hide the pain, but I knew he wasn't well.

"What you like to drink?" asked Mama-san.

"Rum and Coke," I answered.

"How about your friend?"

"I'll just have a Coke," replied Jet.

He dozed off as I started flirting with the bar hooker seated next to me. "Why is your friend asleep?" she asked.

"Jet!" I shouted.

"What?" said Jet, raising his eyelids.

"You're falling asleep. Do you want to go back to the hotel?"

"No, I'll be all right."

"What's your name, sweetie?" I asked the hooker.

"Peaches."

"Is that your real name?"

"Real name, Da`o," said the hooker.

"What's wrong with Da`o?" I asked.

"Name mean peach blossom. I no like. I change to Peaches."

"All right, Peaches, Peaches it is," I said. I continued to talk with Peaches until Mama-san interrupted our conversation.

"You buy tea if you want to talk to Peaches," said Mama-san.

"How much is Peaches worth all night?" I asked.

"Twenty MPC," said Mama-san with a smile on her face.

"Here's ten thousand piastres. Come on, Peaches, let's dance."

"Why you want to dance? You pay Mama-san for boom-boom," said Peaches.

"Because I want to dance," I said, leading her to the dance floor.

Peaches would make more money in the bedroom than on the dance floor, so she escorted me to her room. Having sex with Mama-san's girls was one of the ways of dealing with the war. The military called it *fraternization*—I considered it a way to forget. I wasn't proud of it, but that's the way it was.

Although prostitution was illegal, Vietnam tolerated the exploitation of their women. With very few job prospects, young Vietnamese girls found it necessary to provide sexual services to American troops to survive.

I followed Peaches to her room and watched as she undressed. I could only admire her firmly shaped body and milky-white skin as she slipped out of her clothing.

"Why you look at me that way?" said Peaches.

"Sorry for staring, but you're beautiful," I said.

"Thank you."

"No, thank you. You don't know how grateful I am to be with you tonight." I looked into her eyes, holding her hand.

"You crazy, GI. You can be with any girl in village."

"Not any girl. There has to be something I like before I can be with anyone," I said.

"What do like about me?"

"Your smile. It makes happy."

Peaches and I talked for a minute, and then she climbed into bed, pulling the covers over us.

Afterward, we returned to the rooftop bar, where Jet and Billy were having a conversation. "She's good-looking. How was she?" asked Billy.

"Why don't you pay Mama-san and find out for yourself?"

"Hey, don't take it personally. I was just curious."

"Do you know what this war has done to us?" I asked.

"What?" Billy replied, looking a bit confused.

"We have become selfish individuals who take advantage of a country that has opened its heart to us."

"Where did that come from?" Jet asked.

"When you've been in-country as long as I have, you'll understand," I said to Billy, leading the way downstairs.

"They're just hookers," replied Billy.

"They're not just hookers—they're people with feelings, just like you and me."

"Damn, what's up with One Shot?" Billy asked Jet.

"It's no big deal, Billy. Come on, this is my only trip to Vung Tau. Let's have some fun," said Jet.

"You're right. Let's have some fun," I said.

Jet and Billy followed me to the next bar. An elderly Vietnamese photographer offered to take a picture for a dollar. As he snapped the instamatic camera, Jet mustered up a smile. "How you feeling?" I asked him.

"I'm a little tired."

"You want to go back to the room?"

"No, I'm all right," he said.

After we visited a few more bars, Jet agreed to return to the hotel. I decided to go to the Hong Kong Bar for a visit with Qui.

Qui remained one of my favorite girls because she was the first to spend the night with me in the village. The only problem was I had fallen in love with her.

Qui smiled when I entered the club. "You come back to see me."

"I stopped by to say goodbye. This is my last time in Vung Tau Village," I said.

"You no come back to see me?"

"Sorry, I'm going home soon," I replied.

"Stay with me tonight. I souvenir you," said Qui.

It wasn't too hard for Qui to convince me to stay. From the very first time I met her, I remained attracted to her. I actually believed she was attracted to me. That evening, I left Qui with a kiss and ten thousand piastres. Although it was past curfew, I decided to return to the Palace Hotel anyway.

The following morning, Jet and I were up early. Jet appeared to be feeling better. Getting a decent night's rest had done him good. With Bravo Company returning to the fire base tomorrow, we were ready to enjoy our final day in the village.

Jet had spent his piastres and wanted to convert twenty dollars MPC. I suggested a Lambretta ride back to the R & R center. Jet thought it was an inconvenience and saw no harm exchanging the military currency in the streets.

The military frowned on exchanging MPC in the village because American currency could end up in the enemy's hands. Anytime you purchased drugs from villagers or sold army-issued cigarettes to Papa-san, you were contributing to the black market. Soldiers purchasing appliances and furniture from the PX and reselling to the Vietnamese were likewise dealing in the black market.

I tried to convince Jet not to exchange his MPC in the streets, but he decided to do it anyway. The only way to do it was to find a cowboy. These teenage street thugs were easy to recognize, because they were terrors on moped scooters. They never confronted the GIs because they were no match for the American soldier.

Jet searched the village until he found a couple thugs sitting on their mopeds. "I don't have a good feeling about this," I warned Jet.

"Why?"

"Because these little thugs are VC on wheels."

Jet thought they didn't appear smart enough to cheat him, and decided they were a good choice for the exchange.

Cowboys were experts at cheating American troops out of their money and made a successful living at it. They were notorious for switching rolls of piastres for lesser amounts. Jet believed he could beat them at their own game.

"Jet, let's catch a Lambretta back to the exchange shack."

"Why, when I can do it here?" He walked up to the cowboy confidently.

"What you want, GI?" asked the cowboy, blowing cigarette smoke in Jet's face.

"I want to exchange MPC for piastres," answered Jet.

"Where your MPC?"

"Come on, Jet, forget about it. Let's go," I pleaded.

"Keep an eye on him while I make the exchange," said Jet, looking determined.

"Okay, but I warned you."

Jet proceeded to initiate the exchange. "I'm watching, so don't try anything funny."

"No problem," said the cowboy, showing Jet twenty dollars in a roll of piastres. The cowboy smiled, slowly handing over the roll.

"Everything looks good. Go ahead," I said to Jet.

I focused on the cowboy's hands as they made the exchange. Suddenly, the cowboy switched the good roll for a bad one.

"Jet, forget it. Let's go."

"No, I can beat this little street thug," said Jet.

"Why do you want to deal with these guys?"

Two more cowboys rolled up, revving up their motors. Jet proceeded to make the exchange. I took a step closer, watching the cowboy closely as Jet handed over the MPC.

"Looks good, Jet."

"Are you sure?"

"Yeah, take it."

Certain he'd received the legitimate roll of piastres, Jet released the MPC. Nevertheless, when the cowboys sped away, we realized he had been cheated. Somehow the cowboy managed to switch the legitimate roll with a roll that contained fewer piastres.

Jet and I ran after the cowboys as their mopeds sputtered with exhaust fumes. Jet was serious about catching them; he was running at a full sprint. He pursued them until they split in two directions. Jet followed the mopeds that remained on the street, and I gave chase through the park.

I was just about to give up when their moped sputtered to a stop. The driver tried to restart as I gained on the two cowboys. He was within my reach when the scooter fired up again. Before he reached maximum speed, I was able to tackle the cowboy seated on the back. Tumbling to the ground, I was swarmed by five cowboys. I was kicked and punched until Jet arrived. No match for Jet and I together, the thugs fled into the streets.

Jet and I laughed hysterically as he helped me to my feet. "You were right. I should have exchanged the piastres at the R & R center," he said, catching his breath.

"It doesn't matter now."

"Why?"

"Because I have your money," I said, revealing Jet's roll of piastres.

"How did you get the money back?"

"It fell out of the cowboy's pocket when I threw him to the ground. We better get out of here before they realize it's gone."

Jet flagged down a Lambretta, and we headed back to the Palace Hotel. Because it was our last night in the village, I decided to return to the Soul Bar for one last visit with the girl I cared for the most—Manoi.

"You come see Manoi?" asked Mama-san as I walked through the front door.

"Yeah, where is she?"

"Manoi in back. I get for you."

Manoi smiled as she brushed aside the beads hanging in the doorway. Wearing a long, tight-fitting silk dress, she was attractive as always.

"You miss me?" she asked.

"You know you're my number one girl," I said.

"Sit down and buy me tea."

"I wanted to see you one more time before I leave."

"It still not too late to see Buddha," said Manoi jokingly.

Mama-san brought my favorite drink and played my favorite song: *"Ain't Too Proud to Beg"* by the Temptations.

"It's my last night in the village, and I won't be coming back," I said.

"Stay with me tonight," begged Manoi.

"I'd love to, but my friends are throwing a party at the hotel," I said sincerely.

"Then I stay with you later. What your room number?"

It was sad saying farewell to Manoi. Our relationship went beyond sexual. She was my friend. If there was a girl in the village I was going to miss, it was Manoi. I could only wonder what would become of the girl with the beautiful green eyes and delightful humor.

I wrote my suite number on a napkin and gave her a kiss good-bye. I flagged down a Lambretta and gave the driver instructions to return to the hotel so I could celebrate my final night in the village.

Upon my arrival, everyone was in Stanney's room, enjoying a cold beer and being entertained by detailed stories of past and present members of Blackfoot. Like the actors in a play, everyone had an important role in the security of the platoon.

Prior to our arrival, Blackfoot Platoon had been well led by a group of conscientious leaders. Unfortunately, the death of those soldiers on February 7 was a tragic loss for the company.

A West Pointer had given up a relatively safe position in the rear and volunteered to lead Blackfoot. With the desire to lead from the front, he created a point team consisting of two second-tour grunts. His aggressive style not only placed him in grave danger, it cost him his life. His point man and gun team leader suffered the same fate.

The leadership in place when I was assigned to Bravo Company had the unfortunate task of rebuilding the platoon's morale. The position of platoon leader was assign to Sergeant Tomas. He was a dedicated career soldier who inspired his men to keep his platoon combat-effective. He was a young soldier of Hispanic descent, from Galveston, Texas.

Joe, a jungle-wise soldier, was assigned the position of first squad leader. Although he didn't want the position, he was the only soldier qualified for the job. John, a fearless Puerto Rican from Queens, New York, was assigned the second squad leader position.

After serving three months as platoon leader, Sergeant Tomas was replaced by Lieutenant CJ. Although Lieutenant CJ had never been in command of a light weapons infantry platoon, he proved to be an outstanding leader and became well-liked by his men.

The survivors of the February 7 ambush included Edsel, known as Hillbilly. He entertained the platoon with his humor. The only soldier to offer his support when I first arrived was a Pennsylvanian named Hoskie. Lenny was a slim soldier wearing wire-rim sunglasses. He resembled John Lennon and charmed everyone with his West Virginia accent. Chico was a Native American who proudly served the country who subjected his people. He was from North Dakota. Peter Gun, alias Avocado, was the assistant machine gunner who was sent home after taking a round in the shoulder. Scotty always had a smile, even through the toughest times. Kelly Hicks, with little height but a lot of attitude, was from North Carolina. Theo, alias Mississippi Soul, was a minister from Mississippi. Cartwright was the point man who never led his platoon into harm's way.

Arriving on March 16 was a group of soldiers who transferred into Blackfoot Platoon. There was Al, alias Sweet Al, whose humor always kept everyone smiling, from South Carolina. Charles, alias Bear, was a gentle giant who spoke with a lisp. Sundance had an amazing resemblance to Robert Redford, and hailed from Maryland. Joe, alias the Gun, was a dedicated machine gunner from Ohio, fond of wearing sleeveless fatigue shirts. BJ was his resourceful assistant who always carried a spare bolt. He was from New Jersey.

Houston, from Tennessee, was a philosopher who earned the squad leader position because of his impartial judgment of others. Bodie, alias Teeny Bopper, was an irresponsible seventeen-year-old whose childish behavior earned him his name. Clint, a quick-tempered soldier, was from North Carolina. Zane was the son of Russian immigrants, and joined the military to help his parents financially. He came from Ohio. Rodan, from Minnesota, was an inquisitive soldier with a passion for warm beer. Pate, alias REMF, had a scholarly education that earned him a position as company clerk. Finally, there was Son-in-Law, the unpredictable, drug-addicted soldier whose disruptive behavior jeopardized the safety of the platoon, from Ohio.

Among the veterans and the FNGs were my group, who were expected to fill the shoes of the fearless soldiers killed on February 7. There were seven of us. Duggy, the soldier who humped his M-60 machine gun with pride, from Minnesota. Bart, the boastful assistant machine gunner, snored outrageously, from Iowa. JC, a resourceful soldier, fired his grenade launcher with confidence and accuracy, from Minnesota. Cole was a cheerful soldier who earned the main CP radio operator position for his communication skills, from South Dakota. Stanney had an irreverent sense of humor, from Maryland. Holt couldn't process information as quickly as others, from Iowa.

And then there was the latecomer, Jet, my hometown friend who managed to transfer into Bravo Company to spend his remaining time in-country with me.

The majority of us were leaving soon. This would leave a recent batch of replacements in charge. Although the new soldiers lacked experience, they would eventually become jungle-wise, carrying on as many had done before. The replacements assigned to second squad included Billy, the soldier who refused to carry the machine gun on his first day, from Colorado; Brother Bush, the reserved but intimidating soldier from southern Alabama; Short Round, the cantankerous soldier who earned his alias due to his small height and big ambitions; Brother Shake, a spontaneous soldier who should have been a preacher for all his wisdom; DC, the soft-spoken soldier from the State of Washington; and Donny, the sergeant who would take over for Sundance as squad leader.

There was also a new platoon leader, Lieutenant Tamale, and Blackfoot's latest addition, Rebel—the soldier who couldn't get enough of Vietnam and whose motto was "Kill a Gook for God."

Reminiscing with the soldiers in Blackfoot made me wonder if I would ever see any of these characters again. Although they would remain in my heart forever, they would only be a memory of the war I would otherwise try to forget.

Everyone returned to their rooms for the night, except for Jet, who stayed for a visit. I returned to my room and was surprised to see Manoi sitting on the couch. "Are you happy to see me?" she asked.

"Yes," I replied with excitement.

"I brought my things to spend the night."

"I never thought my last night in the village would end like this."

"Now we can talk, and you don't have to buy me tea," said Manoi jokingly.

I opened a can of beer and pressed the Play button on the cassette player. Manoi sat on my lap as we reminisced about the brothers in Bravo Company who had introduced me to the Soul Bar.

Jet returned to the room, surprised to see Manoi sitting on my lap. "I'm sorry, I'll come back later."

"No, come in. I want you to meet my best friend, Manoi," I said.

"Hi, Manoi, I'm Jet."

Jet sat down and joined our conversation. Although somewhat shy, Manoi enjoyed participating. Then Stanney and Cole entered the room, hoping to continue the party. Manoi passed out beers as Stanney entertained us with his humor. A few minutes later, Bart and Duggy stepped in.

Stanney took the opportunity to pick up the microphone and speak in his delightful humor. "I've known Garcia since we were at Fort Ord, along with the other poor souls who came over to Vietnam with us. He has rightfully earned his infamous title, One Shot. Honestly, he has seen more action than most, and that's fine with me. Although One Shot is a modest individual, his accomplishments exceeded expectations in a war we will never win. He has given new meaning to the phrase, 'I was in the wrong place at the right time.' One Shot won't boast about those 116 notches on the butt of his M-16, but I can say that every time we returned from Vung Tau, there were a considerable number more."

"Thank you for those kind words, Stanney, but let's hear from someone else."

Everyone took a turn speaking until it was time for Manoi to say a few words. She refused to speak. I coaxed her just to say hi into the mouthpiece.

"What do you want me to say, One Shot?"

"Say hi to my friends back home."

"Hi everybody, my name is Manoi, from Vietnam," she said in her soft-spoken Vietnamese accent, quickly placing the microphone back in my hand.

Everyone cheered when Manoi spoke. It would be a time Manoi would remember forever.

The sun was beginning to set, and everyone returned to their rooms for the night. Someone had left a Park Lane on the table. I grabbed a can of beer and asked Jet and Manoi to join me on the balcony.

I fired up the Park Lane and took a hit. I handed it to Jet, who usually didn't smoke. "Here, this will make you feel better," I said, exhaling the smoke from my lungs.

The view of the bay was breathtaking as the sun set on the South China Sea. Although one-sixth of Vietnam lay waste, destroyed by Agent Orange or bombing campaigns, it remained a beautiful sight to see.

I took another hit and then offered my interpretation of what the end of the war meant to me.

"Although the war is coming to an end for us, the war will never be over. We will return to our homes and continue to fight the war within ourselves. Unfortunately, Little Joey will not be going home with us. No one will understand the physical or mental damage we have endured. Here's to Little Joey," I said, wiping the tears from my eyes.

I leaned my head against the wall, passing the Park Lane to Jet.

"Yeah, here's to Little Joey," said Jet, taking another hit.

"I believe everything happens for a reason. It was our destiny to fight in this war, and there's nothing we can do to change it," I said.

Jet and I agreed our stories would have turned out differently if the three of us had remained together. The only thing that didn't change was our friendship.

Manoi placed her arm around my shoulder as we watched the sun disappear behind the South China Sea.

"I'm going to crash," said Jet.

I took one last hit and flicked the butt over the balcony.

"How you feeling, Jet?" I asked.

"I'm feeling no pain. I should have started smoking pot a long time ago," he replied jokingly, heading for his room.

Although Jet was ill, he'd managed to control the pain during his only visit to the village. I had been to Vung Tau Village five times and enjoyed every moment, especially my last. I would remember all the wonderful experiences and people forever. Vung Tau Village had been my sanctuary. I don't know how I would have survived without it.

Waking up with Manoi lying next to me was the perfect way to spend my final morning in the village. She accompanied me to the Grand Hotel for breakfast. Looking into her beautiful green eyes, I could see despair and uncertainty. I gave her a hug and kiss good-bye, knowing I would never see her again.

Manoi turned away and wept.

"What's the matter?" I asked.

"I don't want you to go," she said.

"I have no choice. What can I do?" I said, reaching into my pocket. I pulled out my remaining piastres and placed them in the palm of Manoi's small hand. I kissed her again and said good-bye. I'd never expected Manoi to be the one who was there for me in the end.

Episode Thirty

The Final Mission

December 9. Bravo Company returned to the recently built Fire Base Makowski. With signs of malaria, I convinced Jet to visit the base medic. Unfortunately, the medic diagnosed Jet with a severe case of the flu.

***

December 11. After a brief stay on the fire base, Bravo Company was back in the field. This late in my tour, going on another mission with the rookie platoon leader concerned me. I had trusted Lieutenant CJ and respected his leadership. Lieutenant Tamale hadn't gained the confidence of the platoon as a jungle-wise leader.

Bravo Company was scheduled for a six-day mission. The new platoon leader should have allowed Jet and I to remain on the fire base, but insisted our experience was needed in the field. Everyone knew Jet and I would not to get careless, which also meant looking out for the new platoon leader.

At the end of the day, Jet started showing symptoms of another malaria attack. I was about to turn in when his health took a turn for the worse. Lying on the jungle floor, he was wet with perspiration. "What's wrong?" I asked.

"I'm burning up," Jet replied.

"You don't look good," I said. I poured water on my towel and placed it over his forehead. "Try to get some rest. I'm going to get the medic."

"Doc, there's something wrong with Jet," I said when I found him.

"What's wrong?"

"I think he's having a malaria attack."

Jet was in the fetal position when I arrived with the medic.

"How are you doing, Jet?" asked the medic, kneeling down beside him.

Jet didn't respond.

"He's having a malaria attack, all right," said the medic. "I'm calling a medevac before it gets too late."

"Good luck. You know the new platoon leader won't allow you to call a medevac this late in the day," I said.

"He'll allow it if I say so," said the medic sarcastically.

Jet was hallucinating. Beads of sweat were dripping from his forehead. Suddenly his symptoms reversed and he started shivering violently. All I could do was cover him with his poncho liner.

The medic returned with a discouraged look that meant bad news. "Sorry, One Shot. The lieutenant refused to call a medevac. Jet will have to wait until tomorrow morning."

"Tomorrow morning? He might not make it through the night. This is why the lieutenant can't gain my respect. He doesn't make the right decisions," I replied.

I stayed with Jet until he fell asleep. Since Jet and I were assigned to the last two guard times, I volunteered to pull his watch, allowing him to sleep.

That evening, Jet suffered through several phases of illness. This confirmed that he had become the victim of the tropical disease known as malaria.

Exhausted from staying up with Jet and pulling double guard duty, I made my way to my sleeping position the next morning. Jet was up, having a cup of hot cocoa.

"How are you feeling?" I asked.

"I'm a little weak, but I'm okay. What happened last night?" Jet replied, appearing a little glassy-eyed.

"You suffered a serious malaria attack. You're going to be taken out of the field," I explained.

The point team escorted Jet to the LZ, and he was placed on a medevac. The rest of Blackfoot moved off the LZ and continued the mission. The mission passed slowly without my friend. Although Jet was ill, I was grateful for his safety in the rear.

On log day, Jet returned. Test results confirmed he was infected, but it wasn't serious enough to keep him out of the field. With medication, he could control his disease and return to duty. Besides the physical damage, Jet would have the illness forever to remember Vietnam by.

"Why didn't you take your malaria pills?" I asked.

"I took them in the beginning, but stopped because the big orange pill gave me the shits," he said.

"Who cares if it gives you the shits? It's better than going through those horrible symptoms I witnessed the other day."

You could miss the small white pill every now and then, but you could never miss the big orange one. I always made it a point to take my malaria pills. I had grown up personally witnessing what the infectious disease could do to a soldier—Dad had been infected while stationed in the Philippine Islands.

I was fortunate never to have been infected with malaria, but on the other hand, I took the pills.

407

Besides malaria, Jet suffered from a severe case of jungle rot. Due to our unhealthy living conditions and the way we remained wet during the monsoon season, the rot was difficult to heal. The only sure way to heal the infection was a foul-smelling ointment issued by the field medic. It took time to heal from jungle rot, but it wasn't serious enough to take a soldier out of the field.

After six days of searching for an enemy who no longer wanted to fight, we came to the end of our mission. Ordered to the nearest LZ, the company waited for extraction. Lieutenant Tamale informed us that we were going to tear down Fire Base Jefferies and build another. This meant Bravo Company would be on a newly built fire base for the holidays. Although this was physical work, it was time out of the field.

Fire Base Jefferies had only recently been built. Battalion's next fire base would be built over an existing ARVN fire base located near Xuan Loch. I didn't mind, because my goal was to stay out of the field as long as possible.

The wait at the LZ was unusually long. Everyone became impatient. Curious to know the delay, I decided to investigate. "What's taking so damn long, LT?"

"Delta Company is being inserted into the field. When they're done, they'll pick us up. Sit tight; the birds are on their way," replied Lieutenant Tamale.

"Yeah, right. When you have eleven months in-country, see if you sit tight," I said sarcastically.

I wasn't taking any chances, so I returned to the wood line to secure the perimeter. After a thirty-minute, agonizing wait, the birds finally arrived.

"All right, pick it up, the birds are inbound!" shouted Lieutenant Tamale. "Jet, Cole, Stanney, One Shot, you're on the first bird."

The first bird circled the pickup zone. It was a great feeling knowing we were headed in for hot chow and cold drinks. The bird touched down, and Jet and I were the first to climb aboard. The bird lifted off the LZ as a second approached and touched down.

The pilot approached the fire base LZ, and I jumped onto the skid as I had always done.

"What the hell are you doing?" shouted Lieutenant Tamale.

"What? I always ride the skid!" I shouted.

I ignored the lieutenant and continued to ride the skid. When the pilot touched down, I stepped off and headed for the fire base. It appeared most of the fire base had already been torn down.

Bravo Company stepped off the birds, and Delta Company stepped on. This meant Delta Company would spend Christmas in the field. Unfortunately, the war took no holidays.

"Have fun moving the fire base," said Delta Company's first platoon leader as he walked by.

"Enjoy Christmas in the bush," I replied. The platoon leader smiled and gave me the thumbs up.

Jet and I headed for the big green cooler. Pate, the company clerk, was waiting for our arrival with clean clothes and mail. As usual, the cooler was filled with iced-down beer and cold sodas, a welcome sight after a mission.

Stacked next to the cooler were several cases of C-rations and LRPs. This meant the mess hall had been removed and we were fixing our own meals. I reached for a couple beers, picked up my mail, and headed for the nearest unclaimed hooch.

I always looked forward to good news, but the best news was learning that US draftees had an option to end time in service (ETS). This was an unexpected opportunity to be released from the military early, right at the end of tour, without having to spend an additional six months in service stateside.

Knowing I was being released from military early meant I could plan my future. This called for a celebration. I opened a can of beer, turned on the cassette player, and danced to "*Shake Me, Wake Me*" by the Four Tops.

"Why the hell are you dancing, One Shot?" asked Lieutenant Tamale.

"I'm getting out of the army when I return to the States, unlike you, who has to stay forever," I answered jokingly.

"If you're excited about that, wait until you hear my news."

"What news?"

"The CO is pulling you out of the field."

"Are you serious?"

"I'm as serious as a heart attack," said Lieutenant Tamale.

"I can't believe it. I'm finally getting out of the field!" I felt like jumping up and down with joy.

It was an incredible feeling, knowing I didn't have to return to the field. What a Christmas present. Everyone was congratulating me. Then I realized Jet would have to remain in the field.

"What about Jet, LT? He has as much time in the field as I do," I said.

"Sorry, One Shot. Jet has to go out one more time. It's the CO's decision, not mine."

I was thrilled to be out of the field, but without Jet, there was no more celebration.

There wasn't much of Fire Base Jefferies to dismantle. Delta Company had done most of the work. Our job was to destroy anything the enemy could reuse.

The rest of the day was committed to enjoying our time out of the field. Since there was no longer a mess hall, Jet and I had to prepare our own meals. "I won't have to eat any of this shit anymore," I said to Jet as I prepared my last dehydrated chicken and rice LRP.

That evening, the platoon leader informed everyone that in the morning, the platoon would be convoyed to the new fire base to help construct new sleeping and guard bunkers.

The next day, we awoke early in anticipation of the move. The convoy rolled in at nine o'clock. Everyone boarded the trucks, and the drivers vacated the fire base. All that remained were the memories of another fire base built and torn down.

I took one last look at the deserted fire base as the convoy headed for Highway 1. Most of battalion's fire bases had been located near the highway for easier troop transport and resupply. Fire Bases Tiger, Silver, and Billy had been strategically located deep in the jungle, requiring troop transport and resupply by air.

I could only hope this would be my final convoy ride, as the trucks rolled down Highway 1. I waved at the local villagers along the way as if I knew them. They returned the gesture with a peace or black power sign. As the convoy neared the town of Xuan Loc, the trucks slowed down to turn onto a single-lane dirt road.

The convoy traversed a small creek alongside an ARVN observation post. It appeared to be the lookout point for the fire base, but was unmanned. The convoy rolled into battalion's new headquarters and came to a complete stop. The new base was circular in shape and well built.

Standing tall in the center of the fire base was a stone statue. Everyone climbed off the trucks and noticed the nice sleeping bunkers. They were built like major league baseball dugouts. I located a place to hang my hammock.

"Don't get too comfortable, One Shot. We're tearing down these nice bunkers in the morning to push out the fire base," said Lieutenant Tamale.

"What's wrong with the fire base the way it's built?" I asked.

"I don't make the decisions; I just carry them out. Now finish putting your stuff away and get some chow."

There was already a fully functional mess hall, and everyone headed for dinner. A stroll through the fire base revealed a tremendous amount of labor would be needed to insure security.

After dinner, Lieutenant Tamale gathered everyone in Blackfoot for a briefing. "All right, everyone listen up. Enjoy your evening, because in the morning you're going to start building the new sleeping bunkers. Also, the Bob Hope show is tomorrow, and unfortunately only two of you get to go. My first choice was based on time in-country and performance in the field, and that person is One Shot."

"Jet should be the second choice. He has as much time in-country as I do," I said with conviction.

"What I understand is Jet hasn't been with us very long. Besides, I thought it would only be fair to give one the new guys the opportunity to go," said Lieutenant Tamale.

"Since I was your first choice, I should be the person to decide who gets to go," I replied.

"Don't press your luck, One Shot. Jet doesn't go, and that's my final decision."

"If Jet doesn't go, I don't go," I responded.

"You're crazy, giving up an opportunity to see Bob Hope, but it makes my decision easier," said the lieutenant, looking around.

"Going to see Bob Hope doesn't mean a thing unless Jet and I go together, Lieutenant."

"I'm sorry to hear that, One Shot."

The discussion was over.

The following morning, the two individuals selected to go to the Bob Hope show were on a convoy. I gave my tailored fatigues to the soldier who replaced me. The rest of us were ordered to move our equipment to the other side of the fire base and start building the new sleeping bunkers.

Blackfoot Platoon stood by as bulldozers removed the existing bunkers and prepared the ground.

"First squad, you're assigned to sleeping bunker number one. Second squad, you're assigned to sleeping bunker number two!" shouted Lieutenant Tamale.

Sundance had gone to the rear to begin processing out of country, so second squad was left without leadership. Unassisted, Lieutenant Tamale would have to assign the new leadership position.

"I told the CO about your decision to turn down the Bob Hope show because your friend couldn't go. I don't know if he was impressed or felt sorry for you, but he put you in for an E5 promotion. Effective immediately, you're acting E5 in charge of second squad," Lieutenant Tamale said to me.

413

"Just because I decided not to see the comedian with the big nose?" I replied incredulously.

"No. From what I understand, you deserve it. You've done an outstanding job in the field, and everyone in platoon knows it," he said.

John and Sundance had been my mentors, and I considered myself fortunate to have been led by them. I was stepping into their shoes and didn't know if I was capable.

Lieutenant Tamale informed second squad I was to be their new acting squad leader. Jet laughed when Billy called me Sergeant. After eleven months in the field, I finally had some authority.

"All right, soldiers, let's get to work!" I shouted.

The soldiers under my supervision worked hard until Christmas Eve, looking forward to Christmas Day off. Jet and I put together a small Christmas tree out of a tree branch and decorated it with beer cans and pull rings from canisters of smoke grenades.

Christmas Eve was just another day for Jet and me until the convoy arrived. The truck that stopped closest to our bunker contained C-rations and LRPs, along with cases of beer and soda. When I noticed no one guarding the truck, I decided to give my squad a Christmas present.

"Jet, give me a hand," I said as I looked around us.

"How do you know the beer and soda are for Blackfoot?" asked Jet.

"I don't, but I'm sure they won't miss a couple cases."

I handed Jet a case of Pabst Blue Ribbon and a case of soda, and returned to the sleeping bunker.

"Hey, One Shot, where did you get the beer?" asked Billy when he saw what I had brought.

"Compliments of battalion. Merry Christmas," I said, handing everyone a warm beer.

Jet and I led the squad in an assortment of Christmas carols. When no one could remember the sixth verse of "The *Twelve Days of Christmas*," we decided to call it a night.

The following morning, we awaited the arrival of the flying PX. The flying PX was a smaller version of the regular PX. It flew out to the fire base to sell a variety of items needed in the field. Although each squad was provided with a supplemental package containing toothbrushes, toothpaste, and so on, the flying PX provided less common items such as watches, cassettes, cameras, film, magazines, and batteries.

By the time Jet and I took a position in line, we were practically at the end. We knew that when we reached the front of the line, the popular items would be sold, so we decided to pull rank and take our place at the front of the line.

"Sorry, time in-country," said Jet, placing himself at the head of the line. No one disputed the policy; they allowed us to remain at the head of the line.

We were all getting a little anxious, so I decided to put on a show for the guys. "I have an idea, Jet."

"Yeah, what's that?"

"Let's fake a fistfight," I said and started choreographing the fight.

I stepped back and threw the first punch, simultaneously slapping my thigh to give the impression I had struck Jet in the chest. We caught everyone's attention. Jet returned the punch, slapping his hand to imitate a slap on the face. I took a

415

second swing at Jet's face and he fell to the ground. I faked a kick and then wrestled with him. Everyone was convinced we were involved in a schoolyard brawl.

Suddenly Lieutenant Tamale stepped in and pulled us apart. "What the hell is going on? You guys are buddies!"

Jet and I laughed hysterically, because we had the lieutenant convinced we were actually fighting. "We were just entertaining the guys," I said.

"It didn't look like entertainment to me," he said.

"Seriously, LT, we were only joking around," replied Jet.

"You guys get back to work," said Lieutenant Tamale.

"How about the flying PX?"

"Don't press your luck," he warned with an angry look.

***

December 27. Christmas had come and gone. Jet and I had just spent Christmas Day in Vietnam, and were convinced we were going to spend New Year's as well.

For the next few days, second squad worked diligently to complete sleeping bunker number one before New Year's Eve. Jet and I worked hard during the day and managed to stay out of trouble during the night.

To finalize the construction of the bunker, we placed ammo boxes filled with dirt around the perimeter of the four-foot-deep excavation. Metal plates were placed across the top of the ammo boxes, along with three layers of sandbags.

With the completion of the bunker number one, second squad headed for the mess hall for well-deserved lunch break. A group of soul brothers, actively involved in the brotherhood, were congregating around the mess hall. Curious to know what was going on, I stopped to ask, "What's going on, Brother Shake?"

"We're meeting with battalion regarding our 'fros and shaving profiles," replied Brother Shake.

"Why?"

"The higher-ups want us to cut our hair and shave our beards."

A shaving profile was a medical condition given to an African American soldier unable to shave due to irritation of the skin. Blacks claimed they couldn't shave due to the unhealthy living conditions. Higher-ups believed it was just an excuse not to shave.

Battalion wanted the brothers to cut their hair and shave according to military standards. Blacks believed it was discrimination and were determined to fight for their civil rights.

Now that President Nixon was reducing the troop level in Vietnam, higher-ups were cracking down on the military dress code in the field. Which I thought was ridiculous, since our missions remained search and destroy.

The group of soul brothers and their new recruits were headed for their meeting when Lieutenant Tamale ordered Brother Shake to pull KP. "Why do I have to pull KP? I'm on my way to a meeting," said Brother Shake in an angry tone.

"I've been asked to provide someone for KP, and you're the first person in the platoon I saw, so report to the mess hall, ASAP," replied the platoon leader.

I believed the lieutenant was harassing Brother Shake, so I stepped in. "Go to the meeting, Brother Shake. I'll pull KP for you." Giving me an evil look, Lieutenant Tamale turned and walked away.

"Thanks, One Shot. I owe you," said Brother Shake.

I was no stranger to KP and had pulled it many times. Besides, I didn't consider it work because the duty came with privileges. The spoons in the battalion were aware of my knowledge of cooking in civilian life, and took advantage of my experience.

I helped with the preparation of meals and enjoyed joking around with all the cooks. I prepared salads and dressings, and occasionally boiled and peeled potatoes. What I enjoyed most about the work duty was having the opportunity to eat first.

Brother Shake and other members of the brotherhood met with the officers on the fire base that day and came up with an agreement. The brothers were allowed to keep their afros as long as they wore a boonie hat, and were allowed to keep their shaving profiles as long as they had a medical excuse. The outcome was a stalemate because nothing changed on either side. At least there was a peaceful resolution to it all.

The following morning, Blackfoot went back to work finalizing the construction of the sleeping bunkers number one and two. Everyone in the squad worked hard until lunch break. After lunch, everyone went back to work until dinner.

After dinner, Jet and I returned to the bunker to enjoy an evening of relaxation.

"Here comes the lieutenant," said Jet.

"I wonder what he wants," I replied.

"One Shot, your squad is going down to the observation post tonight," said Lieutenant Tamale.

"You can't be serious, LT. Some of us have less than thirty days in-country," I replied.

"I don't make the decisions, I just carry them out. Prepare your squad to move out, and I don't want to hear anything about it."

"You must have really pissed him off," said Jet.

"Okay, guys, you heard the LT. Get your shit together. We're moving out in five mikes," I said to the soldiers in second squad.

Knowing there was no way to change the lieutenant's decision, I packed an LRP and a couple cans of C-rations for a late-evening meal. I grabbed a couple bandoliers of M-16 ammo and a few grenades.

"One Shot, there's been movement down by the observation post the last couple nights," said the lieutenant.

"Then why are you sending us down there?" I asked.

"It wasn't my decision. It came from the CO. He specifically requested your squad."

"Sure," I said sarcastically.

"Your call sign for the night is 7-6 Whisky, and the main CP is 7-6 Zulu. Got that?"

I was well aware that my actions had compelled the platoon leader to send me down to the observation post, but I hadn't expected him to endanger the lives of other soldiers to punish me.

Everyone in second squad picked up their weapons and equipment and followed me out of the fire base. In anticipation of the anniversary of the Tet Offensive, the fire base was on high alert.

Leading the team, I moved cautiously down the dirt road leading to the observation post. When the team reached the creek, everyone waded across and entered the observation post. Cole, the squad RTO, relayed to the main CP that we had arrived.

There were only eight sleeping bunkers, and everyone quickly claimed one. When the perimeter was secured, we settled down for the night. Jet and I shared a bunker near guard bunker number one, located by the creek.

In anticipation of an enemy attack, Duggy placed the machine gun in the guard bunker along the dirt road. Each watch consisted of three hours. With no moonlight to guide us during the night, it was going to be difficult to locate the assigned guard station.

It was time to head for the guard bunker when the sun began to set. Assigned to the bunker overlooking the creek, I settled in for three hours of guard. A slight breeze rustled through the leaves. I feared what the night might bring.

After three hours, my watch came to an end, and I located my replacement. I tried to sleep, but with the constant firing-off of illumination rounds, it was difficult to relax. When I finally dozed off, the thump of a 60 mm mortar round went off in the distance. Unable to predict where the round would explode, I braced myself.

The enemy mortar round exploded on the other side of the dirt road. Placing my steel pot on my head, I grabbed my weapon and made my way to the guard station. "Did you hear that?" I asked JC.

"Sounds like 60 mm mortar. I already called it in," said JC.

"Keep your eyes open," I said.

A few minutes later, a second mortar was fired off, exploding near the creek. Concerned that the next mortar might land inside the observation post, I prepared for an explosion.

"7-6 Zulu, this is 7-6 Whisky, over."

"Go ahead 7-6 Whisky."

"7-6 Zulu, a 60 mm mortar round has just landed down by the creek, over."

"7-6 Whisky, keep your head down. Illumination rounds are coming your way. Keep us posted. Over."

"That's a solid copy, 7-6 Zulu, over."

Everyone was locked and loaded, ready to fire at anything that moved.

"I'm definitely too short for this bullshit," said JC, placing his grenade launcher in the semiautomatic.

"I know what you mean. Just keep an eye out for dinks," I replied. I had a gut feeling the situation was about to get worse. I had never anticipated being in this position with less than thirty days in-country.

"One Shot, the CO is on the horn and wants to talk to you," whispered JC.

"7-6 Zulu, go ahead, over."

"7-6 Whisky, what's your current situation? Over."

"7-6 Zulu, enemy mortar fire has stopped for now. Over."

"7-6 Whisky, we're going to fire a few mortar rounds in the area. Keep your head down. Over."

"7-6 Zulu, that's a Czechoslovakia. Over." I ended the call and handed the receiver back to JC.

Mortar platoon aligned their mortar tube on a predetermined mark, preventing any rounds from landing near our position. If the enemy was anywhere nearby, hopefully the mission would be a deterrent, and the enemy would leave the area. Everyone remained awake, fearing another enemy mortar attack.

By first morning light, everyone was packed, waiting for orders to return to the fire base. When the call came in, everyone promptly picked up their equipment and headed back to the fire base. First squad was waiting our return. Lieutenant Tamale was standing nearby and didn't say a word.

"What happened down there, One Shot?" asked Houston, the newly assigned first squad team leader.

"The enemy heard I was leaving, so they tried to light my ass up," I said with a grin.

"The lieutenant wanted me to assemble a quick reaction force in case the observation post was attacked," said Houston.

"I can guarantee the lieutenant wouldn't have been one leading the platoon to the observation post."

Episode Thirty-One

Farewell Vietnam

December 31. On New Year's Eve, I managed to get back on Lieutenant Tamale's good side by working hard and finishing the sleeping bunkers on schedule. With the guard and sleeping bunkers ready for use, it was time to bring in the New Year.

After a traditional turkey dinner with all the trimmings, Jet and I returned to the newly built sleeping bunker. We had no alcohol in the platoon. I wondered how we were going to celebrate the New Year. Beer rations were gone, and all that remained were a few sodas at the bottom of the cooler. It appeared to be a sober New Year.

Out of boredom, Jet and I started a game of spades. It would be dark soon, so we formed a few candles out of wax paper from artillery canisters. That way, we could continue the game after the featured movie.

The Graduate, starring Dustin Hoffman and Anne Bancroft, was the featured movie. After catching an eyeful of Anne Bancroft's seductive body, Jet and I headed back to the bunker to continue our game of spades. That's when the evening took a turn for the worse. The artillery sergeant was having difficulty escorting an inebriated friend back to his hooch.

"Need help, Sergeant?" I asked.

"Yeah, my friend had a little too much to drink," replied the sergeant.

"Let us give you hand," I said.

Jet took an arm, and I took the other. Struggling to keep the inebriated soldier on his feet, we waited for instructions from the artillery sergeant.

"Where's his hooch?" Jet asked.

"It's over there. Follow me," said the grateful sergeant.

Jet and I followed him and discovered the drunken soldier was the supply sergeant. We laid him gently on his cot, facedown.

"Thanks for the help, guys."

"No problem, Sergeant," I replied.

The artillery sergeant headed back to his hooch, leaving us alone with the supply sergeant. He had three bottles of Jack Daniels and three bottles of Jim Beam sitting on a shelf. I felt the supply sergeant owed us a bottle for bringing him back to his hooch.

"Are you thinking what I'm thinking?" asked Jet.

"I probably am," I replied.

The supply sergeant was out for the night, so I turned off the light and reached for a bottle of Jack Daniels. Jet and I returned to our bunker, boasting of our discovery.

"Guess what I have?" I said to the guys, holding a bottle of Jack Daniels above my head.

"Where did you get the booze, One Shot?" asked Billy.

"Don't ask," Jet replied.

Everyone cleaned their canteen cups, preparing for a New Year's celebration.

"I want to wish everyone a happy New Year," I said, lifting my cup of booze in the air.

"Thanks for the booze," said Billy.

"Here's to the guys in Blackfoot," toasted Jet.

"Here's to Little Joey," I said, tapping my cup against Jet's. Tears filled my eyes as the memory of my fallen friend crossed my mind.

"Happy New Year," said Jet, giving me a big bear hug.

We celebrated until the last drop of booze was consumed. After everyone in the platoon retired, I wasn't ready to stop celebrating and considered pilfering another bottle of booze. Jet persuaded me otherwise, and we quietly brought in the New Year.

At the stroke of midnight, Jet stood on top of the sleeping bunker and decided to impersonate our basic training senior drill instructor. Energized by Jet's hilarious performance, I followed his act with my impersonation of Lieutenant CJ and Sergeant Tomas.

Jet laughed hysterically as I then impersonated Lieutenant Tamale. He made me aware that the lieutenant was sleeping nearby, but being intoxicated, I was not intimidated by his presence.

Unexpectedly, Jet stumbled, landing near a block of wood. Outraged by his clumsiness, he picked up a nearby ax and took a swing at the block. "Take that!" said Jet, burying the ax in the block.

"Hey, that looks like fun. Let me try." I removed the ax from Jet's hand and took a swing. "That's for all the communist bastards responsible for us being in Vietnam."

"My turn," said Jet.

"Go ahead. It feels great," I said, handing the ax back to Jet.

"This is for all the stinking politicians responsible for this bloody war!" Jet shouted, taking another swing at the block of wood.

"This is for all those lousy draft dodgers!" I shouted.

The lieutenant became annoyed and climbed out of his hammock. "Okay, knock it off. I'm trying to sleep!"

It would have been in my best interest to walk away, but I couldn't resist the opportunity to express my feelings. "Excuse me, sir," I said sarcastically

"Let it go," said Jet.

"I guess the lieutenant doesn't understand the unwritten rule of time in-country."

"I don't have to. I'm an officer," said Lieutenant Tamale.

"I don't need any fucking FNG telling me what to do, especially when you've been in-country less than a month. Unlike you, I didn't volunteer for this job. When you have as much time in the field as I do, maybe you'll understand!" I shouted drunkenly.

"I think you need to calm down and go to sleep before you say something you'll regret. Besides, the dinks can hear you a mile away," said Lieutenant Tamale.

"Okay, LT, I'll calm down, but it's New Year's, and I'm not done celebrating."

"I don't give a shit what you do, just keep the damn noise down so I can get some sleep. Don't make me come over and tell you again. By the way, your impersonation of me was lousy." He slipped back into his hammock.

"I can't believe he expects us to go to sleep. It's New Year's Eve, and I'm going to celebrate," I said to Jet, turning up the cassette player.

Jet and I sat on top of the bunker, listening to music. Then I persuaded Jet to get another bottle from the supply sergeant. We walked quietly past the lieutenant as he slept. Immediately, my eyes focused on a quarter-ton truck parked in the center of the fire base.

"Jet, see that truck?" I whispered.

"What about it?" Jet replied nervously.

"Follow me," I said.

I quietly approached the truck and opened the door. I looked inside and discovered the key was in the ignition.

"Get in," I said.

I couldn't resist the temptation and turned the key. The engine started instantly, and I placed the truck in gear.

"What are you doing?" Jet whispered.

"I'm going to take it for a spin!"

I steered the truck around the statue standing in the center of the fire base, then started down the road. Unexpectedly, a trip flare went off under the truck. Being intoxicated, I didn't realize I had driven outside the fire base. I tried to turn the steering wheel, but the front tires were buried in the sand. When the engine died, I desperately tried to restart the engine but flooded the carburetor.

A cloud of dust and smoke filled the air, making it impossible to see. The entire fire base was lit up with illumination rounds. Then a silhouette appeared through the cloud of smoke.

"Who is driving that truck?" shouted Lieutenant Tamale.

"It's me, sir," I replied, stumbling out of the cab.

"Damn it, I should have known it was you. Who else is with you?"

"Jet, sir," replied Jet, trying to get out of the truck.

"I've had it with you tonight. I want you to get your drunken ass back to your bunker and go to sleep. That's a direct order, and you better obey it. You're damn lucky the CO isn't on the fire base to witness your insubordinate behavior."

"Yes, sir, Lieutenant. You want me to drive the truck back to the fire base?"

"Hell no! Get out of my sight!"

"Jet, I think we really screwed up," I said.

"What do you mean, we? You're the one who got me into this mess. This is your fault," Jet said angrily.

I said I was sorry, but Jet refused my apology. Not only had my disobedient behavior placed my recent promotion in jeopardy, it jeopardized my relationship with Jet.

The lieutenant escorted us back to the bunker to ensure our retirement for the night.

"I told you guys to go to sleep, but you wouldn't listen. You're damn lucky you weren't killed tonight."

"Jet didn't have anything to do with it, sir. I'm responsible."

"I don't care who is responsible! I just want out of my sight and asleep."

Jet and I entered the sleeping bunker and lay down.

"Boy, you really pissed off the lieutenant," said Jet.

"I know, and I enjoyed doing it."

***

January 1. It was the first day of the New Year. Jet and I were up early with major-league hangovers. Wishing the previous night's events had been a bad dream, we were about to suffer the wrath of our punishment.

The members of Blackfoot heard about the previous night's mischief and wished they had stayed awake to witness the display of disruptive behavior. Although everyone thought our behavior was humorous, I wished it never happened.

Jet and I waited with remorse for the lieutenant to arrive with the CO's disciplinary action. "Here he comes," said Jet.

"Jet, One Shot, get some breakfast, then report back to me," said Lieutenant Tamale in a disappointed voice.

"I'm sorry about last night, sir," I said apologetically.

"It's a little too late for an apology."

I tried to eat, but couldn't hold anything down. After breakfast, Jet and I returned to the sleeping bunker.

"Are you ready to burn shit for the rest of your life?" Jet asked.

"I'm as ready as you are, troop," I replied.

After an endless hour of waiting, the lieutenant arrived with the bad news. "First and second squad, go to other side of the fire base and help Aztec. One Shot, the CO has requested you and Jet return to the rear and wait for his return. You will be confined to his quarters until he gets back."

"What's going to happen to us, LT?" Jet asked.

"The CO wants to court-martial you," replied Lieutenant Tamale.

"You're joking. For what? Celebrating New Year's? That's bullshit and you know it," I said in an angry tone.

"You guys went berserk last night, not to mention you almost got yourselves killed."

"We were just having a little fun," said Jet.

"Don't you think a court-martial is a little extreme? We're going home soon. Give us a break," I pleaded.

"I don't want to hear it, One Shot. Those are the company commander's orders. They're sending a bird to pick you up within the hour. Be on it," said the lieutenant.

I knew the lieutenant and I had had our disagreements, and at times I had been disrespectful to him, but I thought there was some level of mutual respect for each other. Uncertain of my future, I began packing my equipment. I had no further use for my bush knife, so I handed it over to Billy.

"What's this for, One Shot?"

"Take care of it."

"Wow! Thanks!"

"I won't need it anymore."

"Take care, One Shot. Everyone is going to miss you around here," said Billy.

One of the new FNGs walked up and shook my hand. "If it weren't for you, I wouldn't have had the opportunity to see Bob Hope."

"Don't thank me, thank the lieutenant," I said.

"Get your shit together and don't stop to talk to anyone," said Lieutenant Tamale.

Jet and I picked up our equipment and headed for the LZ.

"That ungrateful lifer," I said to Jet.

"Look at this way. We don't have to take any more crap from him," said Jet.

Members of Blackfoot Platoon were standing on the sleeping bunker as Jet and I climbed aboard the helicopter. When the bird lifted off the LZ, the guys gave us a farewell we deserved. I returned the gesture, knowing I would never see my fellow grunts again.

The pilot made a pass in front of the fire base and returned to Bien Hoa. My final assault was uncertain because we were on our way to suffer the consequences of the previous night's disruptive behavior.

Pate was awaiting our arrival. He was assigned the task of keeping us confined to the CO's quarters. "You guys are the craziest characters I have ever known," he told us.

"I know I screwed up, but the punishment doesn't warrant a court-martial," I said.

"Yeah, I don't understand why they're being so hard on you, since you're one of the company's most decorated soldiers."

Pate escorted us to the company commander's quarters and reminded us that we were only allowed to leave to eat, pull guard, or use the bathroom.

Confinement with nothing to do but sleep, play spades, and listen to Jet's impersonations was punishment enough. Why couldn't the CO just slap an Article Fifteen on us and send us home?

***

January 4. After three days of stressful confinement, judgment day arrived. Returning from breakfast, Pate informed us the CO was waiting in his quarters.

"I'm tired of the suspense. Let's get it over with," I said to Jet.

I knocked on the door and waited for the CO's response.

"Come in and close the door," he said.

Jet and I walked into the room and stood in front of the CO. Sitting on the bed, shining his boots, he looked up and into our eyes.

"Garcia, what I understand is you are well-liked by everyone in Bravo Company and probably this year's most decorated grunt. You've seen quite a bit of action. In fact, I was told you single-handedly took on the Thirty-Third Regiment when it tried to attack your squad. Jet, you haven't been with us very long, and I don't know much about you, but you seem to be squared away. What I don't understand is why did you screw up like

431

that? Do you even remember what you did? What the hell were you thinking?"

"We were just celebrating New Year's, sir. I know we had a little too much to drink, and I got carried away. I guess the stress of twelve months of combat finally caught up with me, sir," I replied.

"The military is about discipline. Regardless if we're fighting in a war, you didn't demonstrate any discipline on New Year's Eve. Because of your actions, I was considering a court-martial, but because of your list of impressive citations, the battalion commander decided to dismiss the punishment. What do you have to say for yourselves?"

"It will never happen again, sir," I said sincerely.

"You're damn right it's never going to happen again—because as of tomorrow, you're going to begin processing out of country. And believe me, if you screw up one more time, your ass is mine! Understand?" said the CO with a smirk on his face.

"Yes, sir!" I replied with big smile.

"Yes, sir!" said Jet.

The CO stood up and shook my hand. "Garcia, for what it's worth, it's been a pleasure working with you. Good luck, guys. All right, soldiers, get the hell out of my sight."

Jet and I made an about-face and ran for the door. "You think we should to celebrate?" I said to Jet, closing the door behind me.

"Hell no! That's what got us into trouble in the first place," replied Jet.

"I think the CO just wanted to scare us!"

"He did!"

Episode Thirty-Two

Coming Home

January 7. JC, Duggy, Cole, Bart, Holt, and Stanney arrived to begin processing out of country. In the beginning, the tour seemed like an eternity, but now that eight of us were returning home, it was just a serious matter of time.

Jet and I passed the time by playing a game of horseshoes. Jet couldn't resist a wager, making the game competitive. After four victories in a row, Jet and I treated the competition to drinks at the EM club.

After a mess hall dinner, everyone returned for the evening movie. On the way back to the company rear, I left the group to head for the latrine. The direction I took brought me to a group of soldiers waiting eagerly outside the medic's hooch. Curious to know why, I wandered over to check it out.

"Hey, waiting for a shot of penicillin?" I asked jokingly.

"No, but there's a beautiful round-eyed nurse selling a piece of ass for twenty dollars," said the drunken soldier at the end of the line.

"Is sex with a nurse better than a Vietnamese bar hooker?" I asked jokingly.

"Hell, yeah!" replied the drunken soldier.

Not only was I curious to know what the American nurse looked like, I also wanted to know why she would exploit the American troops for money. With the limited number of round-eyed girls in country, I believed she was taking advantage of the soldiers' sexual desires to be with an American girl. I wasn't going to contribute twenty MPC just to see if she was worth it.

I joined Jet and the others watching the movie in progress. I explained to Jet about the American nurse and the soldiers willing to pay her twenty MPC to be satisfied.

"Did you check her out?" asked Jet.

"No, but she couldn't be very attractive," I said.

That evening, my thoughts were focused on the FNGs remaining in the field under the leadership of the new lieutenant, especially now that the other jungle-wise grunts were no longer with the platoon. I couldn't help but wonder what the FNGs were doing at the moment. Were they in the field, turned in for the night, or on the fire base pulling base security? It was now up to the replacements to carry on the battle. I could only hope for their safety.

The following morning, everyone was up early, eager to begin the first day of processing. Clearing finance was first on the agenda, followed by records. Next day, we returned to the storage facility at the First Team Academy Training Center to retrieve our personal belongings.

After our final day of processing, everyone returned to company headquarters to wait for word to be transferred to Tan Son Nhut for the final stage of processing.

The remainder of the day, Jet and I didn't wander to far from the company area, to ensure we didn't get left behind. We were careful not to get into any trouble, especially being so close to leaving the country.

***

January 10. After breakfast, Jet and I returned to company headquarters, where Pate was waiting our arrival. "Hey, guys, your orders are ready to be picked up. You're leaving for Tan Son Nhut in the morning," he said.

After twelve long months, I was leaving Vietnam. The eight soldiers scheduled to be transferred to Tan San Nhut in the morning met back at the barracks. JC opened a bottle of Early Times and started pouring. Jet picked up a guitar and started strumming a song. Everyone enjoyed a stiff drink as we sang along with Jet's amateur guitar playing.

The moment was filled with jubilation and rejoicing, certainly for the eight of us who managed to survive the entire year. Knowing I would probably never see these soldiers again saddened my heart.

***

January 11. With expectations of leaving Bien Hoa forever, the group enjoyed breakfast and then retrieved our belongings—possessions, orders, and memories of a war I would never forget.

We made our way to the pickup point, where a bus was waiting to take us to the Tan Son Nhut Processing Center. We quickly filed in and took seats. An empty seat at the head of the bus reminded me of the only soldier in our group who wasn't going home, Little Joey.

The drive to Tan Son Nhut was chaotic. Taking the usual route down Highway 1, the bus arrived at the center. Everyone piled out and waited for the orientation officer.

"Welcome to the Tan Son Nhut Processing Center, gateway to the world. Processing will take approximately three days, and that's if everything goes smoothly. The first thing you're going to do is take a piss test. This test will determine if you are on drugs. Let me make this perfectly clear. If you are on drugs, you are not going home. If you test dirty, you're going to stay until you test clean. After you turn in your urine, return to the formation for your barracks assignment.

"Tomorrow you will be fitted with khakis, and then you will clear records. In the afternoon, you will return to finance to return your MPC for good old American greenbacks. The following morning, if you passed your drug test, you'll be assigned a flight manifest. Any questions? If not, follow me."

"I don't understand why they would test the grunts for drugs. After serving twelve months in combat, you think they would leave us alone," I said.

"I hope I pass," said Jet.

"Why wouldn't you?"

"Because we smoked a Park Lane on the last night in Vung Tau Village," said Jet.

"That was three weeks ago. They're looking for heavy drug users, not the occasional pot smokers like us," I said.

Jet and I followed the orientation officer down to the test area. We entered the latrine and were issued a cup.

"Okay, gentlemen, print your name and social security number on the side of the cup and return it with urine. There will be two MPs watching you piss, so if you're on drugs, don't think your buddy can take a piss for you," said the MP standing in the latrine.

I smiled at the MP as I filled my cup with urine. When I was finished, I placed the cup on the table and returned to the formation for a barracks assignment. Jet and I located our assigned barracks and claimed bunks.

After lunch, we decided to tour the compound, reminiscing about when we first arrived in country. Jet pointed out the area where we reported every morning until we were assigned to the First Team Academy for eight days of RVN training. That was the last time I ever saw Little Joey alive.

I pointed out the area where Jet and I had experimented with the Vietnamese-grown herb known as consai. I found it too strong to handle and chose to leave it alone.

Continuing to explore, we ventured into an unfamiliar area. Although the rows of empty barracks were capable of housing a large number of troops, we hoped the bunks would never be occupied again.

We enjoyed a typical mess-hall dinner and then decided to take in the entertainment at the enlisted men's club. A mixed drink in hand, I enjoyed an evening of music. When the band announced their final song for the evening, everyone was on their feet, singing along to *"I'm Getting Closer to My Home"* by Grand Funk Railroad. It was obvious everyone in the crowd was going home.

Jet and I headed back to the barracks, only to stop for a breathtaking view of Saigon in the distance. The lights were shining brightly in Vietnam's second-largest city. I could only imagine what would happen if the heavily populated metropolis had already been infiltrated by enemy tunnels and insurgents.

"For some reason, I'm going to regret leaving the country. Now I understand why some soldiers return to the war they learn to hate." I said to Jet.

"There's nothing I'm going to regret about leaving this country," he said.

"There's got to be something you like about Vietnam."

437

"There's absolutely nothing I like about this place. I just want to get the hell out!"

***

January 12. Eager to begin the final stages of processing out of country, Jet and I headed for the mess hall. After a quick meal and a cup of coffee, we went to the clothing depot to be fitted with khakis.

An elderly Vietnamese tailor took the measurement around my waist. I was surprised that I had gained an inch during the year. Our feet were measured for a pair of black dress shoes, and we were given a ticket to pick up our khakis at the end of the day.

The second stop of the day was records. We were issued orders for campaign ribbons and citations, along with our next duty assignment. We had been reassigned to a light weapons infantry unit at Fort Riley, Kansas. This sounded discouraging— returning to the States to play war games after playing the game for real.

***

January 13. Our first stop of the day was finance. It was mandatory to exchange MPC for American currency. It was great to feel the texture of good old American greenbacks. Other than the money spent for airline tickets and a few cash withdrawals, the remainder of my combat pay would be issued when I arrived at Oakland Army Base.

The final stop was the clothing depot to pick up our tailored khakis, campaign ribbons, and citations. Issued separately in velvet-lined boxes were three Bronze Stars—two with *V* devices—a National Defense Ribbon, a Vietnam Service Ribbon with two stars, a Vietnam campaign medal with a *60* device, and two air medals. The brightly colored ribbons were impressive but didn't mean much to me.

The only citation with any meaning was the CIB badge (combat infantry). It was the only one that represented the pain and suffering I had endured throughout year.

***

January 14. We reported to the processing center and waited hopefully to hear our names called for the day's flight manifest. After we had waited two hours in humid, dry heat, the orientation officer stood in front of the formation with the day's manifest.

"Attention everyone, the following individuals have been assigned to flight manifest 890. When your name is called, head back to the barracks, put on your khakis, return your pillows and blankets, and then come back for further instructions. Gentlemen, you are going home."

The officer began calling out the list of names. When I heard my name, twelve months of living with the never ending fear of death was lifted off my chest. An extraordinary cycle of events was ending in the same place it began. I waited eagerly to hear Jet's name, and then we returned to the barracks together to pick up our things and change into our khakis.

Jet helped me properly place the ribbons and citations on my khaki shirt. We returned our pillows and blankets, and then went back to the formation. With great anticipation, we waited with the others for further instructions.

Finally, word came down for flight manifest 890 to report to the final processing area. We followed the orientation officer and gathered under the shade of a canopy. Everyone listened eagerly as the officer began to speak.

"After living with the never-ending fear of death and merciless living conditions, you dirt-eating grunts will be returning home. You will be returning to an attitude of coldness and indifference. Nonetheless, never forget you have served your country valiantly in a difficult, repudiated, and unforgettable war.

"Don't forget to take advantage of your veteran benefits. You have earned these benefits, so use them wisely. If you can't find employment, you are entitled to unemployment benefits up to a year. If you're planning on returning to school, take advantage of the GI Bill. There are medical benefits as well. If you have a service-connected disability, don't hesitate to enroll at your nearest VA medical facility."

The officer concluded the orientation with good news.

"If you are a US draftee, you have the option to ETS when you return to the States."

There was a loud cheer from every drafted soldier in the group. I had no desire to remain in the military and neither did Jet. After an agonizing year of physical and mental damage, Jet and I just wanted to be civilians again.

"Before I can allow you to board the bus, the MPs will inspect your duffel bags," said the orientation officer.

We were escorted to an inspection area, and the MPs instructed everyone to dump the contents of their duffel bags onto the table. On my right stood Jet and on my left stood Sam, the battalion cook I had become familiar with.

I lifted my duffel bag and emptied all the contents onto the table. Lying before me were jungle fatigues, jungle boots, and a fatigue jacket, along with an M-16 ammo can containing two captured enemy flags, an NVA bush knife, a soldier's dog tag, 35 mm photographs, and the dollar bill Grandmother had given me for good luck. The dollar bill had remained in my possession for the entire year, protecting me as Grandmother believed it would.

Jet didn't have much in his duffel bag, so the MP quickly inspected his belongings and released him to board the bus. Sam placed two photo albums gently on the table beside me. The MP rummaged through Sam's personal belongings and then picked up a photo album, staring suspiciously. "This is heavy. You must have a lot of photographs."

"Yeah, pictures of my wife. Would you like to take a look?" asked Sam.

"Don't mind if I do," replied the MP. He was surprised to see photographs of an attractive white girl posing seductively without any clothing. "Hey, check this out," said the MP, staring.

"Do you mind? That's personal," said Sam as the MPs thumbed through his album.

"You have a very attractive wife," said the MP, placing the album back on the table.

"Yeah, especially when she doesn't have anything on," said Sam.

"All right, pack it up and get on the bus," ordered the MP.

I reached over and opened Sam's photo album, looking at the photos taken with a folding instamatic camera.

"Is that really your wife?" I whispered.

"Hell no, I'm not married," replied Sam.

"Then who's the girl?"

"One of my girlfriends willing to help me out. See you back in the world, and don't be late," replied Sam, winking as he headed for the bus.

Sam's ambition was to smuggle scag out of Vietnam. He claimed he could make a lot of money if he could figure out a way to get the white powder back to Mobile, Alabama. He must have figured a way to conceal the scag between the instamatic photograph and the cardboard backing. The nude white girl was only a distraction. That's why the photo album was so heavy.

The MP searched my belongings, discovering my war souvenirs. "I can't let you take the knife home," he said, placing the knife in his fatigue pocket.

"What do you mean I can't take the knife? It's a war souvenir."

"Sorry, can't let you take any weapons home," said the MP with a smirk.

"Why not? Intelligence authorized it."

"Do you want to go home, soldier?"

The MP studied the 35 mm photographs taken during my tour. "Can't let you take some of these photographs home either," he said.

"Why not?"

"It's against military regulations to take certain images back to the States."

The MP confiscated the graphic photographs and continued searching my belongings.

"Okay, soldier, pack your things and get on the bus," said the MP.

"Thanks, REMF," I said sarcastically.

"What did you call me?"

"You heard me," I replied, quickly packing.

I boarded the bus and took a seat next to Jet. When everyone was aboard, the driver fired up the engine and headed for Highway 1. I enjoyed the drive, knowing it would be my last.

The driver entered Bien Hoa Air Force Base, where a Pan American jetliner awaited our arrival. The bus rolled up to the terminal and unloaded. The troops arriving in country were waiting to board the bus, to be taken to the Tan Son Nhut Processing Center. With two-thirds of US troops expected to leave by year's end, I couldn't understand why the military continued to send replacements, especially since President Nixon and Henry Kissinger had announced "peace at hand" with an agreement to end the war.

I hoped President Nixon would hold firmly to his campaign to end the violent, bloody war and bring everyone home. With all the controversy that marked the Vietnam War, I could not see the United States being involved much longer, especially now that the fighting had been turned over to the South Vietnamese Army in the northern regions. Perhaps South Vietnamese president Nguyen Van Thieu and his military command could defend their own country against the determined communist forces coming down from the north.

Staring at the Pan American jetliner sitting on the tarmac, I waited eagerly to hear our flight manifest called. I wouldn't be free of the never-ending fear of death until I was safely heading home.

An hour later, it was time to depart. At 2:15 p.m., our flight manifest was called.

"Manifest number 890 may now start boarding," said the Pan American representative over the loudspeaker.

Jet and I fell in behind the others and headed for the jetliner. Freedom was only fifty meters away. Jet and I hurried to climb aboard. At the top of the stairs, I stopped for one last panoramic view of the countryside.

The airline stewardess placed her hand on my shoulder. "Are you ready to go home, soldier?"

"Yes, I am," I replied. Jet and I entered the plane, taking the first empty seats. I took the seat by the window, and Jet sat next to me. The stewardesses were doing their best to make everyone comfortable.

I stared out the window as the jetliner taxied down the runway. My heart raced with excitement as the captain gave word for the stewardesses to prepare for takeoff, and then the pilot went full throttle.

The jetliner lifted off the runway and everyone cheered. The plane dipped its wing and banked to the left. I looked at the landscape. All that remained were the memories of a war I would never forget.

First stop on our journey was Yokota Air Force Base. We arrived on schedule. The jetliner was on the ground long enough to refuel and resupply the galley. Everyone was allowed to depart the plane, but with the weather overcast and cold, I decided to stay in the warmth of the cabin.

The jetliner continued to Anchorage, Alaska. After another brief refueling stop, the jetliner departed Anchorage International Airport on our way to our final destination—Travis Air Force Base, located on the outskirts of Oakland, California.

Everyone was eager to be back in the States. Jet awakened from a nap when the pilot made his announcement. "Please fasten your seat belts and extinguish all cigarettes. We will be making our descent in a few minutes. Due to low visibility, we have been routed to Oakland International Airport. By the way, boys, welcome home."

The Oakland city lights were visible through a thin layer of fog as we flew over the Oakland Bay Bridge. The runway lights were in view as everyone prepared for the landing.

The tires screeched as the plane touched down on the tarmac. Everyone cheered as if the home team had hit a home run in the bottom of the ninth to win the final game of the World Series—we were home.

Jet and I unbuckled our seat belts and jumped out of our seats, only to wait for the airline stewardess to get the door open. I looked out the window, viewing the Pan American employees preparing to unload the luggage. Because of a general attitude of coldness and indifference concerning the Vietnam War, there was no one to welcome us home.

The copilot helped the stewardess open the door. Our instructions were to enter the terminal and board the waiting transportation. When I placed my feet on the tarmac, I fell to my knees and kissed the ground.

The group of returning soldiers was bused to the Oakland Army Base Deportation Center, where we were received by a lieutenant.

"Listen up, everyone. My name is Lieutenant Miranda. Soldiers remaining in the service may leave the processing center at any time. US draftees wishing ETS will have to go through a twenty-hour administrative process that will consist of filling out forms, a physical examination, and a fitting for Class-A army dress greens," said Lieutenant Miranda.

Late in the evening, the group of draftees followed the lieutenant into a large room. Each man was issued several forms to ensure accuracy of our discharge papers. In the middle of the night, we were directed to the clothing depot.

Once I was fitted and dressed in army dress greens, the final step was getting my cavalry patch sewn on my right sleeve and placing my medals on my coat. Everyone was assigned a barracks in the returnee area, quarantined from the replacements on the base. Jet and I decided on a visit to the mess hall that was serving New York steaks to the returning Vietnam soldiers.

We proudly walked into the mess hall, where a sign hung over the door: "Welcome Home."

"How you like your steak cooked, soldier?" the cook asked politely.

"Medium rare, please," I answered.

"How about you, soldier?" he asked Jet.

"Well done," he answered.

As the cook grilled our steaks, I began reminiscing about where it had all begun twelve long months ago. Little Joey had been in this same mess hall, trying to convince the cooks we had just returned from Vietnam. As we were dressed in new jungle fatigues and boots, it was obvious we hadn't been to Vietnam, but the cooks had generously served us anyway.

"Do you remember what Little Joey said to the cook, when he asked him how he wanted his steak prepared?" I asked Jet.

"No, what did he say?"

"Cooked," I said. Jet started laughing and I joined in.

Jet and I enjoyed the New York steaks and talked about the time we'd spent at the deportation center while waiting to be shipped to Vietnam. "If I had known Little Joey wasn't coming home alive, I would have done anything to keep him from going to Vietnam," I said to Jet.

"Yeah, I'll never forget Joey as long as I live," replied Jet.

***

January 17. After our first peaceful sleep in a year, we began the final hours of processing. We underwent routine physical examinations. Then we were only two more stops from being civilians again. When everyone cleared records and finance, all draftees were directed to a room to pick up our DD214 documents.

Everyone waited eagerly in the unconditioned room. I was about to doze off when the clerk returned to the room with a stack of paperwork. "Everyone, listen up. These are your DD214s. This is your official military record. You're going to need it when you apply for military benefits, so make sure the information is correct. After you have completed your six-year obligation to the army reserve, you will receive an honorable discharge in the mail. This is proof you have officially served in the United States Army," announced the clerk.

I looked over my DD214 as the clerk continued to speak. In section 24, under the heading of Decorations, Medals, Badges, Commendations, Citations, and Campaign Ribbons, I hadn't been given credit for the two Bronze Stars with *V* devices and the Combat Infantry Badge. These were proof of the heartache and pain I had endured during the course of a year. I had paid dearly for these decorations and wanted credit for them.

I brought the omissions to the clerk's attention. The clerk rushed the document back to records, where they verified and corrected the document. Then the clerk returned with my corrected DD214.

"Your decorations are impressive. I wanted to go to Vietnam, but was assigned to Oakland Army Base," said the clerk.

"Right, REMF," I replied. Everyone laughed as I removed my DD214 from the clerk's hand. I had no problem identifying the soldiers who had the cushy jobs in the rear as REMFs, especially the brass who deliberately avoided combat.

"All right, everyone, listen up. You are no longer in the US Army. You are now officially civilians. Although you have a six-year inactive obligation to the US Army Reserve, you have completed your obligation to the US Army, and the president of the United States commends you for it."

The last military order I would ever receive was when the clerk made his final announcement.

"Gentlemen, the only thing standing between you and returning to civilian life is finance. Pick up your pay and you are free to leave."

"All right, let's get the hell out of here!" I said to Jet, rushing over to finance.

Jet and I fell into line and waited to be issued our final pay. When the clerk called me up to the window, I handed over my orders. He stamped the paperwork and opened the cash drawer. The clerk counted thirty-one hundreds and handed them to me.

Holding the bills to my nose, I inhaled the smell of US currency. I rolled the bills tightly and placed the money in my front pants pocket. Jet received his pay, and we headed for the exit.

"I'm going to the restroom," I said.

"I'm going to look for transportation. I'll meet you in the parking lot," replied Jet.

Jet was talking with the driver of a black stretch limousine when I arrived at the parking lot.

"The limo driver can take us to the airport," said Jet.

"How much?" I asked the driver.

"Twenty dollars a person," the driver replied.

Jet and I didn't hesitate to reach into our pockets. I panicked when I couldn't find my roll of hundred-dollar bills.

"What's the matter?" asked Jet as I searched frantically.

"I can't believe it. I lost my money," I replied.

"What the hell happened to it?"

"I don't know," I said, wondering where I could have lost it.

"Did you check all your pockets?"

"There's only one place it could be—the restroom. Wait here, I'll be right back," I said nervously.

I ran back into the building desperate to find the money. I entered the restroom as a soldier was about to enter the stall.

"Sorry, soldier, I'm looking for something," I said, pushing open the door to the stall. I searched the entire stall. In desperation, I went to my knees, searching the floor.

Somehow the roll of bills had fallen out of my pocket and rolled behind the toilet bowl. I quickly jumped to my feet and ran out into the parking lot, shouting, "I found it! I found the money!"

I handed the driver a twenty-dollar bill and jumped into the backseat.

"Damn, you're lucky," said Jet.

"You're telling me, brother. I guess someone up there is still looking out for me," I replied.

I rolled down the window and enjoyed the cool breeze from San Francisco Bay as the driver sped down the highway. Filled with anticipation, I looked forward to being reunited with family and friends.

The driver arrived at the airport terminal at five o'clock. The monitor indicated a United Airline flight was leaving for Bakersfield at 5:20 p.m., departing out of gate C, and was on time. Jet and I ran to the other side of the terminal and purchased two airline tickets.

"You better hurry, they're boarding," said the ticket agent, looking at his watch.

Jet stepped inside a phone booth to call his wife. I took the opportunity to call Dad. With the receiver to my ear, I couldn't remember the phone number I had dialed a thousand times. Jet hung up with his wife and pleaded for me to hurry. Unable to remember my own phone number, I couldn't notify Dad of my arrival.

"You guys barely made it. We were about to close the door," said the stewardess.

Short of breath, I quickly took a seat and buckled my seat belt. A few minutes later, the commuter plane approached the runway and prepared for takeoff. The tower gave clearance, and the pilot went full throttle. The plane lifted off the runway, and we were on our way home.

Approximately forty-five minutes into the flight, the pilot announced his descent into Bakersfield. I was thrilled to be home, but without Mom and Dad to enjoy the celebration, the airport would be a lonely experience.

The commuter plane touched down and taxied over to the terminal. I looked out the window, imagining a warm welcome from Mom and Dad. The stewardess struggled to open the door as Jet and I waited eagerly to exit the plane. With a little nudge from the copilot, they managed to open the door.

"Welcome home," said the stewardess.

"Thank you. I thought I would never see this day," I replied.

Jet was the first to exit. Rushing down the stairs, he ran into the arms of his wife and mother. Knowing I had no one to greet me, I made my way down the stairs a bit slower. Jet's mother extended her arms and embraced me with a motherly hug.

Suddenly, the sound of Dad's familiar voice echoed through the terminal. "I knew he was with Jet. I just knew it!" Dad boasted as they ran toward me. Mom and Dad embraced me as tears of joy ran down Mom's cheeks.

"How did you know I was on the plane?" I asked.

"Jet's mother called. She said that Jet was on his way home, but wasn't sure if you were with him. In my heart I knew you were. I just knew it," said Dad, overwhelmed with the joy of knowing his only son was safe. We all headed home.

Epilogue

April 3, 1975

A strong gust of wind rustled the trees as a heavy downpour dampened the granite headstones. When I returned from my memories and got back to reality, I realized my participation in the Vietnam War was only a microscopic piece of American history.

Although my story is similar to that of others who served in Vietnam, the outcome is what makes my story unique. I could have very easily become a statistic of America's most controversial war, but for some reason I was chosen to survive and tell my story.

In life, timing is everything. Call it fate, call it destiny, or call it just plain good luck, but this is how the Vietnam experience turned out for me.

Author's Note

For over forty years, I had an incredible story to share, but no one cared to listen. Although the criticism and ridicule of America's most controversial war would eventually be forgotten, the physical and mental damage would remain in our hearts forever. The idea was not to think or talk about the war, but to move on with the future. What the United States government neglected to realize was the psychological scars that would manifest from the Vietnam War.

As painful as it was, I was able to cope with the denigration and transition back to a civilian life. The greatest challenge was to talk openly about a subject everyone wanted to forget. With the lack of aid for returning Vietnam veterans, we had to deal with the physical and mental damage on our own, and sometimes it wasn't very pleasant. Especially for the soldiers that made the ultimate sacrifice.